Michael T

Peasants in Africa

£12-50
(£6-25 paper)

Volume 4
SAGE SERIES ON AFRICAN MODERNIZATION AND DEVELOPMENT

Peasants
in Africa

Historical and Contemporary Perspectives

MARTIN A. KLEIN
Editor

 SAGE PUBLICATIONS   Beverly Hills   London

Copyright © 1980 by Sage Publications, Inc.

For information address:

SAGE PUBLICATIONS, INC.
275 South Beverly Drive
Beverly Hills, California 90212

SAGE PUBLICATIONS LTD
28 Banner Street
London EC1Y 8QE England

Printed in the United States of America

Library of Congress Cataloging in Publication Data

Main entry under title:

Peasants in Africa.

(Sage series on African modernization and development; v.4)
Bibliography: p.
1. Peasantry—Africa, West—Addresses, essays, lectures.
2. Africa, West—Rural conditions—Addresses, essays, lectures.
I. Klien, Martin.   II. Series.
HN820.A8P4   301.44'43'0966   79-23415
ISBN 0-8039-1406-7
ISBN 0-8039-1407-5 pbk.

FIRST PRINTING

CONTENTS

ACKNOWLEDGMENTS

I would like to thank the friends and colleagues who were helpful in this project. First, those who read my introduction and one or more chapters: Jack Wayne, Bogumil Jewsiewicki, Jan Hogendorn, Jonathan Barker, Harriet Friedman, Michael Bodemann, Jean Copans, and Jean-Pierre Chauveau; and above all, my friends and students, Robert Shenton and Richard Roberts. John Saul carried messages to Africa and Robert Barde helped with the translations from the French. Donald Crummey, Robin Palmer, Claude Meillassoux, and Ned Alpers brought me up-to-date on recent research. Peter Gutkind was helpful as senior editor and ranking critic. But most of all I owe a debt of gratitude to my wife, Suzanne Silk Klein, who went over the translations, read all articles at least once, and did her best to sharpen and make more precise our use of the English language.

If this volume is top-heavy on West Africa, it is partly the luck of the draw. These were the scholars who responded to our invitation and who came through with their contributions. We hoped for more material on southern and eastern Africa, but the focus on West Africa is not without its virtues. The development of peasantries goes back further in West Africa than elsewhere, and in recent years there has been valuable work done there, of which we present a selection.

INTRODUCTION

MARTIN A. KLEIN
University of Toronto

> My contention is that the social organisation of the peasantry is built, first, around the relations of production as they grow from the economic constraints of agricultural activities, and next, around the necessity of reproduction of the productive unit [Meillassoux, 1973:82].

> Security for him [the African peasant] consists, not in the amassing of capital but in the maintenance of social links with neighbors able to help him in times of need [Richards et al., 1973:4].

> [T]o define poverty requires a distinction to be made between that state in which men are helpless pawns at the mercy of nature itself, and that state in which men are reduced to penury by the actions of men [Haswell, 1975:70].

Defining who is a peasant and drawing up typologies can be a barren exercise, because it blinds us to processes of change and imposes a static picture. It is, however, an essential first step. It is also one on which there is significant disagreement. There are two major schools of thought. The first, which took its lead from Redfield (1956) and Fallers, stresses the relationship between a folk tradition and a dominant tradition and,

therefore, emphasizes culture. They use the following definition of Alfred Kroeber's:

> Peasants are definitely rural—yet live in relation to market
> towns; they usually form a class segment of a larger population
> which usually contains urban centers, sometimes metropolitan
> capitals. They constitute part societies with part cultures
> [Kroeber, 1948:284].

In determining whether African cultivators met this definition,
Fallers claimed that in political and economic terms many did
but that, with the exception of some Muslim areas, they did not
because there was a "relative absence of this differentiation
into high and folk cultures" (Fallers, 1961:110). Fallers'
argument breaks down when extended to the colonial period
because in all parts of Africa there was a Muslim or Christian
great tradition using non-African languages.[1]

More recent authors have accepted the "part society"
notion but have stressed economic and political relationships.
Saul and Woods (1971) explain:

> [P]easants are those whose ultimate security and subsistence
> lies in their having certain rights in land and in the labour of
> family members on the land, but who are involved, through
> rights and obligations, in a wider economic system which
> includes the participation of non-peasants [1971:105].

They go on to place importance on formal colonial rule.[2] Eric
Wolf (1966) does not:

> [P]easants . . . are rural cultivators whose surpluses are trans-
> ferred to a dominant group of rulers that uses the surpluses both
> to underwrite its own standards of living and to distribute the
> remainder to groups in society that do not farm but must be fed
> for their specific goods and services in turn [Wolf, 1966:3-4].

The differences between these two schools lie not so much in
what they see but in what they stress. They discuss the same
phenomena but differ on what is important. Most of the
contributors to this volume would agree with Wolf in seeing the
"part society" aspect of peasant society as derivative—a
result of peasants' relationship to a class that expropriates

their surplus. Most discussions of peasants are in agreement on the following variables:

(1) Peasants are agriculturalists who control the land they work either as tenants or smallholders. Landless laborers are not peasants.

(2) They are organized largely in household units which meet most of their subsistence needs.

(3) They are ruled by other classes, who extract a surplus either directly (rent) or through control of state power (taxes). Peasants do not sell their labor the way workers do; they must provide a part of their production to those who control the coercive machinery of the state. Thus, in Godelier's terms,

> "peasant" societies are class societies within which the peasantry constitutes an exploited class, dominated economically, politically and culturally by a class which no longer participates directly in production [Godelier, 1977:31].

(4) Peasant culture is distinct from, but related to, the larger culture of the dominated group.

Some writers have carefully avoided the term "peasant." Hill has done so because she finds the Hausa peasantry highly differentiated (Hill, 1963, 1972:ch. 13). Hill represents a different approach, which, because it focuses on the unit of production, tends to see the peasant as an entrepreneur or, in Hill's terms, a "rural capitalist" (Hill, 1963, 1970). In fact, Hill has provided as full a description of peasants in Africa as we have, and the differentiation she describes is a process that others see as characteristic of peasant society (Williams, 1976:142). Peasants are not, in fact, an undifferentiated and egalitarian mass. Similarly, Berry (1975b:91) argues that the "growth of cocoa production has created neither a peasantry nor a full-fledged system of agricultural capitalism in Western Nigeria." However, there is not really a contradiction. Peasant society in Africa and elsewhere increasingly has been influenced by capitalist relations of production. Berry, like Hill, has provided a vivid description of what we would call peasants.

Peasants can be distinguished from subsistence cultivators by their involvement in the market and their submission to other social classes; however, exchange is often present in subsistence societies, and the germ of later forms of domination can be found in the limited authority exercised by elders, earth priests, and village chiefs (Meillassoux, 1975b). Furthermore, the individual may operate as a peasant in one year and as a subsistence cultivator in the next, until external forces deny him that freedom. At the other end of the continuum are the capitalist small commodity producers, who often share key attributes of the peasant; most notably, a continued reliance on unpaid family labor (Friedman, 1975; Vergopoulos, 1978). The difference is that peasants still meet most of their subsistence needs, while capitalist farmers are dependant on the market both to sell their surplus and to take care of their daily needs. Here too, the line is often a fuzzy one, and individual producers or communities may straddle the line and be hard to define. The crucial questions, however, are not defining where the line is but describing how cultivators became peasants and why they remain so.

This involves analyzing how the extension of market relations, both precapitalist and capitalist, and the establishment of new forms of domination have affected the rural populations. There are important differences among African peasantries: population density, the existence and nature of landed property, the presence of an identifiable landowner class, and various relations of production, among others. Most African societies differ from their counterparts in Asia and Latin America in that they lack a well-defined landowner class and thus the antagonistic relations that sometimes result in peasant-landowner conflict. "Without rent and landlords, could there be peasants?" Welch (1977) asks. He answers yes, but without going into the wide variety of claims on the land. Well-defined landowner classes existed in Ethiopia (Hoben, 1973; Cohen and Weintraub, 1975) and in various interlacustrine societies (Cliffe, 1977; Fallers, 1961). In Muslim societies across a broad belt of Africa, fief-holders of various sorts collected tribute (Smith, 1960; Hill, 1972) and in other societies there were traditional land claims which gave rights to descendants of those who cleared the land (Labouret, 1941). For most of Africa, surplus was extracted even in precolonial times—not as rent but as taxes; though if we take Wolf's (1966) definition of rent, the difference was unimportant.[3] What is important is that peasants had to produce a surplus for others.

Africa was also characterized by low population densities—although there were striking exceptions, like the closely settled zones around Kano and other large Hausa cities and the highlands of Ruanda and Burundi. In most of Africa there was free land for the taking and in many areas there still is. African land is often poor, but there was a lot of it. Even in the rich areas described by Clarke, Levin, and Chauveau, land was still available into the 1960s. This was a key factor inhibiting the development of landownership. Land was not short; labor was. Slaves, rather than peasants, were the primary source of surplus and the most important form of investment in those societies most involved in market relations. In some societies, however, the difference between slave and peasant was only the heavier obligations of the slave, who often farmed for himself (Meillassoux, 1975a; Miers and Kopytoff, 1977). Mason describes for Nupe a situation in which the primary motive for enslavement was to move refractory peoples to the center of the state where they could be more effectively controlled and a larger surplus could be extracted from them (Mason, 1973). Gang labor systems were probably rare in African slave societies.

Significant peasantification took place in precolonial Africa —as Copans, Chauveau, and De Latour argue—and often shaped later responses to colonial rule. It took place in areas near caravan routes and where there was trade between different ecological zones. It also took place in fertile coastal areas as the European industrial revolution created a demand for vegetable oils, cotton, rubber, cocoa, coffee, and other tropical products (Hopkins, 1973). Thus, the stimuli for change were both indigenous and external, but the processes of change were sped up by the demands of the world economy and by colonialism, which forced change in areas where subsistence production still predominated and hastened it in areas where change was taking place.

MARXISM AND PEASANT SOCIETY

Confronting these processes has left many younger scholars dissatisfied with the older liberal explanations of both the Redfield-Fallers and Hill schools because (1) they focus more on the effect than on the cause, (2) they fail to account for the form and structure of peasantries, and (3) they do not adequately describe the relation of the peasantry to the larger economy. Many—including several contributors to this book —have turned to Marxist analysis. Ironically, they often use Marxist method to argue against Marx himself. Marx was more concerned with the analysis of the capitalist system than with precapitalist modes of production. He regarded the peasantry as doomed, largely because its social structure was amorphous and atomistic and therefore incapable of protecting itself against erosion by capitalism. Peasantries have not only proved more resilient than Marx expected, but have been, in the twentieth century, a more important base for revolutionary action than the proletariat Marx looked to.[4] The search for a more accurate understanding of what has happened to peasants has been part of a larger effort, most developed in France, to break away from the inherited dogmas of earlier Marxist writers. The two bodies of literature most relevant to this effort have been the analysis of precapitalist relations of production (Meillassoux, 1975b; Seddon, 1978) and the exploration of relations between the capitalist metropole and the more exploited periphery. Several chapters in this book are part of an effort to extend this analysis to the evolution of peasantries. Even the non-Marxist contributors to this volume have been influenced by these ideas.[5] It is desirable, therefore, to examine some of the terms and concepts they use.

The most important of these is the concept of mode of production. The original German term, *produktionsweise,* simply means "manner of producing," but it can be divided into two other concepts. The first is means of production: that is, tools, material resources, sources of power, and techniques of production. For African peasants it is the land, the seeds, the simple hand tools most of them used, and their own physical strength. These underwent little change in most of Black Africa during the colonial period. The second concept is the relations of production: These are the social relations which are the basis of the productive system. The central dimension of these relations is how work is organized and who gets what from whom. They involve relations within the household between the elder and his dependants and between men and women; forms of cooperation with the village; the way in which the product is distributed, including relations with the dominant class which appropriates part of the product; and relations with commercial groups which get a part of the product through their control of exchange. Furthermore, these two aspects are organically linked. Changes in man's way of winning sustenance from the environment have generally been reflected by changes in social relationships, and vice versa. Ecology does not determine social relationships, but it does determine the framework within which they are formed. Ecology provides opportunities for change and establishes the confines within which people can seek sustenance.

There is less consensus on the term "social formation." Some use it simply to indicate a social organism. A better definition would probably be that it is a social space within which economic and social relationships are played out. Another would be to see it as a region within which factor mobilization takes place. Either way, it is the arena within which the historical dialectic can operate. Chauveau argues that it can be either highly localized or international. Most social formations, especially precapitalist ones, are marked by the existence of several modes of production, though often one is dominant.

The concept of reproduction is also central to Marx and to contemporary Marxist thought. The basic notion is that a society must be able to reproduce itself. At its most elementary level, this involves the day-to-day and year-to-year needs of the producers for food, clothing, and shelter so that they may continue working. Of equal importance is that producers must replace themselves: The system must produce enough to nurture the unproductive young. The economic system may fail even at this elementary level, as Jewsiewicki's discussion of Leopold's Congo testifies. Finally, the mode of production must be able to reproduce itself

> by replacing the means of production—i.e., the instruments of labour, the raw material, and the auxiliary substances consumed in the course of a year—by an equal quantity of the same kind of articles [Marx, 1887:I, ch. 23].

In other words, for a social order to survive, the producers, the means of production, and the relations of production must be reproduced.

In the various chapters in this book, the problem of reproduction manifests itself most vividly in the way the colonial economy put the costs of reproduction on the traditional economy. The African worker did not, and does not, receive a wage that permits him to support a family or provide for his retirement. The African cultivator does not sell enough cash crops to feed and clothe his family. Both survive because they are underwritten by the peasant household's ability to feed and house its members (Meillassoux, 1975b). This process was most brutal in South Africa, where the economy began by forcing the precapitalist modes of production to subsidize both industry and agriculture and ended by destroying that traditional economy so that black males in South Africa have no choice but to migrate (Palmer and Parsons, 1977; Bundy, 1979). The same dependance on subsistence production is also present with those innovative and successful peasants whom Hill has labeled "rural capitalists." They certainly have been involved in capitalist relations of production, but they have been successful in part because they have been able to meet subsistence needs while expanding cash crop production.

For Marx, another important question was primitive accumulation; this was essentially the starting point for capitalism, the way in which a mass of capital was created by the transfer of value from precapitalist modes of production. Primitive accumulation then led to a process of continued capitalist accumulation, a process of expansion which took it abroad. In the periphery its operation was different from its operation in the industrial center, where capitalism tended to destroy earlier modes of production, albeit sometimes slowly. The basis of the process was the alienation of the worker and peasant from the means of production so that they were forced to sell their labor power. In the periphery the earlier modes were not destroyed. In fact, as we have seen, the profitability of the colonial system depended on the ability of these earlier modes to handle the costs of reproduction. Essentially, then, the process involved not the destruction of earlier modes of production but the articulation of capitalist and noncapitalist modes in a way that made possible a continued transfer of value (Meillassoux, 1975b; Rey, 1976a, 1976b).[6]

There are three levels at which we see processes of accumulation parallel to those which took place earlier in Europe and involving essentially a transfer of value from other modes of production. First, at the level of the enterprise, colonial firms were able to "create themselves" as much through their local profits as through investments from abroad, often using their relationship to the state. Second, the colonial state itself was limited by the reluctance of metropolitan parliaments to subsidize the dreams of colonial proconsuls. Thus, the development of infrastructure and the elaboration of more complex administrative systems depended on the ability of the colonial state to extract wealth from African producers. They were being taxed not simply to pay for the operation of the state but, in essence, to create the state that exploited them. This process is most vividly described for the Congo by Jewsiewicki, but the Congo differed from other colonies only in the magnitude of the problem—and of the solution. The process was brutal in the early years, but increasingly involved the active collaboration of African elites. Finally, these elites also accumulated. The ability of certain families to gain resources—either through early movement into a key cash crop and the establishment of claims to land or through education and resultant government employment—was often crucial. The ruling class of contemporary Africa contains many of the offspring of those who became involved in accumulation or education at an early stage.

In understanding the processes of change a major question is the relationship between the base (Copans calls it the infrastructure) and the superstructure. The base is the material structure of society, the forces and relations of production. The superstructure is the larger framework of ideology, culture, law, and religion, which is often more visible to the casual student. Marxist writers have increasingly rejected as "vulgar materialism" the notion that material factors are always determinant (Friedman, 1975), but most would argue that in the long run the superstructure is the expression of the base— that is, it will reflect and foster the relations of production. Nevertheless, the superstructure is usually elaborate and often shapes both individual action and the way in which changes in the base take place.

Two important conclusions follow here. First, every social situation is in some way unique. Many Marxists have drawn up lists of modes of production, and this exercise is not without value. Comparison often contributes to understanding, and typologies can be useful, but understanding requires more than labeling. The scholar must come to terms with the particular combination of forces and relations of production and with the particular relationship between base and superstructure. Clarke argues particularly strongly against deductive reasoning, but almost all of our contributors are concerned with the close study of particular cases. The analysis they present flows from the study of that case. Second, in studying peasants, we must go to the base. That is, we must look at the forces of production, the land, the technology, and the ecology; and we must define the relations of production.[7] For the Marxist and the non-Marxist alike, it is here that the focus on such questions and processes is important.

COLONIAL RULE AND THE PEASANT

Although the eight case studies presented in this volume cover radically different situations, they pose a series of related questions about processes of change. While the policies of colonial powers tended to be similar, there were crucial differences shaped by colonial interests in the metropole, by political and administrative traditions, and by the resources available to the colonial state. There were also crucial differences between fertile zones with good access to transportation (see Clarke, Copans, Levin, and Chauveau) and interior regions such as the Dallol Mawri (described by De Latour), an area producing little export wealth in the fragile ecology of the savanna; or the Zambian area (described by Muntemba) which experienced rapid economic change only in the wake of the development of the copper mines. Finally, there were differences between West Africa, where the major source of wealth for the colonizers was peasant commodity production, and southern Africa, where hunger for labor converted large areas into labor reserves and strongly distorted the growth of others.

All of this is described by authors who, by and large, do not know each other. Therefore, the similarities among the different areas are striking and might well have been more so if at any point we had all sat down together to compare notes. The various precolonial societies all participated in trade and thus were somewhat involved in market relations. Trade generally involved exchange between ecologically different areas. Most of the peoples discussed below had some form of state which extracted surpluses from those who produced it. There was some specialization, diversified production, and social differences among different groups in the society. Thus, as Copans argues, in many areas the early stages of peasantization occurred before the beginning of colonial rule. The significant exception is that in many societies the ruling class was more dependent on slaves than on free peasants for the production of surplus.

The first phase of colonial rule tended to be the most coercive, in part because the limited resources of early colonial regimes forced a systematic effort to extract wealth from conquered peoples and in part because the resistance of African societies forced more coercive policies. The colonial state accumulated wealth by the systematic expropriation of land, labor, and products from indigenous peoples. Compulsion was widely used. Taxes forced cultivators to produce for market. Forced labor created public works. Rural dwellers were severely punished if they did not deliver quotas of rubber or did not raise cash crops that were assigned to them. The more prosperous areas of West Africa escaped the worst excesses of this early period because they were already deeply involved in producing for foreign markets. Britain was importing 40,000 tons of palm oil in 1855, and Senegal's exports of peanuts reached 140,000 tons in 1900. Even here, taxes and other forms of pressure were used to extend cash cropping into hitherto undeveloped areas (Hogendorn, 1976, 1978).

In other areas cultivators learned quickly that they could sell food or cash crops. In Rhodesia the first mines created a market for food (Palmer, 1977). In Kenya peasant production for export increased until World War I at a more rapid rate than settler production (Wrigley, 1965). Colonial rulers were often reluctant to trust to the free play of the market, and were sometimes threatened by its successes. In both Kenya and Rhodesia the success of peasant farmers kept down the size of the labor supply and eventually led the colonizers to restrict peasant agriculture in the interests of the labor pool desired by white farmers, mine owners, and manufacturers. Elsewhere, the lure of the market was often slower, but by the 1920s it was important everywhere and often caused social tensions. Slaves were freed or were permitted to free themselves. Young men broke away from the control of their elders either to migrate or to set up their own households. The autonomy of village and household gradually broke down, and individualism eroded traditional institutions of cooperation.

Crises play a major role in history. This is striking in the Mawri experience, described by De Latour, where famines in the 1920s and the 1960s, and '70s broke down the capacity of peasants to resist change. The major crisis, however, was the Great Depression, which radically reduced both rural incomes and the possibility of employment in cities and mines. The most striking result was the impoverishment of a peasantry often forced to increase production to compensate for the fall in prices. Workers who lost their jobs fell back on the rural areas. In parts of French Africa peasants pawned their children to be able to pay taxes. Usury increased and the import of consumption goods declined. In French Africa obligatory cultivation was no longer necessary. Peasants had to grow cash crops to pay their taxes and to maintain their already low living standards (Coquery-Vidrovitch, 1977). Nor was coercion needed to get migrants to labor in the cities: From the depression on, the supply of labor tended to exceed the demand.

At the same time, there was a more rapid growth of the African bourgeoisie. In French Africa both the number and value of African savings accounts increased (Coquery-Vidrovitch, 1977:135). The colonial state also became more deeply involved in the rural economy. In the Congo, after briefly considering a policy that would have freed the peasant to respond to the opportunities of the market, the Belgians moved to the regimented and paternalistic policy that Jewsiewicki describes later. Both the British and the French responded with systems of imperial preference, and the French developed a system of support for producer prices (Hopkins, 1973:260-267).

The end of World War II saw a different kind of crisis as colonial regimes found themselves forced to come to terms with the elites they had spawned. Only with difficulty could they rule without the new class of educated Africans. Only with difficulty could they feed the growing cities (see Muntemba) and provide tropical produce for European consumers and industry without freeing peasant initiative from earlier restraints. The Belgians never learned to interact with either peasants or educated Africans—a failure that had disastrous consequences a generation later—but the French and British adapted. Chauveau describes the dramatic reversal in the Ivory Coast. Even in Kenya, where settler resistance was strong, Mau Mau contributed to the development of an independent peasantry (Sorrenson, 1967; Leys, 1975).

The elites contained overlapping groups. Clerks, teachers, and other colonial auxiliaries invested in land and hired either poorer neighbors or migrants from disadvantaged areas. Peasants who saw their opportunities and could mobilize land and labor expanded cash crop production and often used the returns to pay school fees for their sons (and sometimes even for their daughters). In time it became harder for even the enterprising peasant to accumulate. In the more fertile areas private property in land developed and increased until good lands were no longer available. Richards describes a situation in Buganda, where peasants could go into coffee production until the coffee boom of the 1950s forced the price of land so high that only persons with outside sources of income could hope to acquire land (Richards et al., 1973:295). Since independence, most African countries have experienced slow rates of growth, and in some cases production has actually declined, but there has been a significant change in the distribution of wealth. Nowhere is this more evident than in the countryside. Urban-based political, administrative, and commercial elites have established claims to land, and a rural bourgeoisie, combining agriculture with usury and transport and shopkeeping, has asserted itself in many rural areas.[8]

RULE OF THE MARKET

The coercive policies of the early colonial period were successful in breaking down the autonomy of village and household, in incorporating traditional authorities as agents of the colonial state, and in involving Africans in the modern economy as migrant laborers or as peasant producers. The most important early innovation was taxation, collected in money form and nonnegotiable as to amount. Forced labor and compulsory cultivation were passionately detested and often resisted, but they involved few long-range structural changes in peasant societies. Taxes, unlike precolonial levies, had to be paid in specie, and thus the peasant had to earn money. Good year or bad year, the taxes had to be paid. In some precolonial states taxes paid in kind had gone into royal granaries, from which they were dispersed during famine years. This was no longer so.

When the peasant planted at the beginning of the season, he did not know whether the rains would be good, whether his harvest would be large, or whether disaster would strike. He had to produce enough to feed his household between harvests. He wanted a reserve just in case the following year was bad (Comité Information Sahel, 1974:252), and he needed what Wolf has called a "replacement fund" for new tools and equipment and a "ceremonial fund" for the weddings, naming ceremonies, and other rituals that were an important part of social life (Wolf, 1966:5-9). Now, he also needed to earn money to pay taxes, but if the market price for his products dropped or if disaster struck, he had to borrow money. Debt increasingly became a part of the peasant way of life; loans were made, usually at usurious rates of interest (often above 100% or more for a three- or four-month period). Participation in the market had been voluntary; now it was obligatory. Furthermore, peasants increasingly became dependant on the market for small pleasures: a little bit of tea, some sugar, kola nuts, some cloth. Peasant incomes generally remained low. Thus, in a highly commercialized peanut-growing area of Senegal, per capita cash income tended to be between $30 and $50 in the late 1950s. After payment of taxes, this left little for anything else (Brochier, 1968:117-132). A study of three Hausa villages in a peanut- and cotton-growing area in 1966-1967 reported an average per capita income of $34.80

(Norman, 1977). About 40 percent of agricultural production was marketed. A study of a richer coffee-growing area in Uganda reported that 45 of 64 families studied had under 10,000 shillings, or $1,400 family income (Richards et al., 1973:178; see also Jewsiewicki, 1975:ch. 5). Only five households reported over 30,000 shillings of income.

The peasant found himself subject to the vagaries of weather, the demands of an uncomprehending authority, and dependent on the fluctuations of a world market price he could not understand. In describing the way peasants in Southeast Asia have acted under similar pressures, Scott refers to a "subsistence ethic" which

> was a consequence of living so close to the margin. A bad crop would mean not only short rations; the price of eating might be the humiliation of an onerous dependence on the sale of some land or livestock which reduced the odds of achieving an adequate subsistence the following year. The peasant family's problem, put starkly, was to produce enough rice to feed the household, buy a few necessities such as salt and cloth, and meet the irreducible claims of outsiders [Scott, 1976:2].

Scott draws the implication of the peasant situation:

> [T]he peasant household has little scope for the profit maximization calculus of traditional neo-classical economics. Typically, the peasant cultivator seeks to avoid the failure that will ruin him rather than attempting a big, but risky killing. In decision-making parlance, his behavior is risk-averse; he minimizes the subjective probability of the maximum loss [Scott, 1976:4].[9]

The regions described in this book are different from the densely populated and fertile rice lands of Southeast Asia. In Africa the problem was not population density and land shortage, but rather the quality of the soils, a backward technology, and a hostile variable climate. Nevertheless, Scott's insights are valid. The peasant, wherever he lives, inhabits a hostile world where opportunities are few and disaster is always imminent.

Only some kind of modernization could have freed the African peasant from the harsh rule of an unyielding nature, but, generally, colonial regimes did little to modernize African agriculture. White settlers introduced European agricultural methods, but these were generally beyond the means of the peasant, and in those areas of southern Africa where Africans tried to modernize the state actively intervened to protect white farmers from African competition (Palmer and Parsons, 1977; F. Wilson, 1971). Africans were denied the right to buy land in white areas and were generally forced into areas far from transportation with poor soil and generally subject to customary law, which made accumulation difficult (Palmer, 1977). For the rest, Rodney's comment "that the vast majority of Africans went into colonial rule with a hoe and came out with a hoe" is appropriate (Rodney, 1972:239). In few areas were there any significant improvements in agricultural technology. There were only isolated efforts to design appropriate equipment for small-scale farmers or to introduce animal power.[10] The amount of land a peasant can cultivate with a hoe and the size of the yield depends on the crop, the amount of rainfall, and the methods used, but for grain agriculture, four to five acres is probably the most that a strong, hard-working man can cover. If that is planted with millet and conditions are generally favorable, the yield is not likely to be higher than a ton to a ton and a half.[11] That would be enough to feed three to five adults, but conditions are rarely that favorable. Most peasants have difficulty feeding themselves. Not only do they often experience nutritional deficiencies, but many societies have a "hungry season." Thus, Haswell cites a study of eight Gambian compounds in which none of the eight had an average per capita intake of over 1300 calories during the hungriest month of 1949 (Haswell, 1975: 101; see also Richards, 1939). This is about half of the recommended adult diet—and the hungry season is generally a period of very hard work. Whether the peasant has enough to eat or not, he must produce enough income to pay his taxes, to repair and replace tools and home, to fulfill his social obligations, and to buy salt and cloth. Not surprisingly, many peasants find themselves trapped in a cycle of debts or are forced to migrate.

The peasant generally works under rigid time constraints. The season is often short, and seeds must be planted as soon as the rains begin. By the time seeding is finished, the weeds are pushing up. If too much land is seeded, the weeds get ahead of the peasant and yields are low. Generally, he weeds three times, all back-breaking but necessary labor. Harvest time is also often a time of intensive labor. Some crops have to be harvested quickly, while others can be left in the fields. The agricultural calendar is important in determining the reception of new crops. The peasant can more easily add a crop if its work cycle is different from the crops he already farms (Tosh, 1978).

The options are somewhat better in well-watered forest regions, where crops are more varied and work tends to stretch out over a greater part of the year. Yet, even here, as Chauveau tells us, the pressures on the peasants were often harsh. Both Chauveau and Jewsiewicki describe the increasing cultivation of manioc, a crop that demands relatively little labor. For peasants interested in freeing time for cash crop cultivation, manioc is an ideal crop, but it is nutritionally inferior to most other staples. Peasant life was probably best in rich, fertile, and well-watered areas with good transportation outlets; but even here, the pressures of time, technology, climate, and plant disease limited the peasants' potential. In general, there were three ways a man could rearrange his schedule to respond to market opportunities. He could increase the amount of time he worked on his fields, but this was generally limited by bottlenecks like the weeding problem described above; he could cut back on the size of his reserves; and he could shift time from subsistence crops to cash crops.

There was also a tendency to cut back on other activities. Sometimes colonial policy was responsible (see Jewsiewicki); other times, it was the economic pressures of the new agricultural cycle. Precolonial cultivators probably met a significant part of their nutritional needs, especially for proteins, from hunting and gathering. These activities also served as a famine reserve. In areas with low population density there were famine foods which could be called upon.[12] Over time, how-ever, these activities were restricted. In the Congo they were often prohibited. Elsewhere, time was short. As empty lands were cleared and game became scarce, the potential for hunting and gathering became more limited. Similarly, artisanal activity became less important. Weavers have persisted in many areas, but they were often unable to compete with imported cloth. Leather-workers have an even harder time. Blacksmiths are still necessary, though they have had to compete with manufactured tools and are getting most of their income from cultivation. New forms of work have become necessary, though largely limited to slack seasons. Among the Hausa, most peasants have at least one subsidiary occupation (Hill, 1972:72). Although imported cloth has displaced weavers, tailors have proliferated. Young men travel from village to village to sell goods during the dry season, and women supplement agricultural activity by selling goods in various markets.

The market also stimulated an individualism which has eroded traditional forms of solidarity. The household broke down into smaller units. Relations between husband and wife and between father and son were transformed. Thus, Roberts (1978) describes how the Marka tried to compensate for the loss of their slaves by making their sons work harder. The result of this was simply to stimulate the emigration of the sons. In 1975, when I asked two young migrant workers why they migrated from an especially fertile and well-watered district, they answered simply, "because the money is ours." Older men, interviewed on the same research trip about the decline of the household, complained bitterly about the reluc-tance of sons to work with their fathers. "Our dependants are the machines," they claimed, referring to the agricultural machinery being introduced by the Senegalese government (Klein, 1979). Similarly, cooperative work groups are scarcer or are used by the wealthier members of the community. The peasant in difficulty can usually turn only to the village usurer.[13]

AGRICULTURAL INVOLUTION

The term agricultural involution has been used in two ways. In the original application of the term to agriculture, Geertz (1963) used it to describe the intensive wet rice cultivation of Java, where, as population grew, people responded by developing more complex ways of sharing the land and its product. The result was stagnation, a shared poverty, and a structure which was resistant to innovation.[14] Geertz contrasts Javanese agriculture, which is capable of absorbing increasing inputs of labor (albeit with decreasing returns), and the swidden cultivation of the outer islands of Indonesia, which resembled the conditions found in much of Africa. While the Javanese rice farmer moved toward closer communal links and sacrificed potential income for the security of collective poverty, cultivators in Africa and the outer islands moved toward more individualism, a breakdown of communal ties, and increasing economic differentiation. Scott has suggested that this process was most rapid where peasants could increase land under cultivation without jeopardizing their subsistence production. This was especially striking with cocoa, where food-bearing trees provided the young cocoa trees with shade (Scott, 1976:ch. 1). The process depended on the availability of both land and labor: Where the peasant could invest extra labor time (or hire it), he could get the land he needed and raise his income (see Clarke, Chauveau, and Levin).

The condition Geertz (1963) describes for Java—in particular, the ability to absorb ever-increasing amounts of labor on a relatively fixed area of land—does not exist in any significant area of Africa. However, the questions he poses are of interest to any student of peasants: the conditions under which agricultural productivity remains stagnant; those under which it transforms itself; and the conditions under which peasants will seek a communal poverty rather than the risks of change which might bring disaster. These questions are all the more relevant because as good free land disappears, many parts of Africa have seen the end of the conditions that made growth possible.

Other writers would see the process Geertz describes as the result of an economic situation and would define involution in Iliffe's terms as "gradually falling agricultural productivity" (Iliffe, 1971).[15] This is a phenomenon found in many, but not all, areas integrated into the capitalist world through the export of labor rather than the production of commodities. These are the areas Amin has labeled the "Africa of the labor reserves" (Amin, 1972). It includes South Africa, those societies within its economic orbit, and Kenya. Here, decline did not take place overnight. As in West Africa, these areas often saw a substantial growth in production for market. In the middle and late nineteenth century Xhosa, Tswana, and Sotho peasants eagerly adopted both new crops and the use of oxen and plows. Numerous writers (M. Wilson, 1971; Bundy, 1979; Parsons, 1977) have described how, in many parts of southern Africa, there was increasing production for market and the emergence of a prosperous peasantry. Then, at a certain point, production for market peaked, sometimes because of an ecological crisis and sometimes because of population pressure or the policies of the South African government. Unable to meet their needs within agriculture, young men were increasingly forced to migrate; gradually there was a decline not only in the marketed surplus but in yields per acre. Bush was not cleared, plots were not moved, soils deteriorated, and erosion took place. As productivity declined, the young had even less justification for remaining on the land. In many parts of southern Africa up to 60 or 70 percent of the able-bodied males are away at any given time. Only the women, the children, the sick, and the elderly scratch a meager living from the soil, unable to modernize or increase the productivity of the land. For most, there has been a decline in productivity, a dependence on migration, and a breakdown of social institutions. Peasants in much of southern Africa have simply become a reserve army of labor, with rural areas providing a cushion for dependants, which makes reproduction possible at very low wages.[16]

When we move away from the labor-hungry economies of southern Africa, we find that the degree of coercion was less marked, but regional inequality was important almost every-where and was reflected in movements of labor (Iliffe, 1971; Raikes, 1978). Wayne (1975) describes the negative impact of migration on the fertile Kigoma area of Tanzania. In West Africa, Upper Volta and northern Ghana served as labor reservoirs for richer coastal areas (Amin, 1974b). The argu-ment has been made both by Rey (1976b) and by Gregory and Piché (1978) that these migrations contributed to regional imbalances and the increased stagnation of the departure zones. In many cases poor soil and distance from markets forced men to migrate to pay taxes, but this was often compounded by the failure of colonial regimes to invest in infrastructure. Thus, the Senegal river area once produced a surplus of millet, but the French preferred to feed urban populations with rice imported from Indochina. The Senegal River is navigable only about two months of the year, and there were no good road connections between the river and the peanut-growing areas where the market for millet existed. As a result, young men found it more remunerative to migrate either to the city or to peanut-growing areas (Klein, 1979; Adams, 1977).

PEASANT RESISTANCE

The question then becomes: How do peasants respond to all of these pressures that are placed upon them? If we accept that life for the peasant is a constant struggle for survival, then the question which imposes itself is: How does he respond when his subsistence is at issue? Is there, as Scott argues, some kind of moral economy, some norms for what is and what is not a just demand (Scott, 1976)? In the African case, there may well have been such a set of notions regulating traditional relation-ships—for example, between master and slave[17]—but much of what the colonial state did was new (forced labor, obligatory cultivation, taxation in specie), and the state's right to make its demands was established by force.

In much of early resistance it is difficult to differentiate between peasant issues and a simple desire of African societies to protect their autonomy. The expropriation of land and labor in early Rhodesia was so extreme that it would have been surprising had there not been a revolt (Ranger, 1967). Peasant grievances clearly played a role in the Maji-Maji revolt (Iliffe, 1967) and in Mozambique (Isaacman, 1976, 1977), but in much of the ensuing colonial period the questions need to be explored more fully. The chapter by Beinart and Bundy, which ends this volume, has the virtue of relating a varied pattern of resistance to the transformation of rural society. In doing so, they raise a number of issues. First, they underline that in South Africa, as elsewhere, peasant resistance tends "to be localised, limited in aims and achievements, and deficient in organisation and execution" (Beer and Williams, 1975; Ikime, 1966). The question therefore becomes not why they fail, but why they try and when. Second, Beinart and Bundy stress the role of a threat to rural resources—in particular, land and livestock. Here, we see not only the threat to subsistence Scott described as crucial in Southeast Asia, but a threat to economic autonomy. Third, they underline Wolf's observation that the key actor in peasant resistance is the middle peasant who may be forced to send one or more sons to the city to work but who remains rooted in the rural environment (Wolf, 1969:291-292). Finally, Beinart and Bundy suggest that Transkeian peasants move from specific grievances to "a more general rejection of the state's apparatus of political and ideological control." This raises the question of how the peasant breaks out of the atomistic situation they describe in opening their chapter. Part of the answer is clearly to be found in the study of anticolonial revolts such as Mau Mau (Furedi); the Cameroonian revolt (Joseph, 1977); and the rebellions against Portugal, Rhodesia, and South Africa (Saul, 1974). In these revolts the peasants transcended their limitations, but in collaboration with external elements.

Another major question is the peasant response to the increase in both social differentiation and exploitation that has taken place since independence. Where resistance has occurred, the form, grievances, and alliances have varied. In Mali, a classic peasant resistance to a supposedly "progressive" regime took place under merchant leadership (Amselle, 1978). In Nigeria, the Agbekoya movement in Nigeria was led largely by middle peasants and was hostile to both the state and local bourgeoisie (Beer and Williams, 1975). In the Senegal, the "malaise paysan" of 1968 and 1969 was a less violent and perhaps more effective movement which involved a regression away from cash crops and back toward subsistence, thus threatening the economic base of the state (Copans, 1975; Cruise O'Brien, 1979; Barker, 1977).

There are a number of priorities in the study of peasant resistance. First, we need to pay more attention to the ways in which peasants have resisted the spread of the market principle (Wolf, 1969:282). Second, we must look at the various types of economic action tried by peasant groups and studied perhaps most fully for Ghana (Howard, 1976; Southall, 1978). Third, we need to examine the emergence of a distinctive peasant consciousness. Finally, we need to reexamine what is probably the most significant category of social movement during the colonial period: the independent churches. Balandier has linked the development of religious movements to periods of economic stress, though he sees in them not so much an effort to maintain control over their own economy as an effort to recreate a shattered moral order (Balandier, 1953). Bundy and Beinart raise questions in their analysis of the Wellington movement that are worth extending elsewhere.

PEASANT WOMEN

Muntemba considers, and several other authors refer to, changes in the position of rural women. The subject is not one that has been well researched, though it is clear that in most societies women were economically autonomous—that is, they often had defined rights and obligations but controlled some of what they produced. We can, however, make some generalizations. First, women had limited access to education, and thus limited opportunities in moving into urban society. Second, men tended to get involved in cash crops, while women remained in subsistence crops. This led to a third phenomenon: When new inputs like machinery, animal power or fertilizers were introduced, it was the men who received them and it was the men who benefited from the extension services. Women tended to be better off when they were involved in trade on their own account or where they controlled their own production. In general, it is safe to say that colonial rule has often unwittingly affected the relations between rural men and women, generally to the disadvantage of women (Boserup, 1970; Rural Africana, 1975).

CONTEMPORARY CRISES

This book appears at a time when Africa is facing a series of related crises. The first is that, as we have seen, social differentiation has increased at a rapid rate since independence, and, with it, the gaps between social groups have become more visible. The links between the different elite groups vary from country to country, but at the top everywhere there is a ruling class of bureaucrats, politicians, and sometimes businessmen. In many areas these men have invested in land: In Kenya they have taken over the prosperous farms of what used to be the White Highlands. De Latour describes how deputies and functionaries in hard-pressed Niger exploited famine to get control over land. Copans discusses a more unique group, the Mouride *chaikhs* of Senegal.

This ruling class overlaps with and is linked to a rural elite, often recruited from clerks, teachers, and minor functionaries, most of whom combine agriculture with various kinds of rural enterprise. They run small shops, own trucks and taxis, engage in usury, and also farm. Below them is a still large class of middle peasants who have enough land to cultivate and can exploit new inputs like fertilizers and farm machinery. At the bottom is a smaller, but rapidly growing, population of land-short peasants. The number of landless is still relatively small, but an increasing number of peasants must sell their labor to survive, even in what were once labor-importing areas. In

Africa, we do not often see the tendency to share poverty which Geertz and Scott have described for Southeast Asia. African rural areas have been increasingly dominated by an acquisitive and aggressive class of peasant-entrepreneurs.

Second, in those areas where population densities are high or where economic opportunities are considerable, free land is disappearing, if it is not already gone. Where it was once possible for the freed slave, the migrant, or the land-short peasant to clear new land and claim it for himself, that opportunity no longer exists. Communal rights have given way to private property in land, and reserves of free land have often been claimed. Furthermore, even many of the more secure peasants can easily see their positions eroded by misfortune or, worse, by what seems like good fortune—a large and prosperous family. A large farm is an inadequate heritage if there are too many heirs. One result is that many prosperous farmers invest in education for their sons. As class lines grow sharper, the poor find themselves forced into the work force, into the urban unemployed, or into dependant relationships like the *bara* described by De Latour.

The third crisis is essentially a crisis of production. After independence, many African countries tried to expand agricultural production, recognizing that only increased agricultural exports could pay for modernization. In general, they did so without paying adequate attention to food production and to the nutritional needs of their peoples. Some countries have been successful in increasing production—countries as diverse as capitalist Kenya, the Ivory Coast, and socialist Tanzania—but many have stagnated and have been caught up in harsh cross-pressures. Migration to the city has increased, often beyond the capacity of the city to absorb population, and the number of agricultural producers has declined. At the same time, the modernization of food crop production has been inadequate. Zaire imports heavily to feed the urban masses, though the amount of potential arable land in the country is vast. Similarly, Zambia has seen drastic shortfalls in the production of maize and has been forced to spend needed foreign exchange to buy what it could easily grow.

For many years, the crisis of productivity was compounded by a negative trend in the world market. Agricultural exports, which drew rising prices after World War II, have begun rising again in the mid-1970s, but the limited benefits of these increases have been eroded by the prices paid for machinery, oil, and imported consumer goods, increasingly sought by the growing bourgeoisie. All of this has been compounded by intermittent ecological disaster; in particular, the prolonged series of droughts in the sahel between 1968 and 1975 (Copans, 1979).

The position of ruling classes in this is very tenuous. Except in a few mineral-rich countries, their well-being is closely linked to the productivity of the peasant sector, though not always to the well-being of the peasant. While they have in some countries been forced to bend to pressures from below, they have generally used state power to increase their control over the means of production and the distribution of the product. Development policies pushed by the World Bank and various western powers have operated to extend capitalist relationships in rural life, to increase the production of export crops (often at the expense of food), and to further erode the peasant's ability to protect himself. As exploitation increases, the peasant could become an increasingly important actor—or an increasingly pathetic victim.

NOTES

1. Fallers' use of the ethnographic present blurs the fact that he is talking about precolonial Africa. It also contributes to a static picture of societies that experienced dramatic change during the nineteenth and twentieth centuries. Ironically, some of the Muslim societies he referred to can be better seen not as peasant societies, but as slave societies, in that slave labor was the major source of surplus which supported elites (Klein and Lovejoy, 1979; Lovejoy, 1978; Cooper, 1977). Another qualification of Kroeber's definition is that many African peasants are urban and thus travel long distances to their fields. This is especially true of the Yoruba and Hausa. Conversely, the Amhara of Ethiopia at one time had peasants without cities (Gamst, 1970).

2. The Saul and Woods definition was used by many of the contributors to Palmer and Parsons (1977). For a discussion of how this shaped that book, see Ranger (1978).

3. Wolf defines rent as payments in labor, produce, or money made to a superior power (1966:9-10).

4. The reasons for this will appear in the course of various case studies. A very perceptive analysis of the problem is presented in Scott (1977). Scott argues, first, that peasant social structure is not as amorphous and atomistic as Marx assumed; and, second, that what Marx saw as its disadvantages have turned out to be its strengths. In particular, the relative isolation of peasants has made them more immune than other classes to the social and moral hegemony of the dominant class.

5. In the introduction to their collection of essays, Palmer and Parsons (1977) express their debt to French Marxist scholarship, but none of the authors in their book seek to use the insights of those writers. Most operate within the more limited confines of dependency theory.

6. Both dependency theorists like Frank (1969) and Amin (1972, 1973) and articulation theorists like Rey (1976a), Meillassoux (1975b), and Cliffe (1977) and Bernstein (1978) are concerned to explain the continued poverty and exploitation of the periphery, but they do so in different terms. For Frank, there is a "development of underdevelopment" in which the peripheral society becomes capitalist. The articulation theorists argue that exploitation is based on the preservation of the noncapitalist mode and the transfer of value from it to the capitalist mode, which is possible because the capitalist does not have to worry about the costs of reproduction. Frank's term, "underdevelopment," is an unfortunate one because it implies lack of development; as the articulation theorists make clear, the phenomenon is really a particularly exploitative form of development. Nevertheless, if the argument made below by Copans is correct, this articulation does not prevent the extension of capitalist relationships within rural areas.

7. In a rather terse article, Meillassoux (1973) presents an analysis of peasant social organization which successfully links the forces and relations of production. He argues that the social organization of the peasantry evolves from the nature of agriculture itself. The crucial variable in the West African cases he has studied is that labor is invested in the land with the expectation of a later return. This means that there must be both cooperation in production and arrangements for the storage and distribution of the product during the dry months. Kinship organization evolves to meet these needs as well as the reproduction of the productive unit. This kinship structure then provides the conditions and the ideology for the emergence of the state when some kinship groups, often from outside, are able to impose tribute obligations. With the establishment of a market economy, kinship begins to lose its importance, and the product and the producer (as slave) both acquire an exchange value. Eventually, as the peasant economy is incorporated into a larger capitalist one,

> the elements of production are dissociated further and each becomes an object of property: land, tools, means of production, labour force—now distinguished from the producer himself [Meillassoux, 1973:].

Agriculture is no longer dominant; kinship relations give way to wage relations, and the household takes over the function of reproducing the labor force for capitalist society.

8. In Senegal this elite is referred to as *borom barke*. The term is derived from the Berber *baraka,* but has come to mean simply wealth. The *borom barke* generally have some experience outside the rural economy. Their power and much of their income comes from their access to bank loans and their control over rural credit at much higher rates of interest. Many of them grow not cash crops but millet. At harvest

time, peanuts are worth more than millet, but at the beginning of the next growing season, granaries are low and the millet price is high. Millet can be loaned to those who need it at 100 percent for a three- to five-month period.

9. Scott's argument here reflects the work in the 1920s of the Russian economist, A.V. Chayanov, who argued that neoclassical economics could not explain the peasant economy, in part because certain variables could not be calculated but, more important, because the logic of the peasant household was different from that of the firm. Peasants, Chayanov argued, were involved in a tension between the needs of the household and the drudgery of labor. The way in which the individual household struck the balance reflected the relationship between the number of producers and the number of consumers within the household (that is, the nonproductive young, the nonproductive old, and the sick). Chayanov explains, among other things, why the peasant will work even when the marginal return on labor is close to zero and, conversely, why he will not maximize if maximization involves risks to subsistence (Chayanov, 1966).

10. There were a number of capital-intensive projects which involved mechanization, of which the best known were the Niger project in Mali (Suret-Canale, 1971:275-279) and the ground-nut scheme in Tanzania. These projects tended to founder because of problems of maintaining equipment, high costs, and low return on capital. More recent schemes have often involved animal power, light equipment, and the use of fertilizers and pesticides; in effect, modernization within the framework of the peasant household.

11. Pollet and Winter (1968:510) calculate that the average cultivator works a little over a hectare (about 2.5 acres) with a yield of 600 to 700 kilograms of millet per hectare. Meillassoux (1975b:249) figures that an adult male slave produced a little over a ton of millet in a year. Even if we assume that some work harder, that some crops give better yields, and that some areas are more fertile or better watered, the productivity ceiling is very low in hoe cultivation.

12. In Senegal, there are two famine foods. The fruit of the baobab tree, which is widely distributed, can be eaten; and there are thistles that can be ground into a fine powder.

13. The significant exception seems to be solidarity among age-mates. I knew of two cases of young men who could not work part of the season, one because of illness, the other because he had to return to school. In both cases, age-mates helped out.

14. Geertz (1963), following Goldenweiser, used the term involution

> to describe those culture patterns which, after having reached what would seem to be a definitive form, nonetheless fail either to stabilize or transform themselves into a new pattern but rather continue to develop by becoming internally more complicated [1963:81].

15. Scott (1978) has treated as postpeasant society the two types of stagnation: classical Geertzian involution and that characteristic of labor-exporting areas. Scott suggests that there are significant differences in social structure, culture, and political action between the two types.

16. The effects of involution were worst in South Africa, where Africans have been confined to 13 percent of the arable land (Bundy, 1972, 1979; Wolpe, 1972); client areas totally dependent on migrant labor like Lesotho (Palmer and Parsons, 1977:20-26); and distant areas like northeast Zambia (Cliffe, 1978; Hellen, 1968), where ecologically unfavorable conditions or the absence of cheap transportation

leave people little choice. Muntemba describes in Chapter 7 a part of Zambia where some peasants profited from the development of an urban market. This is also true of Tonga areas, where some returning migrants have invested in agriculture (Cliffe, 1978). In the abstract of an article that unfortunately was not completed in time for publication in this book, Ruth First, Marc Wuyts, and David Wield suggest that in Inhambane province of Mozambique the draining of labor to the South African mines limited the possibilities of richer peasants, but that wages from migration facilitated the emergence of a middle peasant sector. The research brigade working on Inhambane has produced Centro de Estudos Africanos, The Mozambican Miner, and Wuyts (1978). On labor migration, see also F. Wilson (1972a, 1972b) and Wolpe (1972). On Rhodesia, see Arrighi (1970) and Van Onselen (1976); on Zambia, Cliffe (1978); and on Kenya, Van Zwanenberg (1972) and Leys (1975).

17. Richard Roberts and I expect to make just such an argument in an article we are now writing.

REFERENCES

ADAMS, A. (1977). "The Senegal River Valley: what kinds of change." Review of African Political Economy, 10:33-59.

AMIN, S. (1972). "Underdevelopment and dependance in black Africa." Journal of Modern African Studies, 10:503-524.

_____(1973). Le Développement Inégal. Paris: Minuit.

_____(1974a). Accumulation on a world scale. New York: Monthly Review Press.

_____[ed.] (1974b). Modern migrations in West Africa. London: Oxford University Press.

_____[ed.] (1975). L'agriculture africaine et le capitalisme. Paris: Anthropos.

AMSELLE, J. L. (1978). "La conscience paysanne: La révolte de Ouolossébougou (juin 1968, Mali)." Canadian Journal of African Studies, 12:339-355.

ARRIGHI, G. (1970). "Labour supplies in historical perspective: A study of the proletarianization of the African peasantry in Rhodesia." Journal of Development Studies, 6:197-234.

BALANDIER, G. (1953). "Messianism and nationalism in Black Africa." Cahiers Internationaux de Sociologie, 14:41-65.

BARKER, J. (1977). "Stability and stagnation: The state in Senegal." Canadian Journal of African Studies, 11:23-42.

BEER, C. and WILLIAMS, G. (1975). "The politics of the Ibadan peasantry." African Review, 5:235-256.

BERNSTEIN, H. (1978). "Notes on capital and peasantry." Review of African Political Economy, 10:60-71.

BERRY, S. (1975a). Cocoa, custom, and socio-economic change in rural Western Nigeria. Oxford, England: Clarendon.

_____(1975b). "Export growth, entrepreneurship and class formation in rural Western Nigeria." Pp. 75-92 in R.E. Dumett and L. Brainard (eds.), Problems of Rural Development. Leiden: E.J. Brill.

BOSERUP, E. (1970). Woman's role in economic development. London: George Allen & Unwin.

BROCHIER, J. (1968). La diffusion du progrès techniques en milieu rural sénégalais. Paris: Presses universitaires de France.

BUNDY, C. (1972). "The emergence and decline of a South African peasantry." African Affairs, 71:369-388.

_____(1979). The rise and fall of the South African peasantry. Berkeley and Los Angeles: University of California Press.

Centro de Estudos Africanos (1977). The Mozambican miner (Research Director Ruth First). Maputo: Universidade Eduardo Mondlane.

CHAYANOV, A.V. (1966). The theory of peasant economy (D. Thorner, R.E.F. Smith, and B. Kerblay, eds.). Homewood, IL: Irwin.

CLIFFE, L. (1976). "Rural political economy of Africa." in P.C.W. Gutkind and I. Wallerstein (eds.), The political economy of contemporary Africa. Beverly Hills, CA: Sage.

_____(1977). "Rural class formation in East Africa." Journal of Peasant Studies, 4:195-224.

_____(1978). "Labour migration and peasant differentiation: Zambian experiences." Journal of Peasant Studies, 5:326-346.

COHEN, J.M. and WEINTRAUB, D. (1975). Land and peasants in Imperial Ethiopia: The social background to a revolution. Assen: Van Gorcum.

Comité Information Sahel (1974). Qui se nourrit de la famine en Afrique. Paris: Maspero.

COOPER, F. (1977). Plantation slavery on the east coast of Africa. New Haven, CT: Yale University Press.

COPANS, J. [ed.] (1975). Sécheresses et famines du Sahel. Paris: Maspero.

COQUERY-VIDROVITCH, C. (1976). "The political economy of the African peasantry and modes of production." In P. Gutkind and I. Wallerstein (eds.), The political economy of contemporary Africa. Beverly Hills, CA: Sage.

_____(1977). "Mutation de l'impérialisme coloniale français dans les années 30." African Economic History, 4:103-152.

CRUISE O'BRIEN, D. (1971). The Mourides of Senegal. Oxford, England: Clarendon.

_____(1979). "Ruling class and peasantry in Senegal, 1960-1976. The politics of a monocrop economy." In R. Cruise O'Brien (ed.), The political economy of underdevelopment. Dependence in Senegal. Beverly Hills, CA: Sage.

FALLERS, L.A. (1961). "Are African cultivators to be called 'peasants'?" Current Anthropology, 2:108-110.

FRANK, A.G. (1969). Capitalism and underdevelopment in Latin America. New York: Monthly Review Press.

FREUND, W.M. and SHENTON, R.W. (1977). "Vent-for-surplus theory and the economic history of West Africa." Savanna, 6:191-196.

FRIEDMAN, J. (1975). "Tribes, states, and transformations." In Maurice Bloch (ed.), Marxist analyses and social anthropology. London: Malaby.

FRIEDMANN, H. (1979). "Peasants and simple commodity producers: Analytic distinction." (unpublished)

FUREDI, F. (1974). "The social composition of the Mau Mau movement." Journal of Peasant Studies, 1:486-505.

GAMST, F. (1970). "Peasantries and elites without urbanism: The civilization of Ethiopia." Comparative Studies in Society and History, 12:373-392.

GEERTZ, C. (1963). Agricultural involution. Berkeley and Los Angeles: University of California Press.

GODELIER, M. (1977). Perspectives in Marxist anthropology (R. Brain, trans.). Cambridge: Cambridge University Press.

GREGORY, J. and PICHÉ, V. (1978). "African migration and peripheral capitalism." African Perspectives, 1:37-50.

HASWELL, M. (1975). The nature of poverty. London: Macmillan.

HELLEN, J. (1968). Rural Economic Development in Zambia, 1890-1964. Munich: Weltforum Verlag.

HILL, P. (1963). Migrant cocoa-farmers of Southern Ghana. Cambridge: Cambridge University Press.

_____(1970). Studies in rural capitalism in West Africa. Cambridge: Cambridge University Press.

_____(1972). Rural Hausa. Cambridge: Cambridge University Press.

_____(1977). Population, prosperity and poverty. Rural Kano, 1900 and 1970. Cambridge: Cambridge University Press.

HOBEN, A. (1973). Land tenure among the Amhara of Ethiopia. Chicago: University of Chicago Press.

HOGENDORN, J.S. (1976). "The vent-for-surplus model and African cash agriculture to 1914." Savanna, 5:15-28.

_____(1978). "Economic initiative and African cash farming: Precolonial origins and early colonial development." In P. Duignan and L. Gann (eds.), Colonialism in Africa, vol. 4. Cambridge: Cambridge University Press.

HOPKINS, A.C. (1973). An economic history of West Africa. London: Longmans.

HOWARD, R. (1976). "Differential class participation in an African protest movement: The Ghana cocoa boycott of 1937-38." Canadian Journal of African Studies, 10:469-480.

ILIFFE, J. (1967). "The organization of the Maji Maji rebellion." Journal of African History, 8:495-512.

_____(1971). Agricultural change in modern Tanzania: An outline history. Dar-es-Salaam: Historical Association of Tanzania.

ISAACMAN, A. (1976). The tradition of resistance in Mozambique. Anti-colonial activity in the Zambesi Valley 1850-1921. Berkeley and Los Angeles: University of California Press.

_____(1977). "Social banditry in Zimbabwe (Rhodesia) and Mozambique, 1894-1907: An expression of early peasant protest." Journal of Southern African Studies, 4:1-30.

JEWSIEWICKI, B. (1975). Agriculture itinerante et economie capitaliste. Histoire des essais de modernisation de l'agriculture africaine au Zaire à l'époque coloniale. Lubumbashi. (mimeo)

JOSEPH, R.A. (1977). Radical nationalism in Cameroun: Social origins of the U.P.C. Rebellion. London: Oxford University Press.

KLEIN, M.A. (1979). "Colonial rule and structural change: The case of Sine-Saloum." In R. Cruise O'Brien (ed.), The political economy of underdevelopment. Dependence in Senegal. Beverly Hills, CA: Sage.

_____(1967). "The organization of the Maji-Maji Rebellion." Journal of African History, 8:495-512.

KLEIN, M.A. and LOVEJOY, P. (1979). "Slavery in West Africa." In J.S. Hogendorn and H.A. Gemery (eds.), The uncommon market. New York: Academic Press.

KROEBER, A.L. (1948). Anthropology. New York: Harcourt, Brace Jovanovich.

LABOURET, H. (1941). Paysans d'Afrique occidentale. Paris: Gallimard.

LEYS, C. (1975). Underdevelopment in Kenya. London: Heinemann.

LOVEJOY, P. (1978). "Plantations in the economy of the Sokoto Caliphate." Journal of African History, 19:341-368.

MARX, K. (1887). Capital. Moscow: Progress Publishers.

MASON, M. (1973). "Captive and client labour and the economy of the Bida Emirate." Journal of African History, 14:453-471.

MEILLASSOUX, C. (1973). "The social organization of peasantry: The economic basis of kinship." Journal of Peasant Studies, 1:81-90.

_____ [ed.] (1975a). L'esclavage en Afrique précoloniale. Paris: Maspéro.

_____ (1975b). Femmes, greniers et capitaux. Paris: Maspéro.

MIERS, S. and KOPYTOFF, I. [eds.] (1977). Slavery in Africa. Madison: University of Wisconsin Press.

NORMAN, D.W. (1977). "Economic rationality of traditional Hausa dryland farmers in the north of Nigeria." In R.D. Stevens (ed.), Tradition and dynamics in small farm agriculture. Ames: Iowa State University Press.

PAIGE, J. (1975). Agrarian revolution. New York: Free Press.

PALMER, R. (1977). Land and racial domination in Rhodesia. London: Heinemann.

_____ and PARSONS, N. [eds.] (1977). The roots of rural poverty in Central and Southern Africa. London: Heinemann.

PARSONS, N. (1977). "The economic history of Khama's country in Botswana, 1844-1930." In R. Palmer and N. Parsons (eds.), The roots of rural poverty in Central and Southern Africa. London: Heinemann.

POLLET, E. and WINTER, G. (1968). "L'organisation sociale du travail agricuole des Soninke (Dyahunu, Mali)." Cahiers d'Études Africaines, 8:509-534.

POST, K. (1972). " 'Peasantization' and rural political movements in Western Africa." Archives Européennes de Sociologie, 13:223-254.

RAIKES, P. (1978). "Rural differentiation and class formation in Tanzania." Journal of Peasant Studies, 5:326-346.

RANGER, T.O. (1967). Revolt in Southern Rhodesia, 1896-1897. London: Heinemann.

_____ (1971). The agricultural history of Zambia. Lusaka: Historical Association of Zambia.

_____ (1978). "Reflections on peasant research in Central and Southern Africa." Journal of Southern African Studies, 5:99-133.

REDFIELD, R. (1956). Peasant society and culture. Chicago: University of Chicago Press.

REY, P.P. (1976a). Les alliances de classes. Paris: Maspéro.

_____ (ed.) (1976b). Capitalisme négrier. Paris: Maspéro.

RICHARDS, A. (1939). Land, labour and diet in Northern Rhodesia. London: Oxford University Press.

_____ STURROCK, F. and FORTT, J. [eds.] (1973). Subsistence to commercial farming in present-day Buganda. Cambridge: Cambridge University Press.

ROBERTS, R. (1978). "The Maraka and the economy of the middle Niger Valley, 1792-1908." Doctoral dissertation, University of Toronto.

RODNEY, W. (1972). How Europe underdeveloped Africa. London: Bogle L'Ouverture.

Rural Africana (1975). "Rural women: Development or underdevelopment." Special issue, vol. 27.

SAUL, J. (1974). "African peasantries and revolution." Review of African Political Economy, 1:41-68.

_____and WOODS, R. (1971). "African peasantries." in T. Shanin (ed.), Peasants and peasant societies. Harmondsworth: Penguin.

SCOTT, J. (1976). The moral economy of the peasant. Rebellion and subsistence in Southeast Asia. New Haven, CT: Yale University Press.

_____(1977). "Hegemony and the peasantry." Politics and Society, 7:267-296.

_____(1978). "Some notes on post peasant society." Peasant Studies, 7:147-154.

SEDDON, D. [ed.] (1978). Relations of production. London: Cass.

SMITH, M.G. (1960). Government in Zassau, 1800-1950. London: Oxford University Press.

SORRENSON, M.P.K. (1967). Land reform in Kikuyu Country. London: Oxford University Press.

SOUTHALL, R. (1978). "Farmers, traders and brokers in the Gold Coast cocoa economy." Canadian Journal of African Studies, 12:185-211.

SURET-CANALE, J. (1971). French colonialism in tropical Africa 1900-1945 (T. Gottheimer, trans.). New York: Pica.

TOSH, J. (1978). "Lango agriculture during the early colonial period: Land and labour in a cash crop economy." Journal of Africal History, 19:415-439.

VAN ONSELEN, C. (1976). Chibaro. African Mine Labour in Southern Rhodesia 1900-1933. London: Pluto.

VAN ZWANENBERG, R. (1972). The agricultural history of Kenya to 1939. Nairobi: Historical Association of Kenya.

VERGOPOULOS, K. (1978). "Capitalism and peasant productivity." Journal of Peasant Studies, 5:446-465.

WAYNE, J. (1975). "Colonialism and underdevelopment in Kigoma region, Tanzania: A social structural view." Canadian Review of Sociology and Anthropology, 12:316-332.

WELCH, C. (1977). "Peasants as a focus in African studies." African Studies Review, 20:1-7.

WILLIAMS, G. (1976). "Taking the part of peasants: Rural development in Nigeria and Tanzania." In P. Gutkind and I. Wallerstein (eds.), The political economy of contemporary Africa. Beverly Hills, CA: Sage.

WILSON, F. (1971). "Farming, 1866-1966." In M. Wilson and L. Thompson (eds.), The Oxford history of South Africa, vol. II. Oxford, England: Clarendon.

_____(1972a). Labour in the South African gold mines, 1911-1969. Cambridge: Cambridge University Press.

_____(1972b). Migrant labour in South Africa. Johannesburg:

WILSON, M. (1971). "The growth of peasant communities." In M. Wilson and L. Thompson (eds.), The Oxford history of South Africa, vol. II. Oxford, England: Clarendon.

WOLF, E. (1966). Peasants. Englewood Cliffs, NJ: Prentice-Hall.

_____(1969). Peasant wars of the twentieth century. New York: Harper & Row.

WOLPE, H. (1972). "Capitalism and cheap labour-power in South Africa: From segregation to apartheid." Economy and Society, 1:425-456.

WRIGLEY, C.C. (1965). "Kenya: The patterns of economic life, 1902-1945." In V. Harlow and E.M. Chilver (eds.), History of East Africa, Vol. II. Oxford, England: Clarendon.

WUYTS, M. (1978). Peasants and rural economy in Mozambique. Maputo: Universidade Eduardo Mondlane.

1

AFRICAN PEASANTS IN THE TOTALITARIAN COLONIAL SOCIETY OF THE BELGIAN CONGO

BOGUMIL JEWSIEWICKI
Université Laval, Québec

This chapter is an analysis of the evolution of peasants in the Belgian Congo. The colonial regime, which was at first remote from the life of the African cultivator, came to involve itself in the details of daily existence to a degree rarely matched elsewhere. The result was the development of a rather uniform and bleak peasant existence. There was not, however, a mass movement among the peasantry leading to a specific peasant program. This resulted as much from the class interests of the African petit bourgeoisie as from the absence of peasant class consciousness (Jewsiewicki, 1978a). My theoretical framework is rooted in the present debate on modes of production, on primitive accumulation in the transition to the capitalist mode of production, and on the mechanisms of the modern world-system (Gutkind and Wallerstein, 1976; Wallerstein, 1974;

AUTHOR'S NOTE: The author wishes to thank the Social Science and Humanities Research Council of Canada.

Jewsiewicki, 1977b, 1979b; Legassick, 1976; Brenner, 1976; Coquery-Vidrovitch, 1978; Frank, 1978; Amin, 1976).

The authoritarian character of colonial regimes is now clear.[1] Modern European colonization in Africa probably constitutes the most extensive western attempt to build an authoritarian and technocratic state on the myth of the welfare state. One result is that a colonial mode of industrial production is now dominant in almost all nominally independent former colonial territories. The following analyzes the evolution of a petty peasant economy dependent on the world market (Jewsiewicki, 1978a, 1979b).

In a number of works (Jewsiewicki, 1974, 1976a, 1977b) I have tried to describe the Belgian colonial system and depict the way in which the various regional complexes were grouped together politically and economically in the Congo Free State. Among the many attempts of industrial systems to impose "rational" management on both human and natural resources, the Belgian colonial experience is especially interesting. From the time of Leopold II, intimate links were established between the colonial state and Belgian finance (Peemans, 1973). Increasingly, Leopold II saw himself less as the civilizing monarch presiding over a coalition of black African states and more as the manager of a vast economic enterprise designed to guarantee the viability of his political creation. The necessity of providing short-term returns to private capital and payments on a loan by the Belgian state pressed Leopold to turn to management by the state. Between 1890 and 1906, many of the country's resources were placed under state supervision: rubber, ivory, and gold. Whether directly exploited or granted to concessionary companies, state monopolies permitted an economic mobilization which was spectacular in the short term but disastrous in the long term. The bad press which the Congo received in the early years of the century did not prevent Leopold from turning to international capital for a new phase (Slade, 1962; Stengers, 1969). In 1906, the creation of three new companies marked the penetration of industrial capitalism: Union Minière du Haut Katanga in copper (UMHK),

Forminière in diamonds, and the Bas-Congo au Katanga Railroad (BCK).

From 1890 to 1906, colonial exploitation was based on merchant capital. The state extracted surplus value by political coercion in the form of products. Industrial exploitation imposed a new task: the reproduction of human resources. As much from internal reasons (exhaustion of resources) as from external (the drop in world market prices), colonial exploitation could no longer be based on a predatory state. Attempts between 1910 and 1920 to turn over the management of human resources to private enterprise failed and the colonial state was forced to take it over directly from 1920. A similar process took place in transport. The second decade of the century saw a transition from commercial capitalism to industrial capitalism. The creation of Huileries du Congo belge (HCB) by Lever in 1911 marked the entry of industrial capital into the treatment and then later into the cultivation of agricultural products.

The second decade saw the development of one of the dominant traits of Belgian colonialism, the interpenetration of the state and finance capital (Stengers, 1974). Belgian finance capital, having suffered extensive losses in Russia (Baudhuin, 1947:II, 402), found in the administration a "patriotic" support in its efforts to "Belgicize" the colony. (Fetter, 1970:72-93). This process was shaped by Leopoldian traditions, by the financial autonomy of a colony forced to finance itself, by the absence in Belgium of strong colonial pressure groups outside of finance capital, and, finally, by the movement back and forth of personnel between the administration and high finance (Lutumba, 1972). Colonial state investment in big companies increased the identification of the state and colonial high finance.

The liberal phase of Congolese economic history (1912-1931) enabled Société Générale of Belgium to establish its financial control (Peemans, 1970; Joye and Lewin, 1961; Vellut, 1979). Once the process of concentration was completed, Société Générale pushed the state to take control of the management of resources in order to end the inefficient and expensive experiments of liberal capitalism. The welfare state was the logical conclusion of this economic concentration (Jewsiewicki, 1976). Thenceforth, the administration managed both society and economy in close consultation with the principal economic interests. Essentially, the country was divided among diverse monopolies controlled by Société Générale and three smaller financial groups (Vellut, 1975). The degree of destructive pressure by capitalism on precapitalist modes of production, the maintenance of social and political structures, the creation of an industrial proletariat, and the planning of the supply of labor and agricultural products were handled by the state.

From about 1920, we can speak of a process of indigenization. This involved the creation of a special legal category of "native," subject to a customary law, not to the Code Napoleon which applied to whites. All Africans were henceforth "natives"; they were required to carry a pass and were tightly regulated in where they could go and what they could do. The process of indigenization gave the administration control over the economic, social, and political evolution of African societies. From 1921, all Africans were eventually required to return to the rural societies from which they came (Franck, 1924). In this, Colonial Minister Franck was influenced by the British experience of indirect rule, by the brutal proletarianization of industrial Katanga, and by the Flemish experience in Belgium. Racial differences hid behind cultural differences. Any African was a native, attached to a particular society and to a particular subsistence economy. During the teens and early twenties, settler agriculture failed, but monopoly capitalism established its control (Jewsiewicki, 1979a). By 1935, legal status was clearly linked to mode of production and was clearly based on race. Any native was permanently a peasant and temporarily a worker. Even the residents of urban centers, which were stabilized between 1928 and 1935, were urban only during their active lives and only as long as industry needed them (Peerings, 1978). Organized by decrees between 1931 and 1933, this division of society into two orders remained until the late 1950s when a division based on class developed.

World War II clearly showed the limits of village economies based on shifting cultivation; it led also to the first experiment with state planning of the industrial and commercial sector. The necessity of guaranteeing an increase in the African agricultural surplus, the growth of the internal food market, and the integration of local markets for food and labor into a national market led to the first Ten Year Plan (1949-1959). The importance of public investment (especially in infrastructure), the role of the state in controlling prices and wages, and the progressive imposition of administrative control over agricultural structures gave the administration the instruments for overall planning. At the same time, the struggles of the largely bureaucratic black petit bourgeoisie led to its assimilation by the colonial bourgeoisie. From 1947, the administration was conscious that it had to tie this African bourgeoisie to itself. The creation of a bipolar class society composed of a bureaucratic bourgeoisie and a peasantry ended the society of orders. It coincided with the passing of political control over local structures into the hands of this black bourgeoisie. This two-class structure, so typical of the colonial system, is still maintained by the way in which the Zairian economy is integrated into the world industrial economy. The mechanisms for the control of the nonindustrial economy remain the same as in the 1950s (Peemans, 1975; Grun, 1976; Young, 1978).

I. COLONIAL PRIMITIVE ACCUMULATION

Belgian Rural Policy in the Congo

The Leopoldian period was dominated by the necessity of financing the military occupation of the country, mineral exploration, and the delimitation of its borders. The status of the colony denied it access to Belgian public funding. Belgian private capital was largely oriented to other markets (Russia, China, Latin America) and was only marginally involved in the Congo (Baudhuin, 1946). The necessity of an immediate return on capital prevented the formation of fixed capital, except in the case of the railroads, and even there an immediate return was expected. In the particular conditions of African shifting cultivation and in the absence of a massive immigration of European labor, the acquisition of land offered no potential return. Extensive concessions of unknown lands stimulated the first offer of speculative stocks on the European market. However, it quickly became evident that these lands would have no value if local labor could not be mobilized.

1890-1928: The Expropriation of Capital Accumulated by African Modes of Production

The policy of exploiting wild produce under monopolies granted by the state involved controlling men through taxes in kind. In Europe, this was justified as control over vacant lands. The real reason was evident: Each mode of production has its own means. The violent elimination of political and commercial adversaries (Swahili, Portuguese, and Sudanese) was essential given the direct link between political control and an economy of plunder. It is clear that this phase could not remain after the military occupation with which it was associated. Extensive exploitation was hindered by the slow speed at which exploitable resources (wild rubber and ivory) renewed themselves and by a rapid decline in the productivity of gathering activity. Labor, even forced labor, was limited as much by the problem of the labor force reproducing itself as by the low productivity of gathering activity.

Industrial investment (the formation of fixed capital) in mining after 1906 led to three other decisions: the taking over of the Congo by Belgium in 1908, the introduction of commercial freedom in 1910-1912 (creation of a labor market), and the elaboration of the legal framework of a capitalist state from 1910 to 1930 (Napoleonic Civil Code). This phase of primitive accumulation permitted the formation of fixed capital in the mining industry, transport, and commerce. The state left capitalist enterprise freedom of action but helped it in mobilizing African labor. The preference which the larger enterprises claimed from 1919 and received in 1925 was related to the importance to local investment of surplus value coming from the exploitation of capital accumulated by African economies: principally men, but also wild palm, cleared land, and other resources. Primitive accumulation continued along these lines, but in regions different from those exploited by the gathering monopolies before 1910. The proletarianization of clans and lineages led to the appearance of the objective conditions for the promotion of a peasant class in the 1930s (Jewsiewicki, 1978a). State and enterprise used noneconomic mechanisms in creating fixed capital (European agriculture), which became the base of the capitalistic economy. A new mode of production was imposed on the traditional ones while primitive accumulation eroded these very traditional modes. The appearance of both a lumpenproletariat and a real proletariat is marked by the strike movement of 1919 and 1920. (Jewsiewicki, 1974:211-212). African commercial agriculture began to appear in those areas where labor levies led to the destruction of social structures or where the market and the prices justified it. Elsewhere, chiefs were able to create plantations by exploiting local social structures and the powers granted them by the colonial state (Jewsiewicki, 1975, 1977a). The dissolution of precapitalist modes of production was accompanied by pressures for the creation of a national market for goods and services. However, some traders and industrial companies created closed economies where vouchers were used for money or where economic relations were based on levies and not on the market. Nevertheless, the economy of the Congo was progressively opened to the direct pressure of the world economy. We see this in the appearance after World War I of a wide interregional market for palm products and regional markets for food and labor. The color bar henceforth prevented the formation of a class-based colonial society.

At the beginning of the 1920s, the labor market barely existed outside of the largely foreign population of the major cities. Forced recruitment speeded up proletarianization. In the previous decade, primitive accumulation was centered in Katanga. It paid a heavy tribute in men both to the mines and to the war in East Africa. The technology both for the Katangan copper mines and for colonial wars (the massive use of porters) demanded a constant flow of labor. In general, labor power compensated for a low level of investment (Peerings, 1978). Through the early twenties, the regions most affected saw the destruction of traditional social structures, depopulations, and a crisis in the subsistance economy. There was also a similar development around the Kilo-Moto gold mines, near the C.F.L. railroad (Compagnie des Chemins de Fer du Congo Supérieur aux grandes Lacs Africains), in the lower Congo, and later in Kwango.

The effects of World War I on the Belgian economy led to both quantitative and structural changes in the Congolese economy. The flow of Belgian capital toward the Congo (1921-1929) led to tight state control over the use of local resources, especially African labor and largely to protect Belgian capital. The slow rate of population growth within the precapitalist modes of production and the limitations of these same economies in extending agriculture imposed limits on primitive capital accumulation. Proletarianization threatened the ability of societies to reproduce themselves and to feed themselves. By contrast, where the market created a demand for both agricultural products and salaried labor, the development of African commercial agriculture became a brake on the rapid expansion of the colonial capitalist economy (Vellut, 1977). Shifting cultivation to which colonization brought no technological changes could not increase production and provide laborers without compromising its own reproduction. With the increase in agricultural prices, the head tax no longer forced people into the labor market. There could be no real surplus labor in the rural economy without technological change in agriculture.

1928-1946:
Simple Reproduction of African Capital
And the New Division of Labor

In the late twenties, certain large companies—especially Union Minière—were ready to subsidize the transformation within their industrial zones of African shifting cultivation into a system of petty producers. The initial investment in a transport network, in technological innovation, and in relocation of villages would have paid for itself by an anticipated increase in agricultural productivity and by the increased availability of labor, which would, in turn, result from a local demographic revolution. These changes would have enabled the companies to do without labor recruitment in distant areas (Jewsiewicki, 1975). The Depression rendered these proposals dead letter: They were too expensive and were politically unacceptable at a time when the state was refusing any change in the status of the native. Instead, the state decided to extend administrative control over the use of men and arable land by African rural economies. New crops were the only technological change which accompanied the system of obligatory cultivation (Mulambu, 1974). These new crops, like cotton or manioc,[2] often had negative effects on men and on the soil and contributed to peasant hostility.

The Depression led to a "rationalization"[3] of colonial exploitation. The administration chose an option, discussed since 1910, of confining Africans to shifting cultivation and temporary wage labor, reserving to Europeans the market for goods and services. From 1935, African rural economies were limited to shifting agriculture under the control of clans and to the social and physical reproduction of the labor force, both rural and industrial. The African producer lost the right to transform agricultural products: to extract palm oil, to husk rice, and, later, to mill manioc and maize. The massive participation of women and children in agricultural labor and public works was guaranteed, though the law spoke only of men. Rigorous and coercive agricultural planning, the control of prices lowered by 50 percent to 80 percent during the Great Depression, and tight regulations of labor movement prevented African participation outside the state-controlled market. The state decided what peasants could grow, what prices they would receive, and what areas would provide labor for the mines. Africans were unable to hire labor because of the 1922 law on labor contracts between Europeans and Africans and a 1933 decree on obligatory cultivation.

African chiefs were denied as state functionaries the right of new economic activity. Finally, Africans as natives were denied the right to register land as private property and immatriculation was stopped. This in turn denied Africans access to credit. These legal measures of the 1930s gave a profound economic sense to the legal indigenization of Africans during the 1920s (Jewsiewicki, 1975). As natives, they were not subject to the Civil Code and therefore could not be the agents of a capitalist economy.

A 1931 decree recognized the existence of African urban communities, but Africans were not conceived as permanent urban residents. The administration and the private companies feared that complete proletarianization in the cities would put the cost of the reproduction of industrial labor on the Congolese capitalist economy and create grave social problems. Urban centers were places for a temporary, albeit often long, stay. The old, the sick, and the unemployed had to return to the villages. The European industrial economy was concerned that the worker remain rooted in his traditional culture and on good terms with his native community: customary law tribunals, "native" chiefs for urban communities, traditional marriage with bride-price, and so on.

This policy permitted the administration to limit the social effects of primitive capital accumulation. It also permitted the maintenance of low wages (Peemans, 1970) by putting the costs of reproduction on village economies which became essentially peasant economies. Only a limited amount of skilled labor was reproduced in the labor camps. The divisions between the rural and industrial worlds, between the white world and the black world, and between the capitalist and noncapitalist world were frozen during the thirties. The division into a society of orders—native, peasant, and worker on one side; white agents of the capitalist economy on the other— was henceforth rigorously applied (Jewsiewicki, 1977b).

In 1919, A. Delcommune, a leading Belgian policy maker, underlined that given fluctuations in the world market and regardless of the inelastic supply of agricultural products, only

Africans could provide these products at a price interesting to commerce. The bankruptcy of a large European enterprise would be a tragedy for the colonial capitalist economy and would reduce the availability of capital and render it more expensive. The unpurchased harvest of hundreds of thousands of Africans would only be a minor incident.

Cotton was organized from 1920 into purchasing zones, each of which contained a monopoly purchaser and tens of thousands of cultivators. The administration set minimum prices and the minimum area each cultivator had to work. The attempts at "collaboration" between African cultivators and European enterprises were thenceforth based on this cotton organization. Africans were to produce product X in quantity Y at a price set by the administration. The enterprise committed itself to buy the product, to transform it, and to export it. The enterprise also committed itself to invest, but these investments were limited to the transformation and marketing of the product, including the transport from the marketing center. This "collaboration" could not bring technological change, although it modified the African division of labor and introduced a new organization. It remained linked to obligatory cultivation and thus to extraeconomic constraint.

The depression profoundly affected the colonial economy, which was saved from bankruptcy only by putting the weight of its difficulties on African rural economies. Their supply of products was increased at a time when the purchasing price dropped 80 percent by comparison to the late 1920s (Jewsiewicki, 1977a). After briefly hesitating between the transformation of African shifting agriculture into a system of petty producers and collaboration between Africans and Europeans, the latter formula won out by 1933. The spread of obligatory cultivation confirmed the collaboration formula. During the '30s, the system for exploiting cotton—including the monopoly purchasing zones—was extended to palm fruits and rice. It was applied to milk products in Oriental Province after European settlers took over African cooperative dairies. The construction and maintenance of the local transport infrastructure was assigned to African rural communities.

Obligatory cultivation coupled with the collaboration formula permitted a more intensive and a more "rational" exploitation of nonindustrial modes of production. A series of measures, both political and economic, during the '30s nearly kept peasants from any occupation other than agricultural production, gathering of wild produce such as palm nuts and copal, and reproduction of the labor force. Traditional craft work, local trade, hunting, and gathering of food products declined and often disappeared. In order to increase productive labor, the administration circumscribed social rituals blamed for "laziness"—for example, initiation schools and dances—except on Saturdays and holidays (Gevaerts, 1945, 1953; Turnbull, 1962). The extension of manioc led to an increase in productivity both for subsistence and for the food trade. There was no discussion of nutritional problems created by this technological change and aggravated by the decline of hunting and food-gathering (Jewsiewicki, 1979c). Finally, in measures taken in the late 1930s, perennial cultures, except for palm oil, were restricted to Europeans. The situation then deteriorated during World War II. Though the gravity of the war-time crisis was exceptional (Jewsiewicki et al., 1975), the situation was a logical consequence of the evolution described. The increasing price of consumer goods coupled with the stagnation of agricultural prices paid to the producer led to a sharp drop in real individual income, although production almost doubled (Thibangu, 1976). Constraint was more necessary than ever in order to maintain and stimulate productive effort. Inadequate resources, the necessity of more work, and the movement of people into wage labor all led to a drastic reduction in the reproduction of the labor force and in the productivity of the soil. Reports on cotton tell of the exhaustion of lands near villages. The press, missionaries, and colonial authorities all complained about the social and demographic crisis. The political dimension of the crisis was shown by the Manono demonstration, the Masisi revolt, and the rural reaction to the Luluabourg mutiny (Gambo, 1974; Lovens, 1974).

1949 and After:
Increased Reproduction and
The Breakthrough to a Class Society

After 1947, the cotton companies demanded the massive transformation of the native peasantry through the *paysannat* system in order to avoid the destruction of capital in land (Brixhe, 1958). Structural changes in both world economy and colonial economy imposed new tasks on the Congolese economy.

The Ten Year Plan of 1949 recognized the need to increase rural revenue. Its authors were explicit:

> [the] internal market should be stimulated by more abundant and more widely distributed revenues, which would be spent locally and stimulate a new cycle of production. . . .
> This vast internal market so avid for consumer goods, so apt to supply its own needs, will be the stable and indefinitely expandable base for a growing congolese economy [Ten Year Plan, 1949:XXI, XXV].

And here is the principle of agricultural development, strangely similar to that of the early 30's:

> Public authority should not be satisfied with maintaining and clearing arable lands: it should assume direct responsibility for the development of native agriculture [Ten Year Plan, 1949:XXXIII].

"Native" agriculture was assigned, however, only a meager 20 percent of the resources planned for "native welfare." The slogan, or catchphrase, was the native *paysannat:*[4]

> The expression 'native paysannat' is suggestive. Even today, rural populations are satisfied to scratch from the soil a meager sustenance. Our present duty is to create a race of peasants attached to the soil and capable of extracting a sufficient profit from it. A short time ago, we tried to group people along the roads. This policy made administration more easy, but it was bad for agriculture. We have to encourage the return to fertile lands; these should preferably be marked out by scientific enquiry [Ten Year Plan, 1949:XXXIV].

The *paysannat,* conceived during a time of crisis, promised a vast transformation of African agriculture, but these plans were soon slowed up. Direct constraint, obligatory cultivation, and "collaboration" were favored by the administration and by Belgian capital. Meanwhile, a colonial research institute (Institut National pour l'Etude Agronomique du Congo Belge) experimented timidly with about a hundred peasants. The formulas articulated during the war were to permit, by careful crop rotation, the maintenance and even an increase in the productivity of the soil. In *paysannats* where annual cultures were predominant individual tenure was ruled out, but in those with perennial cultures it was applied without receiving legal sanction. The *paysannat* formula would have revolutionized African agriculture through a judicious choice of lands, considerable investment, the introduction of fertilizer, partial mechanization, cooperatives, and a vast educational effort. The *paysannat* became a simple agrarian reform replacing direct constraint with a program of crop rotation—largely because it was carried out in haste for essentially political reasons—or to improve cotton yields by integrating it in the cycle of food crops. The capital investment was not available. The *paysannat* was thus a vast fraud designed to reestablish control over the peasantry and improve the quality and increase the quantity of agricultural produce, while keeping the peasant outside the market and under administrative constraint. Compulsory rotation schedules involving specific crops were stretched over about a dozen years, making it difficult for peasants to respond to increases in demand for various products. Increased returns for principal crops because of the increased investment of labor made it possible to keep food prices low and control the cost of reproduction of the labor force. Rural revenues remained low after a brief period of improvement in the early 1950s. Their share of total African revenue dropped between 1950 and 1958. Lower prices made it possible to control the level of African wages and guarantee a return to local capitalist industry.

Although the principle of keeping the different rural regions more or less equal was maintained until 1959, zones of rural economic growth were set up. These were designed to create a rural bourgeoisie of petty producers. An alliance with this group seemed indispensable given the inevitable rate of proletarianization. The Ten Year Plan also involved a new phase of economic growth in which the *paysannats* were to play an important role. Greater control was to be exercised over areas using modern technology and over areas where there was an interaction of modes of production, while the hinterland was increasingly to be left to African petty producers. These petty producers were to take over certain perennial crops such as coffee, cocoa, and rubber, while the capitalist economy continued to control transformation. This new collaboration found its first expression in the cotton decree of 1947. The same type of change was introduced when retail trade was opened to the local bourgeoisie, while European capital concentrated on wholesale commerce and export-import.

Certain rural zones were assigned to annual agriculture, to the reproduction of the industrial labor force, to African petty producers, and to commerce. This division of the labor force was possible because of the demographic revolution which matured in the 50s as a result of better medical care and the application of the Ten Year Plan. These changes were reflected in laws suppressing racial segregation and opening the exploitation of noncapitalist modes of production to the African petty bourgeoisie. The process was too slow and the 1957 decree establishing a new administrative formula in local circumscriptions came too late for the petty bourgeoisie to really take power and effectively control the peasantry and the proletariate.

Once the state was turned over to this bureaucratic bourgeoisie in 1960, the metropolitan administration was no longer responsible for the social and political problems of urban and rural areas. International capital still controlled areas with a high concentration of modern technology and the points of articulation between the local and world economy. In contrast to some other African countries, the petty producers of the Congo, very weak economically and not yet organized politically, were swept up in rural revolts and then crushed. An intermediate group, as much rural as urban, which was developing as a petit commercial bourgeoisie disappeared between 1964 and 1968, and the bipolar structure (modern/traditional) of former colonial society was maintained. Zaire remains the weak point of the neocolonial system; the contradictions of that system are more clearly visible than anywhere else.

II. COLONIAL POLICY IN PRACTICE

The documents which follow were chosen to illustrate the effects of the economic, social, and political ascendancy of the colonial state. Each represents a given period, often related to a specific form of industrial ascendancy over rural society, and gives us a picture of a given form of exploitation. The collaboration formula was first applied in the 1920s by the H.C.B. (Huileries du Congo Belge). The Pende revolt of 1931 led to reforms in its application, but the formula was extended to other regions in the 30s. It was the formula best adapted to this stage of the evolution of the colonial economy and to its integration in the international capitalist economy. The policy was extended and modernized. Roads constructed by Africans facilitated communications, while agricultural agents were increasingly African. An anecdote helps us understand the change. A doctor, who worked for the H.C.B. from 1927 to 1930, told us:

> When I felt that it was necessary to whip someone I ordered a native chief, a decorated chief, to do it because he had that right toward his subjects. [Gordzialkowski, n.d.:105].

The abuses necessary to maintain and increase agricultural production could thenceforth be attributed to the savagery of Africans and to their customs. The marking out of monopoly zones helped the administration with its planning; that is, in using compulsory cultivation to guarantee the supply of export products. Collaboration assured the supply of family labor within a regulated market and cut Africans out of the transformation of agricultural primary products.

Free African Agriculture,
Or Collaboration

By the mid-20s, colonial opinion was increasingly in agreement that all agriculture except plantations must be assigned to Africans, with all other activities reserved to Europeans. This policy was confirmed by a 1933 decree, but this did not prevent the use of African cultivators as temporary wage workers. I have elsewhere shown that African cultivators could respond "rationally" to the demands of the market with increased production (Jewsiewicki, 1977a). Without repeating this material, let me cite a Union Minière report for Katanga. "Encouraged by the existence of a close and sizable market, blacks from these territories (Elisabethville, Jadotville, Bukama) have begun to cultivate the land" (Province du Katanga, 1934:98). The phenomenon was not limited to Katanga: African peasants of the Madimba region (Lower Congo), to take another case, became suppliers of manioc for Leopoldville.

In contrast, I would like to indicate the means necessary to obtain the collaboration of African peasants in those regions where their palm trees were expropriated and they were then forced to work on them:

> The labor imposed by the H.C.B. on the natives with the effective, but not official aid of the administration . . . consists of furnishing palm nuts to the factories. . . . We try to create vital needs that he can only satisfy by earning money, but at the same time, we use pressure, we threaten harassment, and we use methods which are strangely reminiscent of those used by slave traders. . . . Blacks will only work under pressure and not to earn money. Some of them flee to the mission, but they are unhappy because they must also work there. . . . She [the negress] is supposed to remove from the fruit the hard and fibrous parts, which is a considerable work, and then carry a basket weighing 20 to 30 kilograms to the factory. . . .

> To those tasks already mentioned and themselves hard, sometimes going beyond human possibility, there is also a daily walk of 10 to 30 kilometers, half of it with a heavy basket on the head. As with the pounding of manioc, we see old women deformed by

illness, women with children on their backs; pregnant women, and pre-adolescent girls aging prematurely (Gordzialkowski, n.d.: 78-80).

The observations of the H.C.B. doctor should be supplemented by a high colonial official, who was a member of the Commission de la main d'oeuvre indigène and later Governor General:

> [Pressure] sometimes takes forms which are hard to justify, as when the District orders the transfer of an agent to a factory where production has flagged, to remain until the return has "become normal"—without any effort to find the causes of the drop in production. This distaste for the cutter's job is widespread in Kwango. . . .
>
> It is difficult to explain except by the conditions imposed on this category of worker. We demand a constant return from them although palm kernel production is seasonal. They are plagued by supervisors, whose maladroit interference deprives them of any liberty. We carefully measure out the leaves necessary for their participation in tribal life, in agriculture, in the repair of their huts. Finally, carrying the fruit demands the daily participation of women, extra work for them; this makes it more difficult for cutters to get married, which makes the job unpopular [Ryckmans, 1931:40-42].

And here are the methods described by the European chief of an H.C.B. "industrial village" during the same period:

> In order to keep the native population submitted and working regularly, there is a special group of agricultural agents. . . . They are responsible for the increase in production. These functionaries, inundated by circulars and letters, which are always unhappy with the slow growth in production, soon exhaust the legal means of forcing natives to work harder. The agricultural agent has become a policeman, fulfilling his duties without conviction and with resignation [Debczynski, 1928: 249-250].

Compulsory Cultivation
And Colonial Planning

The compulsory cultivation of food crops for local use was no less restraining when combined with other legal obligations. In 1932, a missionary at Rugari (Burundi) wrote in his diary:

During the visit of the Resident . . . I remarked that *the rains being a month and a half late and the natives having waited impatiently to plant their crops, it would be unwise to stop them from doing it* by imposing numerous labor levies which would do nothing to prevent an immediate famine: coffee campaign, manioc campaign, eucalyptus campaign, buckwheat campaign, public works (the dispensary at Kinazi and elsewhere) etc., etc., maintenance of the roads, the quest for tax books demanding a continual coming and going to Muhinga, the transport of manioc shoots by our people to Ruanda (people who did not have enough themselves and who had to go to M. Merz and pay 5 francs for each load and God knows how many loads are necessary to plant a field 50 meters by 25, as ordered). I pointed out that in addition there was in the area an epidemic of abscesses, condemning sometimes as many as five people in a household to inactivity. . . . That many men had left for the English colonies so that all these corvées fell on those remaining, and finally that at any moment, the order could be given to fight . . . locusts [italics in original].

In the same diary, a year later, the 507 taxable subjects of a neighboring subchiefship were distributed as follows:

left for other chiefs	36
left for Bukoba (towards Uganda)	118
too old to work	37
sick or crippled	17
pages of the chief	7
employees of the mission (tax exempt)	19
aides of the sub-chief	16
aides of the local administrative agent	15
	265

Thus there are available for taxes and levies:	242
But, every labor levy is	140
Which leaves	102

Without counting 10 herdsmen watching the cattle and those who bring the workers their food it is almost the whole population which is on their feet, if we except the women, and they speak of ill will [Chrétien, 1973:16-17].

An examination of agricultural planning demonstrates the real goal of compulsory cultivation, the cheap provisioning of the industrial workers, and the totalitarian nature of the system. The colonial administrators were astonished that Africans did not like the system and could find no explanation other than their laziness or lack of economic rationality.

Let us now look at compulsory export crops. The impact of the collaboration system, in which it was central, was profound. The situation described below, without being exceptional, took place during World War II, when the use of direct compulsion reached its peak. Except for the compulsory gathering of wild rubber, it was the same as the situation before the war. The limits on legal compulsion, which were increased to 120 days during the war, generally had little relationship to the reality of the work imposed. Requirements were always shaped by the demands of the local colonial economy, while no norm effectively limited the number of days of compulsory labor. Both before and during the war, colonial functionaries acted arbitrarily. The impact of this system on life and social structure was profound.

> Seed [cotton] is generally distributed in October and November. The native, who has only the slightest idea of the secrets of our calendar and who has been taught by experience and previous disappointments to be distrustful and prudent, remains anxiously in his village. There is no way to leave for a palaver to claim a debt, to mourn an old aunt—because these people are constantly in mourning—to greet an influential relative, or for the service of a White from whom he expects something. . . . Finally, the time comes for the preparation of the cotton field—heavy labor, for which the women and kids are mobilised, then seeding and selection. . . . Some weeds in the field; the whip; not enough land in cultivation: a violation, fine, jail, whip!!! . . .
>
> Cotton demands continuous maintenance because weeds grow quicker than cotton and woe to the Negro if his field is not neat; no more strolls and hunting parties, no more endless palavers at the Chief's court, no more palm wine drinking parties in which each family in turn invites everyone in, little clan feasts. . . . We have invented no better way of destroying native customs, a real taboo for the administration, than cotton. . . . The harvest begins in June, it demands great care and constant presence. In the village, the cotton must be left out in the sun. For this, the

black must make a little granary with a screen in front on pilings. In the meantime, the cultivator must equip himself with large baskets in order to carry the cotton to market. His evenings are busy cleaning the cotton, dry leaves and other dirt must be removed, as must yellow capsules which did not fully ripen. Market days are set in advance and the police come to the villages to alert people. In spite of a real effort by the purchaser, sometimes, for various reasons he is not there on the date set. Those who have no brothers in the market village must tighten their belts.

And it is this which weighs heavily on the black and makes him detest this crop. In setting a low price for the cultivator, we have not taken account of his loss of freedom of movement, this is the insupportable ball and chain for the black. It is manifestly inadequate. In this forced culture, the black takes all the risks: drought (like this year), plant lice, caterpillars, insects, locusts, floods, poor land, the fluctuation of the world market, our savage has everything against him. The purchaser only knows and buys clean cotton. The native who receives only 80 francs has worked as much as he who receives 250 francs. But this alone cannot fully explain the tendancy to desert the village. . . . In addition to the imposition of cotton, the black has an infinity of other obligations. Starting this year, he must cultivate a small plot of peanuts. As it is a crop that he has planted for a long time, and which, furthermore, is remunerative, he submits willingly. Let us pass to the public works which the chiefships must carry out during the year: keep the village clean, which in administrative terms means the clearing of grass, bushes and shrubs within 100 meters of the most distant habitation; clear the banks of any watercourse which goes through the village up to 100 meters above and below the village; construct and maintain a prison, clear the trails and local automobile roads, fix up the resthouse, construct one or more schools. All this is done before a large force of police who question the intentions of the person in energetic and unequivocal terms. However, the black must live and take care of his subsistence. Enough manioc is available—I will explain why further down—he has peanuts, but millet, sweet potatoes, palm oil, beans, tobacco, the maintenance of palm trees, all that demands more work. As we see, the native of the interior is badgered, those harsher would say, tracked down like an animal. And in all of this, what happens to fishing and hunting? My man does not live by manioc and peanuts alone.[5]

The provincial commissioner responded to Geldhof's letter in the following terms:

> We must remember that most native work has a familial character. Women and children from their 10th year participate actively in it.
>
> This allows us, within certain limits, a certain elasticity in execution, although the legal prescriptions in the matter are rather strict as far as the division between subjects and the duration of time spent on work imposed.
>
> If we recall that our estimates of the time needed to carry out tasks is inspired by a normal work schedule, but which is scarcely the custom of rural natives, if we consider that agricultural labor does not necessarily require regularity, that there are empty periods when agricultural activities slow up, if we consider that outside of the compulsory crops there are complementary food crops (manioc, sorgho, maize, millet, sweet potatoes, éleusine, beans), it is easy to understand that, in fact, the native is concerned with work almost the whole year and has only rare occasions to move around or to seek pleasures which once formed the essence of his existence. And when the missionary in the letter to which I alluded above says of compulsory crops "that they deprive the native of 11 months of liberty," excessive language is certainly evident, but the thought expressed means that the native is no longer free to act as he wishes—that is to say, he sees himself more and more obliged to dismiss from his economic, domestic and social life whims, negligence, and improvidence, and to submit to more and more strict rules of order, perseverance and work. There is no doubt that the native feels himself oppressed by a condition he does not understand, of which he does not realize the charitable intentions or the long-range effect. But the way followed cannot be abandoned.[6]

Before looking at the last attempt of colonial policy to control the rural world—the *paysannats*—let us look briefly at two political questions: the personnel enforcing compulsory cultivation and the mechanisms for the control of the equilibrium between the supply of cheap industrial labor and the supply of food. For the first question, here is the autobiography of a Ruandan chief named in 1931:

> I was designated sous-chef and the people of the colline were afraid of me. Every morning I received many pots of liquor. In

those days people had boundless respect for sous-chefs. No one passed me without a formal salutation. They had to bow down before me, then I would respond with a greeting. My wife had cultivated the land before I became sous-chef, but afterwards she no longer recognized what a hoe was. Instead she made people who had not paid up cultivate for us.

My day as a sous-chef consisted of going about the sous-chefferie severely punishing all those who did not make regular offerings to me and by doing that to make my wishes known. They worked hard but were malcontent. It was exactly a year and six months when I ceased to be sous-chef. . . . it was really because people accused me unjustly of making them pay for something without giving them a receipt.

Two days later I was summoned to the Tribunal of the Territory about this. However, the Hutu who had made the complaint did not win the case. The Administrator, though, told me that his decision would remain unchanged. In the few days I had left before my removal from office I went to Kigali to explain myself to the Resident. . . .

I continued my work as before, but I kept after that fellow who had accused me before the Tribunal. I made my overseer make him do forced labor. . . . One of my overseers with more schooling than me kept wanting to replace me. It was he who had tried to get me fired. . . .

A month later I received the letter of the Resident of Rwanda. It authorized me to work in the Territory of Astrida as a Moniteur-café. I worked with an agronomist who was favorably disposed toward me but life became more and more difficult. The salary was not enough to keep me and I no longer received any gratituities in kind. I was like an unemployed person who earned practically nothing a month [Codere, 1973:79-81].

Let us add a few words on the agricultural agents and how they went far beyond their legal obligations.

During his daily report of November 22, a police officer noted:

For his part, the agricultural auxiliary Louis declared. . . "I simply said that the women who were not at work the next day would be brought before the police judge at Mashala."

It is clear from this dossier that the agricultural agent believes that women are legally subject to agricultural work and that the judicial police of Gingne are equally convinced of this.[7]

Finally, the territorial administrators were not always neutral mediators between diverse economic interests. It was easy for the functionary of a totalitarian administration to pass from the legal obligation to work to the use of coercion for illegal tasks:

> Although there was no legal obligation for natives to cultivate manioc or make manioc flour, some territorial administrators forced natives to furnish a fixed amount of manioc flour exclusively to Interfina. In order to do this, they used their control records, they brought women before the native courts, and the natives were forced to construct sheds—storage facilities for the flour.[8]

Governor General Pierre Ryckmans tells how the equilibrium was maintained between the supply of wage labor and agricultural products:

> As long as he is well treated, well fed, better housed than in his village, the native is not hard to please on salary questions. He escapes the corvées, the harassment of local officials, the boredom of the village [Ryckmans, 1937:10].

> [A]ny wage worker is a possible cultivator. It is among the producers that wage labor is recruited and they become cultivators again as soon as they are dismissed. The worker does not only compare his present income to his former income: he also compares what he earns in working for an employer to what he could earn in producing for an exporter. This comparison shows him how much he has lost from devaluation (that of 1935): the cultivator earns in cloth 40% more than the worker who earlier, was able to buy as much as him. We must impose an export tax on the cultivator in order to reduce the gap [Ryckmans, 1936:6].

We can also add here the opinions of the Union Minière representatives:

> We should at all costs avoid the proletarianisation of the masses living around our grand centers. Near the industrial centers we should create prosperous communities of farmers, communities which will be the necessary counter-weight to the maintenance of the moral equilibrium of the workers. Old workers will retire there and they will make it possible for industry to find there the labor that it will need.[9]

Native *Paysannats*

Here are the first political goals of the native *paysannats,* expressed both in relationship to the future evolution of the peasantry and to the necessary modification of previous political instruments.

Vade Mecum of the Assistant Territorial Administrators for Paysannats

I. Preliminary Note

The goal of the paysannats is at the same time social, agricultural and economic.

Social: The social equilibrium demands that industry employ only the number of persons absolutely necessary to its operation. This number will be such that the needs of the urban population for food can easily be satisfied by the production of the rural population. . . . We must attach the cultivator to the soil and must see to it that a lack of resources does not force him to emigrate to the cities where he will swell the ranks of a proletariate whose fate is too tied to economic fluctuations. . . .

Economic: It is essential to create in the Congo a peasant class, attached to its landed property and possessing a balanced income which enables it to deal with economic reverses. This stabilised class is a guarantee of peace within the future middle class of the country, that of the well-to-do peasant, owner of land and buildings, attached by tradition and interest to social peace, hostile to any subversive propaganda, the enemy of political adventure. This population can even be a refuge for unemployed workers who will flow back to their home areas during economic crises. . . .

2. Recreate within Native Society an Atmosphere of Confidence

The T.O.E. [compulsory cultivation] have almost everywhere created a permanent malaise, which expresses itself by defiance, by an increasing instability, by emigration, by a reserve in contacts with the agents of the administration, even a certain enmity in these relationships.

Everyone agrees that the period of compulsory cultivation is ending.

It is not possible, however, without risk to the country's economy, to move hastily to an entirely free agriculture. We must go through a transitional period. Experiments made almost everywhere in the Congo to stabilise the rural economy have been given concrete form under the term "paysannat", which has a different meaning in areas of annual and of perennial crops. . . .

While the territorial agent and the agronomist not attached to a paysannat will continue to demand a gradually reduced obligation in order to bridge the gap, the Assistant Territorial Administrator in the paysannat will loosen the grip, regain the confidence of natives by a moderate and not repressive intervention, and will substitute persuasion for coercion [Geurts, n.d.:1-20].

The confidential report cited below helps us to understand what the *paysannat* became in annual crop areas. It also indicates problems for the future evolution of African agriculture in Zaire. More subtle in form, but no less restrictive than compulsory cultivation, the *paysannat* could not in areas of perennial crops transform shifting cultivation into intensive agriculture without massive investments and, thus, without a considerable increase in agricultural prices. However, the increase in prices was not and is not possible because of the way the economy is integrated into the world economy. Massive investments in agriculture have never been planned, while the ability of the cultivator on the edge of impoverishment to invest is almost nonexistent. The following document is a report of the agricultural service of Union Minière from 1954:

Some Asppects of the Agricultural Paysannat in Kanda-Kanda Territory

The present note, which abridges an inquiry made in September 1954, summarizes conversations we had with administrative personnel, Missionaries, company officials and private persons.

Given the strictly confidential character of the opinions expressed, this note should not be published or cited anywhere. Furthermore, it should be given privately only to trustworthy people.

I. Regime of the Paysannat

The paysannat formula is based on careful respect for an approved rotation of crops and fallow. Installation was possible using two methods:

1. Freely constituted communities taking only cultivators who are interested and worthy, and getting for them as a result aid which would supplement their individual efforts and under an educational form. The grant of certain privileges to better develop the social, economic and political role of the peasant would contribute to the prestige and free extension of the paysannat.

2. A complete region subject to the paysannat after studies of the political structure, landed property, and the productive value of the latter.

The second formula was chosen and applied by the government. In order to deal with the inertia of the masses and the opposition of many natives to the paysannat, the only possible method in this case was the imposition by force. . . .

The peasants now find themselves surveyed, grouped as much as possible on their clan lands; not all, which produces some friction. The blocks are not all homogeneous in soil fertility. Some have received rich fields, others poor ones without much chance of improvement.

Many cultivators who were poorly surveyed continue to cultivate small fertile depressions (for food crops), in addition to the assigned lands which increases their total returns. . . .

V. The Paysannat at Kanda-Kanda and European Commerce

Until the present, the peasants have successfully kept the sale prices of their products high. They find these prices fair and in relation to the prices they pay for things they buy. . . . European traders buy few of the products (except cotton bought by Cotonco). It is clear that they do not know how to profit from a system of combined buying and selling, which has made the' fortune of many traders.

Result: more and more white traders are leaving the country to settle elsewhere.

In our opinion, the growth of trade in native hands should be considered a good thing in itself and evidence of the development and entrepreneurial spirit of these peoples.

VII. The Potential Future Evolution of the Paysannat in Kanda-Kanda Territory

All of the people consulted agreed that in the present situation it is no longer possible to retreat. According to them, it is necessary to continue to use constraint and to hope that with the development of peasant needs, the introduction of new methods of tillage, chemical fertilizers and transport, restrictions can gradually be relaxed after a number of years. If the less well endowed leave, they hope that the great majority will want to remain. The methods of constraint used by the government which have succeeded only in alienating the better endowed peasants will not bring that date closer and will no longer permit us to hope for a success by the creation of new free communities. . . .

We can predict that in Kanda-Kanda territory, the production of food will increase during the coming years. The natives of this territory (planters and wage-laborers) are all well nourished. Local consumption of flour will thus have only a slight increase. Export will only be possible when the native agrees to accept a lower price for his products. The tendency to sell maize in the form of beer and alcohol at more remunerative prices will increase unless the Government takes severe and drastic measures.

VIII. Conclusion

The Kanda-Kanda territory has always been a region densely populated by native cultivators settled on lands of average fertility for the province of Kasai. The future of the paysannats centers seems gloomy and dangerous [Debra, 1954:1-10].

NOTES

1. Julien's recent book (1978) presents undeniable support for this interpretation; he shows the direct nature of an administration often used as an example of indirect administration. The reality of indirect rule in Nigeria was recently questioned by Nwabughuogu (1979).

2. Manioc was not a new crop, since it had been grown in some parts of Zaire since the eighteenth century. However, as a staple food crop, manioc increased rapidly only in the 1920s and '30s at the expense of plantain, sorghum, and millet. It guaranteed a higher productivity for the soil and for labor in a purely quantitative sense, though it has a lower nutritional value (see Jewsiewicki, 1979a).

3. I use the term "rationalization" in the same sense as the marginalist economists. Within their definition, behavior is seen as rational within the context of time and place (Godelier, 1966; Hollis and Nell, 1975).

4. The *paysannat* consisted of a commitment (collective or individual) by the African cultivators to follow a rotation established by the agronomist or, in his absence, by the administrator, on the land whose use was given to him as a member of the *paysannat*. Membership in the *paysannat* guaranteed each member the use of a plot of land for life without promising the right of his son to inherit. In order to provide homogeneous and easily accessible areas, *paysannat* lands were often taken from kinship groups to which members of the *paysannat* did not belong. The *paysannats*

had easier access to public funds for infrastructure and for such social investments as wells and dispensaries.

    5. B. Geldhof to M. Schennicke, May 15, 1943. Archives de la sousregion du Tanganika à Kalémie.

    6. Inspection Report, Prov. Commisioner, Manono Territory, July-August 1943. Archives de la division Régionale des Affaires Politiques du Shaba, Lubumbashi.

    7. Procureur Général to Procureur du Roi, March 27, 1945. Archives du Parquet à Lubumbashi, dossier Kivu-Agriculture.

    8. Procureur Général to Governor General, March 15, 1945. Archives du Parquet à Lubumbashi, dossier Tanganika-Agriculture.

    9. Province of Katanga (1934) Conseil de Province.

REFERENCES

AMIN, S. (1976). Impérialisme et sous-développement en Afrique. Paris: Anthropos.
BAUDHUIN, F. (1946). Histoire économique de la Belgique, 1914-1939. Bruxelles: Bruylant.
BRENNER, R. (1976). "The origins of capitalist development. A critique of Neo-Smithian Marxism." New Left Review, 104:27-59.
BRIXHE, A. (1958). Le coton au Congo belge. Brussels: Ministère du Congo belge et du Ruanda-Urundi.
CHRÉTIEN, J. P. with the collaboration of E. MWOROHA (1973). "Rapport sur les migrations du XXe siècle en Afrique orientale. Le cas de l'émigration des Banyarwanda et des Barundi vers l'Uganda." In Commission Internationale d'Histoire des Mouvements Sociaux et des Structures Sociales, Enquête international portant sur quelques grands mouvements migratoires internationaux de la fin du XVIIIe siècle à nos jours. Paris. (mimeo)
_____(1978). "Des sedentaires devenus migrants: Les motifs des départs des Burundais et des Rwandais vers l'Uganda (1920-1960)." Cultures et développement, 10:71-101.
CODERE, H. (1973). The biography of an African society. Tervuren: Musée Royal de l'Afrique centrale.
COQUERY-VIDROVITCH, C. [ed.] (1978). Connaissance du Tiers-Monde. Paris: Union Générale d'Editions.
DEBCZYNSKI, A. (1928). Dwa lata w Kongu. Warsaw: Dom Ksiazki Polskiej.
DEBRA, A. (1954). "Rapport. Quelques aspects du paysannat agricole dans le territoire de Kanda-Kanda." Union Minière du Haut Katanga. Département M.O.I./Service agronimique, Elisabethville, October 6, 1954, Personnel archives, Gécamines, Lubumbashi, dossier service agronomique.
FETTER, B. (1970). The creation of Elisabethville. Stanford: Hoover Institution.
FRANCK, L. (1924). "Quelques aspects de notre politique indigène au Congo." Etudes de colonisation comparée. Brussels: Goemacze.
FRANK, A.G. (1978). L'accumulation dépendante. Paris: Anthropos.
GAMBO, A. (1974). "L'extension du kitiwala au Kivu et dans les Haut-Zaire (1940-1960). Cas de révolte de Masisi." Memoire de licence, National University of Zaire, Lubumbashi. (unpublished)
GEVAERTS, F. (1945). Vademecum à l'usage des fonctionnaires et agents territoriaux de la Province de Stanleyville. Stanleyville: Direction Provinciale AIMO.

_____(1953). Vade Mecum à l'usage du service territorial. Léopoldville: no publisher.

GODELIER, M. (1966). Rationalité et irrationalité en économie. Paris: Maspéro.

GORDZIALKOWSKI, H. (n.d.) Czarny sen. Lwow-Warsaw: Ksiaznica-Atlas.

GRUN, G. (1976). "Policy making and historic process: Zaire's permanent development crisis." Presented to African Studies Association, Boston.

GUERTS, M. (n.d.). Vade Mecum de l'administrateur territorial assistant paysannat. Archives régionales du Shaba à Lubumbashi, Dossier Paysannat.

GUTKIND, P.C.W. and WALLERSTEIN, I. [eds.] (1976). The political economy of contemporary Africa. Beverly Hills, CA: Sage.

HOLLIS, M. and NELL, E.J. (1975). Rational economic man. Cambridge: Cambridge University Press.

JEWSIEWICKI, B. (1974). "Histoire économique et sociale du Zaire modern. Une conception." Likundoli, 1:205-220.

_____(1975). Agriculture nomade et économie capitaliste. Histoire des essais à modernisation de l'agriculture africaine au Zaire à l'époque coloniale. Lubumbashi: UNAZA.

_____(1976). "L'experience d'un Etat-Providence en Afrique Noire." Reflexions historiques, 2:78-103.

_____(1977a). "Unequal Development, Capitalism and the Katanga Economy, 1919-1940." In R. Palmer and N. Parsons (eds.), Roots of rural poverty in central and southern Africa. London: Heinemann.

_____(1977b). "The great depression and the making of the colonial economic system in the Belgian Congo." African Economic History, 4:153-176.

_____(1978). "Reflexions historiques sur la prise de conscience politique par la paysannerie africaine au Zaire à l'époque coloniale." Presented to the African Studies Association, Baltimore.

_____[ed.] (1979a). "Contributions to a history of agriculture and fishing in Central Africa." African Economic History, 7(special issue):559-572.

_____(1979b). "Le colonat agricole européen au Congo belge, 1910-1960, problèmes politiques et économiques." Journal of African History, 20: 559-572.

_____(1979c). "Zaire enters the world system: Its colonial incorporation as the Belgian Congo, 1885-1960." in G. Gran (ed.), Zaire: The political economy of underdevelopment. New York: Praeger.

_____VELLUT, J.L. and LEMA, K. (1975). "Documents pour servir à l'histoire sociale du Zaire. Grèves du Bas Congo en 1945." Etudes d'histoire africaine, 5:155-188.

JOYE, P. and LEWIN, R. (1961). Les trustes au Congo. Brussells: Société Populaire d'Editions.

JULIEN, C.A. (1978). Le Maroc face aux impérialismes. Paris: Editions Jeune Afrique.

LEGASSICK, M. (1976). "Perspectives on African underdevelopment." Journal of African History, 27:435-440.

LOVENS, M. (1974). La révolte de Masisi-Lubutu (Congo belge, janvier-mai 1944). Cahiers du CEDAF:3-4.

_____(1975). L'effort militaire de guerre au Congo belge (1940-1944). Cahiers du CEDAF:7-8.

LUTUMBU-LU-VILU (1972). Histoire du Zaire. Kinshasa: Ed. Okapi.

MULAMBU-MVULUYA (1974). Cultures obligatoires et colonisation dans l'ex-Congo belge. Cahiers du CEDAF:6-7.

NWABUGHUOGU, A. (1979). "The role of propaganda in the development of indirect rule in Nigeria, 1890-1929." Presented to the 9th Annual Conference of the Canadian Association of African Studies, Winnipeg.

PEEMANS, J.P. (1970). Diffusion du progrès et convergence des prix. Congo-Belgique, 1900-1960. Louvain and Paris: Nawelaerts.

_____(1973). "Capital accumulation in the Congo under colonialism: The role of the state." In L. H. Gann and P. Duignan (eds.), The economics of colonialism, vol. IV. Colonialism in Africa 1870-1960. Cambridge: Cambridge University Press.

_____(1975). "The social and economic development of Zaire since independence: An historical outline." African Affairs, 74:148-169.

PEERINGS, C. (1978). Black mineworkers in Central Africa. London: Heinemann.

Province du Katanga (1934). Conseil de Province. Elisabethville. (mimeo)

RYCKMANS, P. (1931). Rapport de la Commission de la main d'oeuvre indigène: Congo-Kasai. Brussels: Ministère des Colonies.

_____(1936). Discours du Gouverneur Général Ryckmans à l'ouverture du Conseil de Gouvernement. s.l.: Gouvernement Général du Congo belge.

_____(1937a). Discours prononcé par le gouverneur genéra Ryckmans à l'ouverture du Conseil du gouvernement. Léopoldville: Gouvernement Général du Congo belge.

_____(1937b). Discours prononcé par le Gouverneur Général Ryckmans à la séance d'ouverture du Conseil de Gouvernement. Léopoldville: Gouvernement Général du Congo belge.

SLADE, R. (1962). King Leopold's Congo. London: Institute of Race Relations.

STENGERS, J. (1969) "The Congo Free State and the Belgian Congo before 1914." In L. H. Gann and P. Duignan (eds.), Colonialism in Africa, 1870-1960, vol. 1. London: Cambridge University Press.

_____(1974). "La Belgique et le Congo. Politique colonial et décolonisation." In Histoire de la Belgique contemporaine 1914-1970. Brussels: La Renaissance du livre.

Ten Year Plan [Plan décennal pour le développement économique et social du Congo Belge] (1949). Bruxelles: Ed. De Visscher.

THIBANGU KABET (1976). "Demographie, main-d'oeuvre et niveau de vie en territoire de Likasi pendant l'effort de guerre 1940-1945." Bulletin CEPSE, 112-113:31-79.

TURNBULL, C. (1962). The lonely African. New York: Simon & Schuster.

VELLUT, J.L. (1975). "Le Zaire à la péripherie du capitalisme: Quelques perspective historiques." Enquêtes et documents d'histoire africaine, 1:114-151.

_____(1977). "Rural poverty in Western Shaba, c. 1890-1930." in R. Palmer and N. Parsons (eds.), The roots of rural poverty in Central and Southern Africa. London: Heinemann.

_____(1979). "L'impérialisme colonial belge, 1920-1940." Journée d'étude: L'expansion belge aux 19e et 20e siècles. (unpublished)

WALLERSTEIN, I. (1974). The modern world-system. New York: Academic Press.

YOUNG, C. (1978). "Zaire: The unending crisis." Foreign Affairs, 57:169-185.

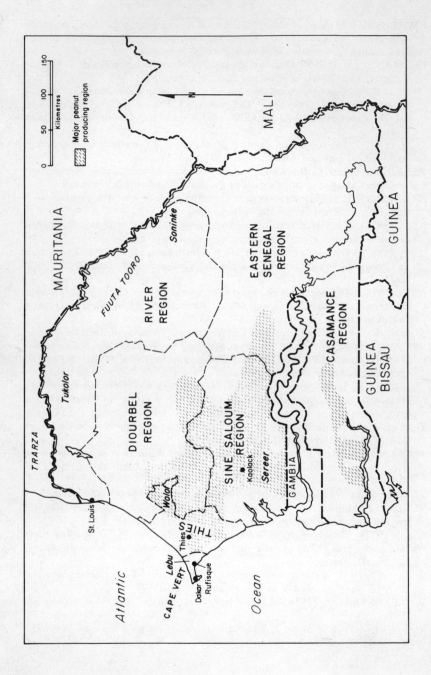

2

FROM SENEGAMBIA
TO SENEGAL:
The Evolution of Peasantries

JEAN COPANS
Centre d'etudes Africaines,
E.H.E.S.S., Paris

A little known and distorted history. We never heard the man from the village speak in those days. Others spoke in his name, people who despised or feared him, who suppressed his anger or treated it as sacrilegious madness. The tensions caused by the uneven distribution of power and profit determined not only the evolution of the production system. It also subjected the entire peasantry to a state of cultural deprivation [Duby, 1975:31].

Natural phenomena (photosynthesis, soil biochemistry) more or less controlled or modified by the peasant societies, ensure the functioning of the whole and its "productivity." In fact they introduce *inertia, constraints, blockages, displacements*. . . . The three sub-parts that compose the agrosystem: the ecological milieu, the peasant society, the plant and animal production are structurally displaced in relation to one another for the elements that constitute them evolve at different speeds [Bertrand and Bertrand, 1975:103].

AUTHOR'S NOTE: We wish to thank S.J. Copans and M. Klein for revising the English draft of this chapter.

The search for modes of production has made a major contribution to anthropological literature (Copans, 1980a). More and more historians and sociologists, political scientists, and even anthropologists are coming to consider the monoethnic approach to African realities as a dead end. Social scientists are questioning the study of closed groups presumed to be more or less homogeneous and autonomous. The transformation of the scale of research is taking place not only because we have more data at our disposal but mainly because historical entities involve groups traditionally defined as sociologically distinct. The uneven evolution and development of social formations has been acknowledged as an object of anthropological inquiry. This enables us to examine the long-term evolution of groups such as agricultural producers or peasants.

I. DO PEASANTS HAVE A HISTORY?

History of Infrastructures
Or of Superstructures?

Anthropology and sociology have always concentrated on rural and agricultural societies in Black Africa, but a cursory review of this literature reveals a fundamental discrepancy between the anthropological view of contemporary peasantry and the history of past peasantries. This discrepancy is both methodological and theoretical. Written and oral sources do not emphasize the same phenomena that fieldwork allows us to observe and describe. Different intellectual and professional traditions determine ideological bases and topical preferences that seem to be value-free and objective. African history is economic and rural only to the extent that the infrastructure, the agricultural producer, is the stake of political power. It is when power has an economic basis (tribute, commerce, raiding) that we have a glimpse of the agricultural universe. History is the history of dominant groups, of the institutions of power, including power within the economic sphere. It tells us little about the nature, the functioning, and the evolution of the productive systems themselves. For periods before 1600, the only options are extrapolation and induction, often using contemporary ethnography or silence.[1] Even after that date, the history of trade, of the exchange of products, of slavery, and, therefore, of modes of levying and production is only partially a history of the infrastructure, of rural production, and of peasantries. It is more a history of processes of circulation than of production; of "circulators" than of producers. But it is this type of history that has pushed us to raise the questions we are putting forward in this chapter.[2] Anthropology and other social sciences such as geography and economics have their merits. Work organization, consumption patterns, land tenure, demographic trends, and the various social forms that connect these factors are common objects of inquiry. Microlevel approaches produce case studies of the productive processes with quantitative data.

In fact, to study producers means to study relations of production and productive forces. Until now, natural environments and their organization have been the domain of descriptive and regionalist geography (Pelissier, 1966). Nevertheless, ecological perspectives and agrosystem theories are becoming more accepted. It is possible that African history will some day inspire the type of questioning we have quoted in the head-notes.

Peasant history is essentially a rural history. This means that a serious study of the peasantry must take into account other factors pertinent to the society as a whole. Therefore, the following domains must be examined:

— The intimate relationship between agricultural production and craft specialization.

— Social status of producers, which reflects a complex system of stratification. In Senegambia, this involves free men, slaves, and members of artisan castes.

— The institutional surplus that can be created to support commercial and urban groups.

— Slavery and ethnic migrations considered as a form of the circulation of the labor force.

Diop (1979), in his detailed thesis on the Wolof, devotes only 70 pages (out of 770) to the traditional economic structure of the peasantry, the castes, and the global society (the relationship between slaves and peasants as producers and the nobles and rulers). This general description concerns four centuries (fifteenth to the nineteenth). Although Diop is mostly concerned with kinship and the larger social structure, his work shows how difficult it is to produce an anthropological history of the peasant producer prior to the massive economic changes of the colonial period.

Many anthropologists, historians, and economists recognize the difficulties, the dead ends, and the theoretical illusions which must be faced if we are to describe the social and production system of the peasantry: the social and family division of labor, the units of consumption and production, the work calendar, and so on. It is difficult to produce a detailed historical account of these themes. The known historical sources have not been analyzed from these new points, and for many questions the data are lacking. The study of slavery has yielded promising results, including even statistical evaluations, but the demographic study of the majority of producers is still underdeveloped. Therefore, in order to view peasantries in historical perspective, we must establish the following facts:

— The social, multiethnic, regional, and international levels of the relevant social formations;
— the periodization which ranks these formations throughout the various stages of both African and world history; and
— the priority that the natural and social systems of production establish over kinship and political structures.

Periodization and Social Space

Theories of the development of underdevelopment and dependency have often insisted upon the importance of periodization of the forms and phases of capitalist expansion. Although some of these theories recognize the autonomy and relevance of African history, its resistance to penetration and domination, and the very fact of change within African societies, they stress the domination of the western world since the late fifteenth or early sixteenth century. The economic relations between Africa and the west, which centered on the export of slaves, gave way to an export of commodities demanded by industrializing Europe. This sharp break has been described by Hopkins (1973:125-126):

> Legitimate commerce therefore enabled small-scale farmers and traders to play an important part in the overseas exchange economy for the first time. In so far as firms of this type and size are the basis of the export economies of most West African states today, it can be said that modernity dates not from the imposition of colonial rule, as used to be thought, but from the early nineteenth century.

This transition from predatory trade to productive trade was thus the decisive change from the point of view of the ordinary African producer. But any periodization of the development of social formations shows an uneven pattern (Copans, 1978), as is well demonstrated by Meillassoux's (1978) work on slavery. Trotsky (1962:21) has written:

> This universal law of unevenness of rhythms produces another law that we can call a law of combined development: it implies the bringing together of various stages, the combination of distinct phases and the mixing of archaic forms with the more modern ones.

The natural environment of African social formations was a *multiethnic space.* The position of each group, the network of relations between them, the installation process, and the contacts between them for trade and for war were constraints on the system of production. Space is seldom viewed as a social factor in itself, but scission, overlapping, expansion, or migration cannot be reduced to a mere expression or symbol of more fundamental social determinants. Social formations, modes of production, and class also operate within a spatial dimension. But Africanists do not agree on the level of social reality that should be studied first. Bomba, a historian (1977: 26) considers that the relationships between ethnic groups can best be studied through the history of family and descent groups; that is, by the genealogical method. Amselle (1977: 274-275), in the conclusion to his study of a Malian trading group, the Korooko, writes that whatever the social group under study, "the relation to the environment constitutes a direct element of its formation and maintenance," and therefore,

> instead of studying isolated societies, we must establish for each period "chains of societies" whose networks appear when we take into account the modes of relations between each of the elements.

These remarks reflect the nature of his research on a group whose occupation is the circulation of goods between various social formations. Curtin (1975), in his remarkable work, describes a trading area, but does not provide any history of modes of production.

We must therefore ask whether a history of social formations from the point of view of the producers is possible if we wish to avoid the pitfalls of direct explanation in terms of one unique causal dimension, whether it be international economies, complementary ecological zones, conflicting political spheres of influence, or simply cultural differentiation.

Circulation and Production: Remarks about Articulation

Contemporary Marxism presents various interpretations which lead in each of these directions. Let us consider a class culturalist view. Anderson, in *Lineages of the Absolutist State* (1976), suggests that we should differentiate precapitalist modes of production by the variety of their superstructures. For Anderson, the plurality of modes results from systems in which the state expropriates surplus and gives importance to various forms of property. He focuses on superstructures on the one hand and circulation on the other, but there seems to be just one mode of production. The vagueness of analysis of Senegambian modes of production results from just such an orientation. This is explained by the limitation of available sources[3] and by the success of circulation-articulation theories.

Some dependency theorists have singled out long-distance trade as the most significant precolonial economic phenomenon

(Coquery-Vidrovitch, 1972). An effort to generalize this interpretation would lead us to the idea that all Asiatic, feudal, or tributary modes of production can be considered as modes of articulating autonomous groups. Peasant producers would thus be articulated to dominant groups through relations of circulation controlled by the state (levies, offerings, slave raids, and so on). Most present efforts of "Marxist" anthropologists to construct a peasant mode of production do not oppose this effort to separate production from other social relations. We would like to argue that even before African agricultural producers became involved in production for the world market, they were being separated from the control of their means of production. We also reject the interpretation which sees small autonomous groups of producers as an agricultural proletariat. A precolonial peasantry existed, produced a surplus, and was involved in exchange of subsistence goods.[4]

The history of colonial, then of capitalist, peasantries cannot be understood without reference to these precolonial processes, because capitalist peasantries are not the direct product of colonial peasantries. An essentially uneven development has taken place in agriculture. I cannot present these phenomena in detail, so I shall proceed in two stages. First, I shall describe the dominant traits of Senegambian history and the process of specialization in production, which was both regional and social.[5] I shall then examine some specific problems concerning the various peasantries; and in the conclusion, I shall deal with the potential evolutions of the past quarter of a century.

II. MAJOR TRENDS OF SENEGAMBIAN HISTORY

State Building from the Eleventh To the Fifteenth Centuries

For Barry (n.d.), Senegambia was "until the first half of the 16th century a dependent zone of the Sahel and the Soudan"

(p. 1). From the north came political and religious influences, including Islam, which was important along the Senegal River from the eleventh century, and state formation, which developed during the same period. Trade went north to the nomadic peoples of the desert and to North Africa, and east to the Mali empire, which sought control of sources of salt in Senegambia. The states which subsequently controlled Senegambia were formed during this period.

Toward the Domination of Imperialist Trade: Sixteenth to Nineteenth Centuries

"Political disintegration constitutes the most important fact of the second half of the 16th century" (Barry, n.d:5). The coming of first the Portuguese, then the Dutch, British, and French, modified the direction of commercial movement and then greatly increased the slave trade. This, in turn, led to a popular Islamic attack on states that collaborated with the foreigners. During the long mercantilist period, trade with Europe increasingly dominated the region. Both states and trading groups became oriented to the demands of the Europeans as trade moved up the two axes of the Senegal and Gambia Rivers. The same goods were in demand (slaves, gum arabic, and gold), but the routes and terms of trade were changed. The means of production were subjected to political pressure: first war for slaves, then the increasing use of slaves to produce other products. The circulation of subsistence goods became secondary, even though it remained important in some areas, especially the desert-side regions, where pastoralists came south every year in search of grain. The principal produce became the producer himself as a potential slave. There was a demarcation between regions which produced goods and those which produced slaves. This new specialization in the slave trade imperilled the normal conditions of subsistence and of reproduction of the population. The end of the slave trade therefore coincided with a pronounced agricultural crisis.

Toward Commercial Agriculture and Territorial Occupation: The Nineteenth and Twentieth Centuries

The new needs of industrial Europe, primary goods for industry, and a market for its products, led to the reorganization of the Senegambian space. From about 1840 peanuts led the way, with the central regions of Senegambia spearheading the development because they had suitable soils, adequate rainfall, and a large population. Colonial intervention created a new political framework, and the construction of railroads and ports facilitated the export of the produce. The major changes occurred between 1890 and 1930. The Wolof, Sereer, and Lebu of the central regions became more important producers than the Tukolor and Soninke of the river. Islam played an important role, particularly the Mouride religious fraternity, which encouraged the cultivation of peanuts and organized the movement of population from densely populated areas into frontier zones adapted to peanut cultivation. Military aristocracies were displaced and the peasants came to be central to the economic development of both Senegal and the Gambia.

Nation Building, New Internal and External Markets: Second Half of the Twentieth Century

Soil exhaustion, price fluctuations, droughts, and the cost of importing food products have led to a new development strategy. The diversification of crops and the production of food products for export are producing a new social and spatial allocation of work. The more developed zones are not capable of carrying out the new policies. Maraboutic estates and large private farms have appeared during the last ten years, but this solution does not offer any long-range hope because of the high cost of labor.

The new strategy involves the integration of what were the peripheral regions, the Senegal River, eastern Senegal, and the Casamance into a new national and international division of labor. These peripheral regions are in the forefront because of links between the Senegalese state and international financial and agricultural institutions. In these peripheral regions, the use of salaried labor is possible. This would be difficult in the Peanut Basin, where the transformation of peasants into a landless labor force would be expensive and likely to produce a crisis.

III. SUBSISTENCE, LOCAL MARKETS, INTERNATIONAL MARKETS, DEPENDENT MARKETS

The first period was marked by the installation of agricultural peoples coming down the Senegal and Gambia Rivers and south from Mauritania. Very little is known about the formation of peasant and pastoral traditions beyond a general picture of the exploitation and transformation of the natural environment. We need to understand more fully the appearance of flooded valley agriculture along the Senegal River, the development of grain cultivation in the savanna, and the relation between agriculture and other forms of production (fishing, gathering, pastoralism, and crafts). The emergence of large state structures suggests systems of production capable of generating agricultural surpluses. These came from different sources: local surpluses, exchange between complementary ecological zones, and the trade of foodstuffs, for example. The myth of subsistence is a dangerous one in African history and anthropology. We believe, in opposition, that the development of trade and production in the precolonial period explains why European intervention did not in the beginning bring about any radical change.

Local trade led, in fact, to interregional and international trade (we should, of course, keep in mind the spatial scale of these social formations, and understand these expressions as relative, especially "international"). Regional specialization was at the same time linked to the development of social inequality. The cities of the Saharan and Sahelian trade, the merchant groups, and the ruling classes of kingdoms and empires were able to develop because agriculturalists produced a surplus capable of feeding nonproductive groups. The development of a slave economy after 1675 contributed further inequalities which were very important:

(a) Social inequality was basic to the organization of production. Exploitation is the real motor of "progress" and of economic development within both precapitalist and capitalist relations of production.
(b) Slavery made possible the organization of a labor force in areas of low population.
(c) Groups could produce both for the market and for specialized groups that organized the state or the market.

Slaves became integrated with peasant units of production quite late. Until then, they were more often dependent on politically dominant groups and often had more nonproductive functions—that is, political and military—than productive ones. We thus had a society marked by a social division of labor and specialization.

From the seventeenth century on, Africa's historical frame of reference changed. Whatever the form of change—the long crisis along the Senegal River during the eighteenth century, colonial peanut cultivation among the Wolof (1890-1960), or the new economic order of the 1970s—systems of agricultural production were intimately linked to the political structure and to the commercial networks organized by it. During the first period, as Hopkins (1973) has explained, trade was limited to enclaves and did little to change the structures of production, consumption, or technology (p. 120). Though international trade was to bring fundamental transformations, direct producers were not yet called upon to produce for the international market. Until 1840, Senegal's exports were mostly slaves from the Sudanic interior and gum arabic, which was gathered by the Trarza Moors (Curtin, 1975). The organization of agricultural production remained more or less unchanged. The political superstructure that encapsulated the peasantry intervened only to increase the tribute in goods and men, but not to change the conditions of production.

International trade introduced various secondary contradictions, especially at the level of the direct producers.
Competition between those who could satisfy European demand provoked intense struggles among ethnic groups, states,
and social classes. There was even the paradox of dominated
groups, especially free peasants, being sold as slaves by their
own dominant class. Such behavior obviously jeopardized the
conditions of reproduction. There was also a general increase
in exactions: (a) an increase in levies by the state; and (b) an
extension of the labor market and an increase in the cost of the
social allocation of labor. There also appeared a contradiction
between two kinds of levies; those which concern the product
and those which concern the producer. According to Amin
(Barry, 1972:18), "the export of goods . . . does not necessarily
have devastating effects; it can on the contrary promote
progress." For Meillassoux (1978), "the major difference is
that between regions submitted to the intercontinental trade in
the products of work and regions where the export of the
laborers themselves prevailed" (p. 136). Meillassoux continues: "In the coastal regions, traders first bought men and
this demand cancelled the demand for products and hindered
production." In contrast, Hopkins (1973) points out that
regions like Senegambia exported both goods and labor force.
He argues that a diminution in the number of laborers
provoked a diminution of demand and perhaps a transformation of the sexual division of labor, allowing a greater role to
female labor (1973:121-123).

Though agricultural production was adequate in both the
premercantilist and mercantilist periods, the systems of production began to undergo transformations. Between the sixteenth and nineteenth centuries, the autonomy of the producer
was more and more endangered by ecological problems, a
demographic imbalance, increased enslavement, migrations,
flight, famines, and an increase in the demand for subsistence
goods by both warriors and aristocrats. These increasingly
threatened the system of reproduction and created a situation
ripe for revolution. The European capitalist was unable to

profit directly from this situation, not so much because of the failure of agricultural colonization early in the nineteenth century or because of the conflicts between administrators and traders (Barry, 1972). The agricultural producer was still subject to the arbitrary demands of a predatory state, which left him a limited surplus for trade. He could only be freed to meet the demand for peanuts if the burden of the traditional state were reduced or eliminated.

IV. FROM DEPENDENT PRODUCTION TO DEPENDENCY IN THE SYSTEM OF PRODUCTION

The future of Senegal is rooted in the spontaneous and voluntary cultivation by the natives living in their villages and in their families. It is there that we must protect them, encourage them, civilize them and improve their methods if necessary. We do not have much confidence in large estates [L. Faidherbe (1865) in Pasquier, 1955:194].

At the present the only certainty we have is that any significant increase in groundnut production in the cultivated regions of Senegal is dependant on an immense increase in cattle. As long as herds of cattle are so few, we shall have to rely upon the natural potentialities of a virgin soil, i.e., since it is so rapidly exhausted, upon a vigorous expansion of cultivation in regions still uncultivated [Engineer-General Bélime (1931) in Mersadier, 1966:857].

This is not the time to digress upon the dangers of mono-production. Senegal equals peanuts and to save peanut production is to save more than Senegal. Let us be done with this kind of academic solution which consists of proposing to Senegal an assortment of exports. It is upon peanuts that the colony is founded, it is upon peanuts that it must live [Gouverneur R. Delavignette (1931) in Mersadier, 1966:856].

During the nineteenth century a radical change took place, a change which originated outside African societies. The turning point was 1840. At about that date, the gum trade began to decline, the Atlantic slave trade came to an end, and the commercial production of peanuts began, though it was not until about 1890 that new relations of production were fully developed.

Some figures (in metric tons) on the export of peanuts from Senegal make clear the magnitude of this development:

1840	1
1848	3,606
1892	46,790
1897	96,000
1906	150,000
1914	310,000

Unlike previous changes, these occurred primarily at the level of the peasant producer, since it was he who met the demand of the European market. In the process, the center of French attention shifted from the riverine peoples, who bore the brunt of the slave trade and the first French military expeditions to the peoples of central Senegambia. These zones had more secure rainfall, were more central, and were closer to Dakar, the new port which took over the functions of St. Louis, in the mouth of the Senegal River.

During the nineteenth century there were several attempts to introduce the plantation system, which had been so successful in the New World; first in the 1820s under Baron Roger, and then during the 1860s, when the American Civil War created a worldwide shortage of cotton. These projects failed, mostly because of the absence of a "free" labor force.[6] Thus, the quest for useful products for the metropolis was accompanied by a search for the social form best adapted to their production. Political alliances with local dominant groups in Waalo and in the riverine Fuuta Tooro were expensive and did not permit an adequate reorientation of agricultural production. The answer was reliance on the peasant household. There were two dimensions to this.

First, the destruction of the former political rulers and their military forces brought to an end the various levies and arbitrary exactions upon producers and products. The Islamic brotherhoods took over many of the functions of the traditional state, but instead of preying on the peasant, they directed his efforts toward cash crop production. Agricultural colonies, called *daara,* were recruited by clerics from among former slaves and land-short people in the more densely populated areas. These groups cleared and planted underpopulated areas

(Cruise O'Brien, 1971). The old levies in kind were replaced by a head tax, first levied in 1891, which created a need for specie, and thus, a further incentive to produce for market. Second, this evolution was encouraged by the freeing of the slaves, thereby creating a pool of free labor which flowed into new regions of production. The pressure on the peasant was increased by the fluctuations in the world market price. When high, they encouraged him to shift more of his labor time into peanuts. When low, he was forced to contract debts at exorbitant rates of interest, and to pay those debts, to increase his production.

This period displays a complex sequence of causes. One can find a stimulating presentation of the most important factors of change and adaptation in Brooks' paper (1975). Brooks describes the increase in production through the clearing of new land and the shift in labor time from millet to peanuts. He then describes problems of transport, of subsistence for new workers, and of new taxes—in particular, the head tax. There was a deterioration of the sociopolitical system and, therefore, of economic forms of domination. Klein (1972, 1977) shows that while the slave trade consolidated the elites because it provided revenue for the traditional state, the development of peanut cultivation furnished money and arms to the peasantry. In fact, slave traders put slaves to work and became peanut producers. On the other hand, *marabouts,* by protecting peasants from the demands of the military elites, also became peanut producers. These groups therefore took over some of the functions of economic direction in the new system of production. On the other hand, key factions of the formerly dominant groups, both nobles and slave warriors, underwent a process of peasantization. Whereas in the precolonial system the slave was integrated into the kinship system, the new economic system made the former slave an independent and free agricultural producer. These transformations resulted in the lightening of former burdens and the possibility of a more direct relationship between agricultural producers and those who controlled the external market. These new relationships did not suppress the existence of locally dominant groups and the economic demands by these groups on the peasant. The persistence of former land tenure dues and the increase in payments to *marabouts* were both important demands on the peasant. Most of these phenomena developed during the last third of the nineteenth century.

Many scholars have argued that something had to be done to replace the Atlantic slave trade (Wallerstein, 1976; Hopkins, 1973) and that the productive factors had been underutilized (Vanhaeverbeke, 1970). Such an explanation underestimates on the one hand the level of agricultural production before the middle of the nineteenth century and suggests on the other hand that the increase in peanut production was the result largely of colonial policy which offered new means of production to the direct producers (transport, tools, prices). Such an explanation ignores a whole range of questions: relations of production, labor process, and accessible land for commercial and subsistence production.[7]

The trader was freed from taxes so that the laws of the market might operate more freely. But political change and price fluctuations imposed a more drastic interventionist policy. Transportation was developed and services were provided to producers. The development of peanut production was not simple and direct. The Casamance (the southern region of Senegal) before 1860 was a major exporter. Until World War I, millet was a more important cause of migration into new lands than peanuts. The first Murid *daara* concentrated on subsistence agriculture. Administrators perceived from the beginning the contradiction between subsistence agriculture and the expansion of peanut cultivation. As one wrote in November 1879:

> All they can think of is cultivating peanuts and some millet to feed themselves. But they often lack the latter which allows the traders of Rufisque to exploit them twice: first, by purchasing their nuts for almost nothing, second, by selling rice at an exorbitant price [N'Diaye, 1968:475].

The regional and ethnic specialization on peanuts was therefore the result of a complex history in which the emancipation of the labor force was in contradiction to the control of this labor force within a monetary and market economy. The emancipation of the labor force increased the peasant's control over his means of production, but he was at the same time subject to external constraints which limited the productivity his land—in particular, ecological degradation which resulted from the cash crop economy and control by the colonial state of tools, seeds, and other inputs. This evolution toward a complete liberation then takes on the form of migrations. Insufficient liberation makes it necessary to seek a "foreign" labor force, but only for regions where land is plentiful. Total liberation, on the other hand, would have embarrassed the colonial administration because if slaves had become salaried workers the producers could not then have organized agricultural production and assumed the cost of reproducing the labor force. Pseudoprecapitalist forms like that of the Murid brotherhood are a perfect example of this historical period (Copans, 1977). The Murids have their ideological roots in *sufism,* a mystical tradition within Islam, which has often been important on the fringes of the Muslim world. It is a political and economic system which linked the saints (*marabouts*) directly to their followers (*taalibe*), who were mostly peasants. This brotherhood, like other Senegalese brotherhoods, developed in response to social and economic disruption during the French conquest of Senegal. Formally, it could be analyzed as a kind of pseudofeudal and precapitalist system, both because of the ideological basis of power and the importance of the personal link between the *marabout* and his follower; but from very early, it adapted to the international market economy and cash crop production.

Several answers to the same constraints can be found within the same ethnic and regional situation. The direct relation between the family labor process and the world market explains the increasing individualism of decision-making and the separation of systems of production from tributary superstructures (Comité Information Sahel, 1974:71-96). The individualization of the units of production was paralleled by their submission to various state agencies. These agencies mediated between the producer and the world market, but they represented the interests of the foreign economy more than those of the local producers.

Once the conquest was finished, the colonial apparatus adopted a more and more direct approach. Territorial administration placed the highest priority on peanut cultivation, which developed systematically until the Depression forced a thorough review of its institutional structures (Mersadier, 1966). The peasantry had to cultivate in an extensive manner. The capitalist market economy brought about the following changes: (1) individualization of the labor process, (2) the reproduction of the system of production more and more mediated by money, and (3) a policy of assistance imposed by the colonial administration.

The evolution of the Senegal River region is a direct contrast to the peanut basin. Adams (1977b) has documented this history well. The abandonment of the Senegal River as a commercial axis and therefore as a transport route for peanuts cultivated there has limited the desire to cultivate it. People living there have not responded in identical ways: The Soninke resorted to emigration before the Tokolor did. Under colonial rule, the once-productive Senegal River area speedily became peripheral. The Niger was chosen as the site of an irrigation scheme; the Senegal was neglected because of its lower population density and the supposed potential of forced colonization. In fact, the administration was obliged to use forced labor (Magassa, 1978). No foodstuff production was encouraged in the river area, although it would have complemented the peanut basin, where the amount of land devoted to food products was reduced in order to concentrate on peanuts.

The Depression saw a radical drop first in prices and then in peanut production, and Senegalese peasants began to shift back into subsistence production—as much as their debts and tax burdens permitted. The colonial administration, threatened by a sharp decrease in its revenues, responded by trying to increase productivity—in particular, by a modernization of the means of production of the family units of production. In fact, it was only after World War II, with the Porteres Plan of 1950, that this new policy could be implemented. Until that point, the productivity of the peanut basin depended heavily on *navetaans*, seasonal migrants who came every year from eastern Senegal, Mali, and Guinea. As parts of the peanut basin became overpopulated, the demand for these migrants began to decline.

The first mechanism used to increase productivity was the Sociétés Indigènes de Prévoyance, first set up in 1907 and gradually extending throughout French West Africa. By 1912 there were ten in the major administrative districts. Though they could best be described as credit unions, the S.I.P. were much more bureaucratic entities whose very conception was rooted in the French centralizing tradition and which were tightly controlled by the administration. At the beginning, they advanced selected peanut seeds with a limited interest rate (25 percent, which compared favorably to the 20 percent or more demanded by private traders). After the 1930 crisis the S.I.P.s' functions were expanded: They could buy and sell peanuts and sell or lease agricultural machinery (Suret-Canale, 1971:235-244). Agricultural modernization proceeded very slowly, but it has had an effect on the social organization of work. As modernized technologies were adopted, the collective labor process disappeared (Copans et al., 1972).

With independence in 1960, the S.I.P.s were transformed into cooperatives and an effort was made to root them in traditional cooperative values (Schumacher, 1975). However, they speedily became bureaucratic entities which bought the annual crop; advanced seed, pesticides, and fertilizer; and sold agricultural machinery on credit. The state took over the marketing of the peanut crop in 1962, buying directly from the cooperatives. The cooperative policy was closely linked to a policy of rural animation, or community development, designed to identify natural leaders and use them to stimulate modernization of agriculture. This policy did not produce dramatic results, and the government speedily moved from a strategy based on the mass of peasants to one based on model peasants and large producers (Copans, 1979, 1980b). The instrument of this policy was a French consulting firm, Société d'aide technique et de Coopération, which was entrusted with raising production in a selected area. It tried to do so through extension services which provided knowledge and new inputs (fertilizer, animal power, light machinery) to those producers with the capacity and the will to mobilize enough land and labor.[8] As in a capitalist-developed economy, small producers are not able to master the financial, technological, land, and labor needs of an integrated capitalist system of production in agriculture. Only the large producers can make it, and in peanut country, these are not the peasants; they are the *marabouts,* the petty traders, and the state.

The crisis of the 1960s was made all the more difficult by French entry into the European Economic Community. The Depression reforms had included a policy of agricultural price supports, which guaranteed to markets in the metropole colonial products at prices well above the world price. The terms of French entry into the E.E.C. required an end to these supports. Thus, the policy of boosting productivity was partly a response to a drop in the price paid to the peasant, but the peasant had to buy the new inputs on credit, which placed the burdens of modernization on his reluctant back. The "malaise paysan" of the late 1960s essentially involved an effort to shift some production back into subsistence, though this was difficult because rice had replaced millet as the standard urban diet and debt often forced peasants to maintain peanut production even at low prices. The process was compounded by an ecological disaster, the droughts of 1968-1974, and by the rapid increase in migration to the cities. The process of reproduction of social relationships is shaped by continued imperialist domination, consolidation of the dominant bureaucracy, and ideological conflicts between classes. A double process of proletarianization has taken place. First, though some still possess "free" access to land, the peasantry is increasingly separated from the control over the means of production and the labor process. Second, a new class of proletarians has appeared, who are completely separated from their agricultural milieu. This group comes primarily from the Senegal River region, but there is an increasing land-short population in the peanut basin.

Raikes has suggested that this kind of proletarianization is often accompanied by the growth of a "Big Farm," or estate sector involving large tracts. Thus, production comes to be centered in tracts of thousands of acres employing labor on lands that hitherto supported hundreds of small producers. This alternative can take the form of private producers—for example, important Murid *marabouts*—and private entrepreneurs in the frontier regions called the Terres Neuves. It can also take the form of a public investment as in the Senegal River, where the state is developing irrigated agriculture. The origin of the wealth necessary to develop these new farm structures is exterior to agriculture. With the *marabouts,* it comes from their religious functions. With the private entrepreneurs, it comes from trade, transportation, and usury (Copans, 1979; Dubois, 1971; Rocheteau, 1975, 1977).

A generalized proletarianization coupled to exploitation by a state bureaucracy has the advantage of limiting social differentiation at the top and therefore of not increasing the competition between specific factions of the dominant classes. Such a solution allows the state bureaucracy to preserve, if not increase, its own resources, which are threatened by either a stagnation or decrease in peanut production; this condition can result from low world market prices, from peasant resistance to efforts to increase production, or from drought and the degradation of the conditions of production.

To the extent that the form of labor process capable of maintaining a certain level of surplus can no longer be found (except marginally on the estates of the *marabouts* or big producers), the State apparatus must find other regions and other forms of production if it wants to maintain the material basis of its domination.[9] The cost of importing foodstuff, the stagnation of cash crop production, not to mention the degradation of exchange rates, bears heavily on the state budget, either in the form of high import bills or a sharp decline in the revenues of the marketing board. Furthermore, this strategy enables it to develop its own means of political and ideological control in an independant manner, whereas in the peanut basin it has to compromise with the Muslim brotherhoods and other dominant local groups which consolidated themselves during over a half-century of colonial rule.

V. CONCLUSION: THE END OF PEASANTRIES?

Only the analysis of the social process of production—a process which presents itself as the unity of the immediate production process and of the circulation process—allows us to grasp and perceive the relationship of domination—submission between the non-specifically capitalist forms of production and the social relations of production. Any theoretical position which would view things not from a social but from a sectoral and local point of view by considering on the one hand only a determined part of production and on the other, only one of the phases of the complete production process, any such position therefore would not be capable of determining the exact position occupied by the producers from the sectors where non-specifically capitalist forms of production predominate [Faure, 1978:22].

The tendency revealed by capital to extend its field of extortion of surplus labor to the totality of social production, even where it seems particularly absent, constitutes the unifying link between the various forms of production within a social formation dominated by the capitalist mode of production.

The new international economic order is still based in the case of Senegal upon the exploitation of the agricultural producers and on the organization of the labor process and the relations of production. Historical differences, both regional and ethnic, explain the recourse to one or another type of relation of production. Uneven development and the transformation of social relations from their noncapitalist origins explains this permanent reshuffling of forms in the spatial context. All of these development projects and operations correspond to a permanent quest for the optimum social conditions permitting the best exploitation in a given situation. The exploration of the various forms of production is the specific manner in which the neocolonial dominant groups constitute their hegemony today. It also expresses the triple interplay of contradictions: among imperialisms, between imperialisms and dominant national or local groups, and between dominant and dominated classes (Copans, 1977, 1978).

Contradictions between the ethnic and state labor process, between the formal and real subordination of the labor force to capital, are fundamental. Although capitalism dominates the whole of the Senegalese economy, Senegal is not a capitalist society, and many precapitalist social and ideological relations function with some semblance of autonomy. This is even true at the household or kinship level and within the labor process itself. But on the other hand, it is not in the interest of the state to polarize these contradictions within one social field, that of the nation. Whereas the European bourgeoisie rose to power through a progressive expansion and control of a demarcated territorial market, the dominant classes of underdeveloped countries cannot behave as such because they are dependent on external markets and bourgeoisies and because their power stems partly from the weakness and heterogeneity of the dominated groups and classes. The variety of the local indigenous groups is also a factor of unequal social fragmentation. A national unification of these within the frame of two specific classes of the capitalist mode of production is of course impossible and dangerous to the imperial and foreign interests. The policy of regional development is not the result of a new policy toward underdeveloped countries. It is characteristic of efforts to establish a new and indirect mechanism for controlling the direct producers, a mechanism originated by the central power and not by regional, local, or ethnic dominant groups. This new framework is still a "divide and rule" strategy, but the state tries to draw closer to the peasantry by proposing specific solutions to their "problems."

Labor processes do not exist in isolation and are not simply technical devices, as many experts would have us believe.

New social relationships must be worked out that correspond to the labor processes and to constraints imposed by the dominant mode of production. It is the interplay between these various relations of production established at the level of elementary social groups that creates both the labor processes and the groups of producers. Such a situation ultimately shapes the conditions of reproduction, that of international strategies concerning "law and order" and the evolution of peripheral capitalism.

The only option the peasants seem to have is that of accepting the new regional division of labor or of refusing and migrating to the city. Proletarianized on the spot or in the city, the agricultural producer is less capable of protecting his interests. Class struggle as it exists in Senegal is expressed in contemporary political and ideological struggles. The peasantry as such will disappear by the end of the century. Agricultural producers will not all become salaried workers—far from it. The peanut basin will remain unchanged, but the development of the national apparatus for exploitation, of a centrally organized division of space and allocation of labor will submit the direct producers more and more to the demands of international capital and the national bourgeoisie. The various experiments of the past generation are defining a new peasant marked by obedience to the orders, know-how and technologies of the technicians. The "bureaucratic" peasant is not a myth. He is almost a reality, but he is no longer a peasant.

NOTES

1. We disagree with Becker's criticism of Curtin (1975) on the point that a more systematic use of oral tradition would permit a better understanding of the past. Probably, but whose past, and how far back?

2. We are thinking mostly of the works of Curtin (1975), Meillassoux (1978), and Hopkins (1973).

3. Archeology in Black Africa is still more or less in its infancy (at least on a quantitative level) but could probably bring about a complete transformation of our view of the past if it benefited from a great impetus.

4. An uncritical use of Meillassoux's domestic mode of production could lead to dangerous generalizations. As for the illusions of referring to the notion of Petty

Commodity Production and for the limits of the notion of mercantilist economy and trade in noncapitalist formations, see Amselle and LeBris (1979).

5. I quote in this section an abridged version of an earlier paper (Copans, 1978:100-102).

6. A. Adams (1977a:150) quotes the Baron Roger on this point: "It is precisely because the negroes are used to working for themselves that it is difficult to get them to work on our fields. These men are very independent in spirit; they say with reason that they are free like us and their chiefs have very little authority" (letter of January 12, 1820—see also Barry, 1972:253).

7. Hopkins draws our attention to those factors (1973:126,n5) and adds: "Female labor appears to have been particularly important in preparing groundnuts and palm produce for export."

8. S.A.T.E.C. has subsequently become S.O.D.E.V.A., an agency of the Senegalese state which has almost completely taken over agricultural education. The strategy of focusing on the stronger peasants has remained the same (Schumacher, 1975:119-20).

9. The specific evolution of these "new" regions (involution in the Senegal River valley, relative preservation of Casamance societies) and therefore the nature of the social relationships (for example, the importance of salaried work) has facilitated the penetration of multinational capitalism in the form of large state-managed estates and sophisticated technology. A prospective view of the Senegal River projects can be found in Adams (1977a:191-197; 1977b:55-59).

REFERENCES

ADAMS, A. (1977a). Le long voyage des gens du fleuve. Paris: Maspéro.
_____(1977b). "The Senegal River valley: What kind of change?" Review of African Political Economy, 10:33-59.
AMSELLE, J.L. (1977). Les négociants de la savane. Paris: Anthropos.
AMSELLE, J.L. and LEBRIS, E. (1979). Quelques réflexions sur la notion de "petite production marchande." Colloque I.E.D.E.S.: La petite production marchande en milieu urbain africain. Paris. (mimeo)
ANDERSON, P. (1976). Lineages of the absolutist state. London: N.L.B.
BARRY, B. (1972). Le royaume du Waalo. Paris: Maspéro.
_____(n.d.). Evolution des Wolof, des Serer et des Toucouleur; relations avec les européens; début des révolutions islamiques (Futa Djalon, Futa Toro); migration Mende dans l'ouest du Haut-Niger du XVIe siècle au XVIIIe. Dakar. (mimeo) (Chapitre 10 du volume V, 'Le Soudan occidental,' de l'Histoire Générale de l'Afrique)
BECKER, C. (1977). "La Sénégambie a l'epoque de la traite des esclaves. A propos d'un ouvrage reçent de Ph.D. Curtin, *Eèonomic change in Senegambia in the era of the slave trade.*" Revue Française d'Histoire d'Outre-mer, vol. LXIV 64:203-224.
BERTRAND G. and BERTRAND, C. (1975). "Pour une histoire écologique de la France rurale." In G. Duby and A. Wallon, Histoire de la France rurale, Vol. 1. Paris: Le Seuil.

BOMBA, V. (1977). "Traditions about Ndiadiane Ndiaye first Buurba Djolof, early Djolof, the southern Almoravids and neighboring people." Bulletin I.F.A.N., series B, 39:1-35.

BROOKS, G.E. (1975). "Peanuts and colonialism: Consequences of the commercialization of peanuts in West Africa, 1830-1870." Journal of African History, 16:29-59.

Comité Information Sahel (1974). Qui se nourrit de la famine en Afrique. Paris: Maspéro.

COPANS, J. (1977). "Politique et religion—D'une relation idéologique interindividuelle à la domination imperialiste: Les Mourides du Sénégal." Dialectiques, 21:23-40.

_____(1978). "Ethnies et régions dans une formation sociale dominée: Hypothèses à propos du cas sénégalais." Anthropologie et Sociétés, 2:95-115.

_____(1979). "Droughts, famines and the evolution of Senegal (1966-1978)." Mass Emergencies (special issue on "Natural Disasters and Economic Development" edited by W.I. Torry, forthcoming).

_____(1980a). "Mode of production, social formation or ethnic group: Some silences of Marxist anthropology." In D.E. Goodfriend (ed.), Contemporary French Marxist thought. (forthcoming).

_____(1980b). "The Murid models: Daara, villages and farms (Senegal)." In P. O'Keefe (ed.), Villages in the environmental context of development: An assessment of needs, resources and future research. (forthcoming).

COPANS, J. et al. (1972). Maintenance sociale et changement économique au Sénégal. I. Doctrine économique et pratique du travail chez les Mourides. Paris: O.R.S.T.O.M.

COQUERY-VIDROVITCH, C. (1972). "Research on an African mode of production." in G.W. Johnson and M. Klein (eds.), Perspectives on the African past. Boston: Little, Brown.

CRUISE O'BRIEN, D.B. (1971). The Mourides of Senegal. Oxford: Clarendon.

CURTIN, P.D. (1975). Economic change in precolonial Africa. Madison: University of Wisconsin Press.

DIOP, A.B. (1979). La Société Wolof. Tradition et changement. Doctoral thesis, Université René Descartes, Paris V. (mimeo)

DUBOIS, J.P. (1971). L'émigration des Serer vers la zone arachidière orientale. Dakar: O.R.S.T.O.M. (mimeo)

DUBY, G. (1975). "Avant-Propos." In G. Duby et A. Wallon, Histoire de la France rurale, Vol. I. Paris: Le Seuil.

FALLERS, L. (1973). "Are African cultivators to be called 'peasants'?" In L. Fallers, Inequality: Social stratification reconsidered. Chicago: University of Chicago Press.

FAURE, C. (1978). Agriculture et capitalisme. Paris: Anthropos.

HOPKINS, A.G. (1973). An economic history of West Africa. London: Longmans.

KLEIN, M.A. (1972). "Social and economic factors in the Muslim Revolution in Senegambia." Journal of African History, 13:419-441.

_____(1977). "Servitude among the Wolof and Serer of Senegambia." In S. Miers and I. Kopytoff. Slavery in Africa. Madison: University of Wisconsin Press.

MAGASSA, A. (1978). Papa-commandant a jeté un grand filet devant nous. Paris: Maspéro.

MEILLASSOUX, C. (1975). Femmes, greniers et capitaux. Paris: Maspéro.

MEILLASSOUX, C. (1978). "Role de l'esclavage dans l'histoire de l'Afrique occidentale." Anthropologie et Sociétés, 2:117-148.

MERSADIER, Y. (1966). "La crise de l'arachide au début des années trente." Bulletin I.F.A.N., series B, 28:826-877.

N'DIAYE, F. (1968). "La colonie du Sénégal au temps de Brière de l'Isle (1876-1881)." Bulletin I.F.A.N., series B, 30:463-512.

PASQUIER, R. (1955). "En marge de la guerre de Sécession. Les essais de culture de coton au Sénégal." Annales Africaines, 2:185-202.

PELISSIER, P. (1966). Les paysans du Sénégal. Saint-Yrieix: Fabrègues.

RAIKES, P. (1978). "Rural differentiation and class formation in Tanzania." Journal of Peasant Studies, 5:285-325.

RANGER, T.O. (1978). "Reflections on peasant research in Central and Southern Africa." Journal of Southern Africa Studies, 5:99-133.

REY, P.P. (1971). Colonialisme, néo-colonialisme et transition au capitalisme. Paris: Maspéro.

ROCHETEAU, G. (1975). "Pioniers Mourides au Sénégal: Colonisation des terres neuves et transformations d'une économie paysanne." Cahiers ORSTOM, series Sciences Humaines, 12:19-55.

_____(1977). "Mouridisme et économie de traite. Dégagement d'un surplus et accumulation dans une confrerie islamique au Sénégal." In Essais sur la reproduction de formations sociales dominées. Paris: O.R.S.T.O.M.

SAUL, J. and WOODS, R. (1971). "African peasantries." In T. SHANIN (ed.), Peasants and peasant societies. Harmondsworth: Penguin.

SCHUMACHER, E.J. (1975). Politics, bureaucracy and rural development in Senegal. Berkeley and Los Angeles: University of California Press.

SURET-CANALE, J. (1971). French colonialism in tropical Africa. London: Hurst.

TROTSKY, L. (1962). Histoire de la Révolution Russe. Paris: Le Seuil.

VANHAEVERBEKE, A. (1970). Rémunération du travail et commerce exterieur. Louvain: Université catholique, Faculté Sciences economiques, sociales et politiques.

WALLERSTEIN, I. (1976). "The three stages of African involvement in the World Economy." In P.C.W. Gutkind and I. Wallerstein (eds.), The political economy of contemporary Africa. Beverly Hills, CA: Sage.

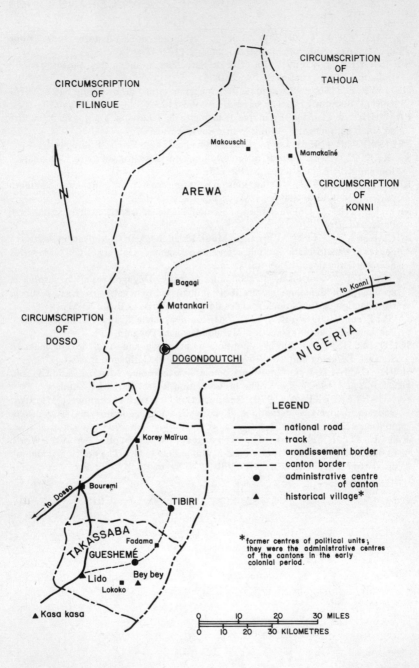

CIRCUMSCRIPTION
OF
FILINGUE

CIRCUMSCRIPTION
OF
TAHOUA

N

Makouschi

Mamakaïné

AREWA

CIRCUMSCRIPTION
OF
KONNI

Bagagi

Matankari

to Konni

CIRCUMSCRIPTION
OF
DOSSO

DOGONDOUTCHI

NIGERIA

LEGEND

national road

track

arondissement border

canton border

administrative centre
of canton

historical village*

Korey Maïrua

to Dosso

Bouremi

TIBIRI

TAKASSABA

GUESHEMÉ

Fadama

*former centres of political units;
they were the administrative centres
of the cantons in the early
colonial period.

Lido

Bey bey

Lokoko

Kasa kasa

0   10   20   30 MILES

0   10   20   30 KILOMETRES

3

SHADOWS NOURISHED BY THE SUN:
Rural Social Differentiation among the Mawri of Niger

ELIANE DE LATOUR DEJEAN
Paris

THE PRE-COLONIAL PERIOD

The *dallol Mawri*[1] was first inhabited by the Gubawa, who had gradually become sedentary while continuing as hunters and gatherers. Moving about in small groups, they constituted a society without a central political organization, following "the rules of clan organisation, under the direction of priest-elders responsible for ancestor and nature cults." (Piault, 1975a:54). The arbitration and resolution of conflicts occurred through a kinship system subject to religious and magical norms.

> The various clans forming the Gubawa group, interrelated through marriage alliances and with access to areas of land large enough to prevent land disputes, based their relationships on prior occupation of the land, expressed in kinship terms and manifested by the complementarity of the priest-elders' sacrificial functions [Piault, 1975a:54].

Editor's Note: Thanks go to Robert Barde for the translation.

In the sixteenth century a group of warriors from Bornu settled in the region at Matankari, establishing a hierarchical system based on war under the authority of the ruler, the Sarkin Arewa. An extreme simplification would suggest that the Gubawa remained masters of the cults and the earth, while the Arewa took charge of defense and political management. Adept at war, the Arewa gave the Gubawa protection and opportunities for pillage; the latter, in turn, ensured the secular legitimacy through the presence of its priests, the Yan'Kasa,[2] during the ruler's investiture. There was not, as one might think, an equal division between the religious and the political:

> The sovereign's legitimacy, bestowed by the assembly of priests, is considered by the latter as a form of nomination, whereas it is actually an enthronement giving the ruler access to the sovereignty he has seized by force, operating within the context of Arewa succession laws, according to a theoretical rotation of power among the four royal lineages [Piault, 1975a:55].

However, not all Gubawa held religious power—only a few important priests had that responsibility. Likewise, not all Arewa held political power—only the sovereign, his immediate family, and his entourage had such privileges. The other Arewa lineages and clans were scarcely differentiated from the Gubawa commoners. Further, the theoretical principles of royal succession could be violated by anyone who had the power. The ruler could be confronted by a superior force and dethroned through violence or trickery. If such an attempt failed, the unfortunate aspirant was forced to leave the country. His defeat confirming the ruler's ability, since the sovereign was identified with the prosperity and happiness of the society, the challenger had to be banished as a trouble-maker. Many unlucky claimants fled to the southern *dallol* and founded little principalities along lines with which they were familiar. While the north retained its political unity around Matankari, the south split up into several small autonomous political centers, each headed by a Sarkin Arewa.[3]

War

The Arewa attempted to create an organization in state form without modifying modes of labor which existed before their arrival, thus juxtaposing differing relations of production. Those in power constituted an aristocracy for whom war was the economic, political, and ideological underpinning (de Latour Dejean, forthcoming). Peasants, too, participated "of their own free will." Their presence was not required but booty was substantial, desirable not only for survival but also as a demonstration of courage, giving them access to privileges previously barred to them.[4] The object of battle was pillage and the capture of slaves; it was never a question of conquering territory. Suzerainty extended only over men, never over land.

In slave relationships, which concerned only the ruler and his notables[5] and not society in general, slaves were both a means of production and a medium of exchange. They supplied the surplus labor necessary for the dominant group's prosperity. In this manner, the aristocracy did not intervene in the lineage mode of production, leaving the peasants the burden of forming a labor force useful to the army. The lineage system was necessary for war, which in its turn became indispensable. The dislocations war provoked upset the agricultural cycle and the organization of labor, thus forcing the peasants to find some external means of making up the resulting shortfalls. If the establishment of a centralized authority and the creation of tributary relations of production with peasants was accomplished easily and without destroying the preexisting social organization, then war, the basic source of wealth for the aristocracy, allowed internal exploitation to be limited. To be sure, peasants were compelled to perform unpaid labor (in theory, each village had to give up one day each year), pay fines (arbitrary rather than systematic, sometimes quite onerous for an individual), and serve in the army (reimbursed through a share of captured booty). But this surplus labor, extracted in a haphazard way, was, for the average person, quite small. Taken as a whole, the value thus extracted was important to the sovereign and his household, but the meaning of these functions lies in ideology. They were neither the cause nor the means of the peasants' subjugation, but rather the end result, the concretization, hence the manifestation of the ruler's power. War, whether offensive or defensive, blurred social contradictions and unified aristocrats and peasants against the outside, the latter profiting from surplus labor extracted from other peoples. But at the same time it kept the hierarchy intact. The prejudices it engendered were directed mainly at the poor. At the same time, it justified and reinforced domination by the royal clan, which seemed indispensable for successful military endeavors from which everyone benefited and necessary as protectors in case of enemy attack. Identified with force, the royal clan was the hinge between the world of man and that of the gods, the ultimate expression of life and of death, as well as their vector. War and the internal organization needed for it welded this society from bottom to top, using lineages that perforce maintained their coherence in the face of danger and the constant need to ensure their collective existence. In sum, it could be said that this system was founded on social inequalities based on relationships of dependence that varied according to internal or external relations of force.

At the dawn of colonization Mawri society had, as we have just seen, a limited orientation toward trade, a division of labor dictated by kinship, and a social hierarchy reinforced by war. Conditions were not propitious for the emergence of a market economy. The French administration never considered directly replacing the existing hierarchy because it wanted to minimize its investments while maximizing exploitation. Penetration by the capitalist system was thus carried out in stages which we shall study: first through a historica' approach to colonial policy; then from a theoretical viewpc ,nt, attempting to shed light on those mechanisms of transition from one social formation to another, which alone can account for the evolution of social differentiation.

THE COLONIAL PERIOD

The ten years following the conquest were devoted to "pacification." The entire Niger military territory was shaken by various revolts. Islam was the apparent cause, but the violence of colonial occupation was the real one, along with the weakness of forces left to guard the new outposts. The top brass viewed the situation "shrewdly" and coldbloodedly:

> According to Captain Angeli, as things now are in this country we cannot administer it through ordinary means. Above all, our forces must be uncontested, and they are not. . . . While awaiting the instructions which I have requested, I felt it necessary to order the commandant of the Dosso post not to remain totally inside the fort, but to mount sorties only with sufficient force, to avoid risks, in a word to remain on the defensive, but not an absolutely passive defensive. Any offensive against a hostile village is forbidden, however. Further, he is not to venture more than one day's journey from his post, two at most, when he feels he will have nothing to fear.[6]

The pax colonial laid down a stream of obligations and prohibitions: abolition of slavery, suppression of war, requisitions, and taxes. These initial measures were designed to remove barriers. By depriving the aristocracy of its principal means of subsistence (warfare and slavery), while leaving it intact and with some of its prerogatives, the French government abolished its power without eliminating its authority. As we saw earlier, this society had found internal coherence and a kind of balance within a balance based on war. With the latter eliminated and replaced by constraints of another type, this edifice, with all its values based on notions about force and personal identification with a family or ethnic group, staggered in its search for a new equilibrium. The point on which it would be centered was provided by colonial policy which oriented choices in the direction of agricultural development.

1910-1930. Measures were taken to protect agriculture (for example, encouraging the growing of manioc, which was safe from locusts), commerce, and men (vaccination campaigns). Military requisitions of men and goods were made without any apparent modifications in the conditions or nature of production. There were requisitions of labor, foodstuffs needed by posts, attempts to buy wild produce (gum arabic, kapok, and karité) or livestock, and, finally, a head-tax payable in cash after

1906-1907. One of the important means of extortion was territorialization. These administrative boundaries (see map on p. 104) were a new phenomenon for a society in which political ties were hitherto based not on territory but on allegiance to a sovereign. The Mawri found themselves enclosed and controlled within a space and directly subject to a *canton* chief, who became an intermediary in this exploitation:

> Native chiefs no longer feeling restrained, assume arbitrary authority. They pressure their people too much, and to avoid it the latter cross the border without our knowledge.[7]

Mawri country, previously closed to trade, began to be visited by Dyula,[8] Nigerian traders or foreign merchants:

> Does not the general progress of our commerce in a year in which the agricultural situation would have been particularly hard and troublesome, bear witness to the benefits that our domination brings to the natives in assuring them secure roads and in giving them the confidence so necessary for trade?[9]

The people themselves moved about to sell a portion of their harvest or herds to pay taxes. Money gradually replaced barter, which did not really die out until 1935-1940.

> The quantity of bronze coins in the Territory is never enough. Transactions among natives are numerous and for small amounts. The rarity of this money creates a rise in the cost of living and is the cause of an even more maddening economic phenomenon: the market being deserted by the natives who, faced with the difficulties they encounter in obtaining change for silver coins, tend to revert to primitive commercial methods such as barter.[10]

The kinship system, which was never totally self-sufficient, sought to guarantee its own reproduction through the market, whereas before it did so through war. This always remained true, as is shown in peasant answers to questions about the impact of colonization—put with typical military subtlety by the head of Dogondoutchi subdivision:

> Old people to whom I asked the question: "What would you do if the whites tired of your laziness and your stubbornness and left you?" "That's simple," they answered: "we would take

shelter in our mountains; the chiefs would go to war and any
man who wandered or came hunting in the places where today
we peacefully farm would be taken prisoner by our horsemen."
"So you think you are freer today than before?" "Naturally.
With the tax paid and granaries filled we can do as we please
and go off to work or trade, in any direction. Never have we
known such peace and tranquility." The Black, even when one
knows him well, likes to flatter, but there is a good deal of truth
in what he says.[11]

Undoubtedly, with less serenity than professed by this
elder, lineages spread out to conquer virgin lands and grew in
number. During this period the French let the system seek a
new equilibrium and adapt itself to market conditions, but the
peasant economy was only marginally integrated into the
capitalist market.

1930-1960. During the second period of colonization, the
establishment of new relations of production took place. It
opened with a great famine that began at the end of the 1920s
and worsened in 1931, provoking substantial emigration:

These emigrants are mainly women and children who go
wherever they can find something to eat. Heads of families,
men who are able to work, remain in the village and take charge
of the sowing. . . . Few taxes are paid.[12]

In the wake of this famine, which upset market mechanisms
and spurred a return to barter, governors and governed found
themselves at an impasse. The colonial state had to intervene
directly in the affairs of peasants who, on top of their
difficulties, saw their numbers increase. Protective measures,
such as the spread of manioc cultivation, were reinforced in an
authoritarian way. Around 1933 orders were issued to create
grain reserves, first for millet and then for groundnuts. The
goal of the latter, pursued throughout the Sahel, was to counter
the legendary "native lack of foresight." These forced reserves
were looked upon with extreme disfavor by the "natives" in
question, who, though they may have seemed lacking in
foresight, had foreseen something else with their harvest,
especially when the harvest was so small:

[the] control and constitution of reserve granaries were rendered more difficult. . . . 3) by the bad faith of natives who do not want to set up grain reserves and who multiply the difficulties: harvests concealed and stored far from villages, fleeing into the bush when I approach, requests for "deals," threats to flee to Nigeria, etc., etc. All these maneuvres facilitated by the inertia of village chiefs. In this connection I have been obliged to explain that this millet is the personal property of each family group having participated in filling the granaries and is not destined, as some fear, to supply canton chiefs or *cercle-guards* on trek.[13]

French authorities then launched plans for spreading cash crops, notably peanuts, around 1935. The latter were first introduced in 1911. After successful pilot projects, seeds were distributed in several villages. A slight increase took place during the 1920s, but fell off during the famine of 1931. After 1933, with bad times behind them, there was a substantial rise. Trade in groundnuts was conducted by the Sociétée de Prévoyance, which had first loaned seeds to peasants according to the size of the family. Big commercial establishments like FAO and Karam-Karam then bought what was produced and had it processed in France. By 1937-1938 practically every village was involved, and year after year the subdivision's production continued to grow:

All the villages visited had sown peanuts. Under these conditions it was difficult to ascertain whether the amounts fixed by the Commandant de Cercle had actually been planted, most seeds not having sprouted yet. I have seen recently-sown fields . . . but the natives are always careless about weeding. . . . This has been pointed out to them and they have been warned that they are liable to administrative sanctions.[14]

Cotton, long grown in small quantities by the Mawri, also attracted attention. Despite efforts to develop this crop, results were mediocre. Propaganda, threats, sanctions, and financial pressures imposed these industrial crops almost as obligations. The need for money grew. Taxes were raised and the appearance of foreign products—notably from Nigeria, where England was dumping cloth and trade goods—stimulated people to spend. The market finally created an exchange economy that exceeded even the dreams of the administration. In effect, foodstuffs and livestock, which had been subject to protectionist policies pursued by the French colonial government during this period, were exported to Nigeria and Dahomey without the authorities' knowledge.

> Furthermore, I can state that in areas where we have been able to make peasants understand the need for grain reserves and family cassava fields, famine has been averted. Unfortunately the Mawri are not yet at this stage. Transactions with Nigeria remain at a high level. Despite surveillance, millet is illegally exported to Sokoto where it is sold for a high price, which explains why there is precious little to be found in local markets. . . . The price of animals [in Sokoto] is coming down following a substantial influx of Tuaregs from Gao who cross the border illegally. Most recently more than 300 head of cattle and 500 sheep arrived in Sokoto. A cow is worth 5 to 7 pounds, a sheep 15 to 20 shillings. All cloth entering the territory comes through the black market, for each individual has a right to only one piece of cloth for garments.[15]

The colonists thus tightened their grasp on the economy, while leaving peasants with the burden of reproducing the labor force. This had the effect of accelerating and crystalizing processes already underway. Increases in trade and in the use of money were preludes to new social relationships. Parallel to this was the creation of an educational system and positions as auxiliaries in the administration or in the private sector which were to create a future ruling class.

1960 to the present. The decolonization process got underway at the end of World War II. Supported by merchants and notables, the R.D.A. (Rassemblement Démocratique Africain)[16] launched a power struggle against the French administration, eventually replacing it in 1960 without changing its methods of operation. After independence, development options and social structures remained the same, except that the state assumed a larger role. The group that took power was legitimated only by the French military presence and the economic support of French business interests in Niger. Development continued to be controlled by the international market and the inflow of foreign currency. Although it relied on the masses, the R.D.A. still remained a party of cadres seeking tighter economic and political control within the country. Members of the government and senior civil servants attempted to take over major offices in the "traditional" sector. This last tactic was made all the easier as the colonial government had always favored the most subservient royal families, fixing a direct line of succession in defiance of customary rules. The heirs enjoyed privileges that brought many of them into close contact with the new state. Such was the case among the Mawri. In the *canton* of Takassaba the *canton* chief was a government minister under the Hamani Diroi regime; in Tibiri he was a deputy; among the Arewa many members of the royal lineage had important positions, both political (deputy, mayor of Niamey, party secretary) and administrative (chief agricultural officer, subprefect). Only the *canton* chief was recruited exclusively from traditional elites.

This old aristocracy, already initiated into various speculative practices, sought to forge a permanent material base on which to anchor its domination, first through whatever means money could buy, then through violent appropriation of the means of production. By combining speculation with a reappropriation of land which was both commercial and feudal, the aristocracy set an example imitated by businessmen and civil servants of various backgrounds. Thus, a unified dominant class emerged. The great famine that began in 1968 and lasted six years helped greatly, just as it permitted western imperialism, then in a crisis of readaptation, to blaze a new trail toward a more profitable mode of exploitation.[17] In effect, this famine, in accelerating the liquidation of the last forms of resistance put up by the "traditional" mode of agricultural and pastoral exploitation, was a timesaver for the dominant classes. This transition is today still far from complete. Neither agriculture nor livestock are "capitalist." The contradictions have yet to be resolved. This phase always entails difficulties, factionalism within the power structure,[18] popular resistance, and periods of stagnation.

Here, as elsewhere, the capitalist system penetrated by fits and starts. First came conquest, a violent imposition corresponding to the need for raw materials and outlets for the growing industries of western countries. Having destroyed the most troublesome precolonial legacies, there was a period of reorganization during which the foundation of another system was laid by directly utilizing the colonized society (requisitions, forced labor). Contradictions within the old structures surfaced quickly and a crisis followed: the famine of 1931. The state responded despotically with obligatory conservation of human and material resources and forced cultivation of cash crops. Peasant surpluses and energy were thus easily seized by a rapidly monetarized market. In this context forced labor was no longer necessary. Shortly afterwards it became obvious that direct rule was becoming too costly, morally and politically as well as financially. Independence was imperialism's easy way out. But the resistance of modes of production not yet totally crushed was compounded by the crisis of international capital, which provoked new convulsions that explain the catastrophic consequences of the 1968-1975 famine for the peoples of the Sahel. Here, again, the local and international bourgeoisies seized the occasion to further their domination, this time by depriving the peasants of the means of production because they could be exploited more efficiently as proletarians—but not without hesitations, false starts, or difficulties.

But this is only a general historical overview seen in terms of colonial policy. Now we must shed some light on the mechanisms underlying the destruction of precapitalist modes of production. How, from the peasants' point of view, was this transformation accomplished? What laws favored one system's domination of another? To answer these questions we will bring out the basic processes in the passage from one social formation to another, at a later stage analyzing modalities and concrete application (struggles, resistance, turning points). This abstract point, studied in its dialectical relationship with the real world, will help us discern the causes of previously noted phenomena as they appear over time.

THE LINEAGE-TRIBUTARY MODE OF PRODUCTION

Let us briefly recall the three modes of production in precolonial Mawri society: slavery, tribute, and lineage. It is the latter which determined the configurations of the rural economy. One way or another, slaves ended up being integrated either into a lineage or into jobs that gave them the same rights as free men, though they were considered "bastards" throughout their lives:

> The mode of production is not dominated by slavery; the lineage mode of production remains predominant, marked by sexual division of labor, work in age-sets, as well as by the pooling of production [Piault, 1975b:327].

As we have seen, the tribute mode of production was juxtaposed on the lineage system. Value appropriated by the dominant group was sufficient neither for that group to be supported by it alone nor to destroy preexisting production processes.[19] The aristocracy not only preserved the laws of the lineage structure, but assimilated themselves into the organization of agricultural labor and kinship. Princes worked their fathers' fields and performed the same work that might fall to any unmarried young man. Court dignitaries were exempted from these tasks; but they had, in addition to their slaves, sons and nephews who took care of the necessary production:

> The tribute mode of production dominates a community fraught with inequalities; i.e., a non-market surplus (goods or labour) is extracted from peasant producers, either by the lineage's elders or, at a higher level, by the political group formed by the ruler, his household, and his council [Piault, 1975b:327].

The entire productive system was subservient to lineage principles, ones that we shall study in their pure or abstract form in order to understand the consequences of the establishment of the capitalist market.

This mode of production is characterized by the absence of merchant capital. Subsistence predominates, trade affects only surpluses or certain specific jobs, often complementary. Most income is from agriculture, with millet the principal product. This crop requires organization to manage stocks. One harvest must feed people for an entire year, provide seeds for the next, and allow for a reserve. Hunting and gathering can become integral parts of the agricultural cycle when there are shortfalls. Herding provides animals either for transport (donkeys, camels, horses) or for luxury additions to the diet, but they are above all a means of saving up for marriage or a medium of exchange. Economic organization relies on sexual division of labor and on work done by age-sets. Men do most of the farming. Women have supplementary fields, but must fetch water and wood and perform domestic chores. Women and youth are subject to the head of the family; he controls production but redistributes it to the collectivity, having no personal or private right to it himself. Control of the bride-price, and hence the circulation of women, gives him his power. He also settles internal conflicts. The assembly of lineage heads constitutes a council for directing village affairs, and their dependents can seldom appeal their decisions. If one of them should die, he will be replaced by his younger brother or his eldest son, who thus assumes the same prerogatives. The only real wealth is human, and there exists scarcely any possibilities for accumulation. The system produces little surplus, something difficult in the absence of trade. There is a permanent search for balance with a harsh natural environment, which figures prominently in religious beliefs:

> Nature is neither specifically hostile or beneficent; man is part of it, and to assure his subsistence without destroying the equilibrium he must return to the environment what he takes from it. . . . Nature is not to be subjugated and domesticated, it is not set aside for man; nor is it the object of constant appropriation, of the systematic attempts to transform it that lead Western man to destroy the universe in making it fit for his use [Piault, 1975a:1].

Land is seen as free, without any limitation on access. Each person takes an area corresponding to the size of his family and changes only when soil is worn out. Rights to the land continue as long as it is actually cultivated. Both simple and complex systems of cooperation unite people through their production

units, either within a lineage or outside of it. *Gaya* is a
collective action, at someone's request, for important under-
takings such as the first and second plantings, building granaries, and constructing houses. Whoever wants to may come:
neighbors, relatives, or friends. The beneficiary of a *gaya* must
in turn provide food and call in *griots*.[20] In the same way that it
adopted kinship structures, so the established power made this
mode of collaboration its own. The terms and surface forms are
the same, but to the degree that the requesting party occupies a
socially dominant position that excludes reciprocity, the sense
is not quite the same. The *gaya* becomes forced labor. Later we
shall see that its application varied over time according to the
ruler's strength. Parallel to the *gaya* is another form of self-
help found among individuals, often within the same lineage. It
is a matter of lending a hand: *Tanyo* (to help), which involved
mutuality within a determined range of time, is an exchange
between heads of households, frequently through the seconding
of their juniors, without any provision of goods in return. In
addition to labor, aid between villages or kin takes the form of
gifts and countergifts, notably millet.

Along with agriculture there is artisanry. Certain family
groups practice the crafts that have been handed down through
the generations: blacksmiths, *griots,* and weavers. This system
does not preclude social differentiation, but it is practically
never the result of accumulated wealth. Rather, social differentiation is based on the ability to harness a maximum amount
of human energy, to which are added values linked to the
presence of a predatory state: strength, courage, authority,
power, prestige, and ostentation. The needs of agriculture,
which regulate this social organization, simultaneously make
it vulnerable. Social relationships largely oriented toward the
group itself presuppose self-sufficiency, but the natural environment is particularly forbidding and uncertain. With the
absence of diversified production and the lack of tools, this
system runs the risk of upheavals when its precarious equilibrium is lost. The solution is to wait, to migrate, and/or to be
discovered by the outside.

This last transformation is in contradiction with the principles of self-sufficiency and requires adaptation, or it creates deterioration or even destruction. This "outside" has, in fact, always imposed itself on segmentary societies which eventually break down when confronted by powerful structures or armies. We have seen how the Arewa brought pressure to bear on the Gubawa, who had to use warfare to alleviate the resulting disequilibria. Now we shall see how the capitalist system established its rule over the Mawri, but with means and objectives that left no room for adaptation. Here we shall analyze the processes set in motion, which must not, under any condition, be confused with a chronological ordering of the unfolding of events.

Pillage. The first phase was a test of strength. Colonialism established a single centralized government, and imposed obligations (head tax, forced labor and sale of products, unpaid porterage, and requisitions) in order to subjugate the population and to break down or modify anything (Arewa sovereignty, councils of elders, or religious leaders) likely to siphon off goods and men. The principle was established that authority flows only from the colonial administration. The latter can thus seize anything the colonized society produces—livestock, wild produce, and millet—without interfering in the organization of the production process.

When the whites arrived, they bought hides. This ceased under Gao.[21] They bought all sorts of hides in great quantities. They took them to the east.[22] They bought animals which they drove to the east. During the reign of Koché[23] they asked peasants to bring millet *(zaka)*[24] to the chief who took it who-knows-where. During Gao's reign, the whites also bought kapok and cotton; that stopped under Arzika. Under Koché peasants sold animals, millet, and calabashes to pay taxes [Magagi, village of Dubelma].

We would build houses, carry tree trunks, we would go look for straw to make *seccos;* we carried earth to repair offices and houses. Two or three years later we were ordered to transport millet on donkeys from villages to Doutchi, from Doutchi to Niamey, guarded by a *dogari.*[25] This was gift millet. It was up to the people from whom millet was demanded to transport it to Niamey; arriving in Niamey they were all given 15 F. [Chief of Marnakainé village].

New structures were erected, in addition, military posts were set up, transport routes were marked out, coins began to be used in transactions, and people began to learn French. This framework and the pillage it unleashed stimulated the beginnings of a new social differentiation.

Divisions crept into the royal lineages. Whoever was in power when the whites arrived remained there if he represented a sufficiently large collectivity and if he collaborated. In this he was favored by French law, which recognized only direct succession, and by economic advantages, which gave him the means to maintain his position. In a similar vein, the burden of requisitions was not felt by everyone in the same way. The chief and his entourage received a commission on taxes, thus giving them access to cash at a time when money was still rare but of increasing importance. In addition, their new intermediary position between the French and the population enabled them to make numerous, and profitable, exactions. They were not subject to the forced labor which affected one person per family each year for a period of ten days to several months. They were exempted from it when they put their children in school or when they acted as monitors, inspectors, and overseers. This is mentioned by GubéGao, a member of a royal lineage in the North:

340 workmen were put at my disposal to go work in Niamey, making a landing strip for airplanes. I was head of the crew, seven horsemen accompanied me. We were gone six months.

On the other hand, these obligations were very onerous for peasants, with a slight advantage going to large families which could spread these new burdens more easily among their members.

The Market Absorbs Surpluses

Once the necessary foundation had been laid, the market economy was in a position to appropriate a portion of the value produced by the population. The development and protection of agriculture and herding and the introduction of peanuts and cotton should have enabled peasants to reproduce their labor force and leave a surplus for taxes. Taxation was the key to this strategy. With the state demanding payment in cash, peasants were under pressure to sell part of their harvests, their animals, or their labor by emigrating toward the coast. Money thus obtained also allowed them to purchase western goods which eventually replaced locally made items. Enameled bowls replaced clay pots, decorated calabashes, and wooden platters. Imported cloth supplanted the *pagnes* made by African weavers. White salt invaded the market, displacing the black salt from local saltworks. Cube sugar replaced honey.

At first the alienated surplus was not large enough to endanger the reproduction of labor. Their own system and their resistance to new impositions enabled peasants to retain reserves assuring a complete agricultural cycle. Peanuts were presented to peasants as a workable, useful safeguard. With their harvest they could pay their taxes easily, diversify their consumption patterns by purchasing foodstuffs or goods they did not make, have savings in the form of livestock, and create reserves with the millet they would not have to sell. Scales were set up in two centers where peasants came in November to sell their crops. As long as a production unit was in this first phase—that is, as long as the capitalist system intervened only at the end of the production chain without disturbing it—the latter would yield a surplus. Peanuts were actually the result of supplementary work, performed in addition to the community's essential work. It was the same for other goods: foodstuffs, livestock, and labor in amounts or at times that would not jeopardize the internal organization. This was so for livestock when it was for a specific need, such as forming a marriage dowry; for grain brought to the market in small calabashes in the months following the harvest; and for migrations affecting only one or two younger sons who left during the dry season—or even small jobs that everyone performed in the area once their own chores were done.

Everything was as if the market and the "traditional" sector agreed to peaceful coexistence and mutual support. In fact, it was nothing of the sort: The former had already imposed its rule over the latter.

Social differences became more marked and took on different forms when confronted by the market.

Accumulation. Those who found themselves in the right place at the right time—the aristocracy, merchants, artisans in a profitable trade, or those who simply seized the opportunity—had things very much in their favor. They were able to develop land, had easy entry into trade, practiced various forms of lending, and used to the fullest their position as intermediaries between peasants and the market. Peanuts played an important role in this process:

> When peanuts arrived for the first time, the whites gave them out as gifts, not even 1 kg. per family. Then they made loans. If people borrowed by the can, they took two cans and had to repay three; if it was by the sack, they took one sack and repaid one and a half. Each village had a granary. Then in November or December, a month after the harvest, the whites would buy. People's borrowing was limited by the size of their family, they checked cards [census-tax cards]. It was rich people who could borrow the most [Hodi, village of Tibiri].

Money made from this cash crop allowed those who could take advantage of it to appropriate land very rapidly.

> It is because of peanuts that there is a shortage of land. People used land for peanuts. They clear it, then it belongs to them; they then plant millet and so on because peanuts need to be rotated yearly to get a good yield. Everyone cleared brush or felt obliged to plant peanuts because of the tax, but would have preferred to plant millet. If some people planted more peanuts than millet, they resold peanuts to buy millet. There weren't many of them, but they got rich more quickly than the rest. We, the others, didn't want to grow peanuts, it's a waste of time. It is better to grow one's own millet than to waste time going to buy it. You can't make *fura* [millet gruel] with peanuts, and if you come home and all you find is peanuts, you have to wait until you sell them. When land began to run out, people planted peanuts in their own millet fields. They were forced to plant less millet, and peanuts grow best by themselves [Hodi, village of Tibiri].

Old Chefu sums it all up: "Those who buy have cars, those who sell don't even have a donkey."

By the same token, livestock spawned a large-scale trade, notably with Nigeria, from which kola nuts were imported. The processes and consequences were the same as for industrial crops. Money was continuously reinvested in commerce. Speculation produced substantial profits. That began a cycle of accumulation: creation of herds, food stocks, and control of paid labor. At the same time, the wealthy continued to profit from their networks of clients and dependents.

Pauperization. Conversely, small producers, even if they were still preserving their nonmercantile activities, felt the repercussions of the economic transformations taking place around them. Drains on the lineage economy, peanuts, taxes, migrations, and sales of various products finally ate into reserves, used up the arable land and reduced pasture lands. While population increased due to improved health care and more marriages, lineages crumbled. Youths had the means to create their personal income by selling crops from their own fields, and above all by selling their labor.[26] They had less and less need of elders in putting together a bride-price, and gradually escaped their control. Conversely, an elder with fields too small to support his consumption unit would send his older children away (this second case occurred less frequently than the first). The head tax accentuated this movement toward individualization made possible by market mechanisms that offered elders and youth the opportunity for private appropriation of goods.

> During each census, they give each married man his family card, everyone pays his own tax, you take care of yourself and you want to pay the tax quickly without bothering your parents. Sons seek their fortune in town; sons get married and leave and the father can't feed his daughter-in-law and grandchildren by himself. He gives plots of land to his sons but they no longer want to work and think only of realizing their dreams in town [Ibrahim, village of Birnini Lokoyo].

> There is no more family unity, every young married man thinks himself self-sufficient. No one wants to share the work to help someone else, even if it's his next of kin [Mayaki, of Dogondoutchi].

Older people always explain the disappearance of the *gandu* by saying that the young are lazy, an argument refuted by young people who complain about the harshness of the elders' authority. However that may be, the transition to small independent production was accompanied by substantial parceling of land. The fields were divided as people separated.

In the end, the formal subjugation of the lineage-tributary mode of production meant abandoning to the market a portion of exchange value which, at first glance, did not seem to greatly affect economic and social organization. Yet, its destruction began there. Without its "shock absorbers" (grain reserves and labor force), trying to adapt to the market, its equilibrium precarious, this society became extremely vulnerable to the slightest fluctuation in prices, to climatic changes, or to trouble of any kind. A crisis such as the last drought would, as we have seen, allow capitalism to enter its second stage of domination.

THE MARKET ABSORBS THE ESSENTIALS

Pauperization. Within the framework of conditions imposed on them, peasants sought to surmount the contradictions confronting them. This recourse led them into even greater subjugation. Take, for example, the case of a farmer who planted his medium-sized fields with millet and peanuts. If the price of peanuts dropped (as was often the case), he had to sell some goats to pay his tax; the following year he tried to sow more peanuts, but at the expense of his millet field. During the consecutive sowing periods his granaries were empty; he looked for work to make ends meet. But this work kept him from spending the necessary time on his own fields. The coming harvest would be even poorer. Thus, one way or another, he had to fall back on the market to find the necessary monetary compensation. The market became a trap. Peasants at first were forced to resort to it, abandoning only what seemed to them the least indispensable, then, at the first sign of trouble, reestablishing the equilibrium by selling a little bit more. This "little bit more" might actually put them back on their feet, but only temporarily. The trap was often already set. Let us return to our peasant. He started selling his animals to pay his taxes. A means of saving, livestock at first made up for shortages and lost their role of savings for a bride-price, which, in turn, took the form of money, prompting a greater and less easily resolved need for cash. When additional money was supplied by the sale of peanuts, the consequences took the form of food imbalances and problems related to land. If this income was derived from outside work, it could result in a smaller harvest.

The second phase of subjugation to capitalism began when the market siphoned off what was necessary for the reproduction of labor; in our example, it is when there was a shortage of millet. Aware of the causes of instability, Mawri farmers tried to eliminate the most serious one—peanuts. They resisted administration pressure and, aside from certain merchants or producers with large resources, they finally stopped growing this crop during the last drought. But this slowdown had an immediate corollary in the commercialization of millet. From here on, peasants met their need for money by selling foodstuffs that were in increasingly short supply, especially when there were crop failures. Pushed to the limit, many of them were forced to emigrate for longer periods (a loss of human resources to the local economy) or to seek work as day laborers during the rainy season—this time, directly to the detriment of their own fields.

> Someone who leaves his field, even for a day, if he hasn't finished his field, it's a loss for him, it's difficult to catch up later [Gumba, village of Lokoko].

Finally, if all these expedients do not suffice, there is a last resort: The land itself can be sold.

> People travel to make money, otherwise they lose their land. That often happens. These days, you pawn more, otherwise you sell everything [Dashigow, village of Guéshémé].

Space does not permit a detailed discussion of land problems (de Latour Dejean, 1975). Let us recall that in the traditional system land was not individually appropriated and was allocated to those who worked it for as long as they continued to do so. When the introduction of cash crops coincided with a relative shortage of land in the southern *dallol,* land acquired an exchange value (insofar as it was productive) and a price (which rose as land was occupied). Land gradually became alienable private property. This metamorphosis of the land system led to numerous violent conflicts:

> Twenty years ago, the bush was like a young girl; anyone could court her. Now it's like a wife; once you've married her you have to guard her, no one can violate her [Maï Angoal, hamlet of Sarkin Tudu].

And there can be unwanted divorces: There are numerous forms of land alienation, mortgages being the most widespread. It can mean, as with sale, that it is lost forever. But landless peasants are still rare, and this market process is mostly confined to rich lands in the south. The phenomenon is practically nonexistent among the northern Mawri. In sum, after selling what they produce, farmers give up their labor force to compensate for the resulting shortfalls, which leads to new imbalances that the sale of land attempts to solve. In other words, capitalism gives the peasants weapons that often backfire.

Peasants also seek help from the traditional system. Gifts and mutual assistance within lineage segments provide some breathing room, but it is more a collective sharing of poverty than a means of combating it. There is still community solidarity at the distribution level, but it is never reestablished at the production level. A solution is for a bachelor to become a *bara,* a dependent of someone who has money. That person, in exchange for work performed, feeds his *bara,* pays his taxes, and, after a certain length of time, gives him a wife. Such "voluntary slavery" obviously avoids the need to make money and the anguish of not being able to put together a dowry. In certain cases it can even allow the *bara* to benefit from the work of day laborers hired by the master if he has been given a *gamana* or has been allowed to return to the family lands for short periods.

I am a *bara* of the medic, I'm from another village. I was at school and I refused to take the exam because I was beaten at school and I didn't see why I should continue. I went back to my parents' for a year and my father asked me to leave and find work to bring in money for my family. I came here to the medic who gives me money when I go to visit my parents. I have been here for six years. I till the fields—there are three of them—I help the medic in the dispensary, in the dry season I tend the garden. I don't work Sundays but on that day I wash the laundry. I have never refused to do a job for the medic. He pays my taxes, clothes me; when I ask him for spending money he gives it to me or he doesn't. He is going to get me a wife. I don't have a *gamana,* he gives me too much work and I would not have the time to work one. I can't just up and leave, because I've been with him for six years. Maybe I'll stay with my wife, if I don't find a job [Tankari, village of Tibiri].

Becoming a *bara* does not actually solve problems; it is a last resort that ultimately strengthens the power of the rich.

Accumulation. Landowners, as we have seen, established themselves as intermediaries between the peasants and capitalist institutions. The cycles of accumulation which they controlled were reinforced by accumulated monetary surpluses which made possible a continued appropriation of labor power and the constitution of large landholdings. This more permanent intertwining of new social relationships was facilitated by the last crisis. We may recall that during the period of formal subjugation, trade focused principally on livestock and peanuts: The drought made their exploitation almost impossible. Aside from fluctuations in the world market, price instability led to overgrazing and irregular harvests, as peanuts required a regular and relatively abundant rainfall.

Dealers turned immediately, and profitably, to the commercialization of millet. With drought speculation increased, taking advantage of regional disparities and seasonal variations. In effect, there was a lucrative trade between the bush and the towns, between towns and the city, or between regions with a favorable climate and parched regions. The same was true for other foodstuffs. Bought during the harvest, when prices were at their lowest, they stored and then resold during the planting season to yield what was frequently substantial profit. At the same time, there was a proliferation of systems for lending with interest to peasants:

> Many people went into the peanut business, sowing large fields and speculating. Those who got rich that way are today dealing in millet, *pois de terre,* and beans. They get even richer. There are three places here where dealers buy millet brought in by farmers in the bush. There they wait for trucks to take it away [Yargu, village of Guéshémé].

Former peanut dealers were not the only ones to start dealing in foodstuffs; many well-off farmers or small traders did so as well:

> I began by selling my millet during planting, then I bought a bit more and took it all to Niamey. Profits rose these last two years with the intensification of the drought. The drought in other regions enables us to make a profit, either in those regions themselves or in Niamey, which wasn't supplied like it was before. When you go into the disaster zones you sell wholesale to merchants in that region. People there sell their animals so they can buy. But I don't sell during the rainy season, I take care of my fields [Mallam Kondo, village of Tibiri].

Even civil servants started investing in agriculture:

> In any case, agriculture is profitable because the price of millet has risen enormously. Last year I spent 12,000 CFA on labour. I borrowed land [not a problem for a civil servant, as people know that he will leave and is unlikely to stay more than ten years[27]] and my harvest was 110 bundles = 1 ton and 100 kg = 33,000 CFA here and 55,000 CFA in Niamey. The price of millet helps solve the rural exodus problem, as the loafers in Niamey can no longer feed themselves in Niamey and are forced to go back home. Prices began to fluctuate five years ago. It is due to lack of rain. Good millet land was in the north. For five years the north has received no rain, while rain falls in arid regions like this. So prices have increased greatly and there is much speculation in foodstuffs. The south can barely meet its needs and northerners descend on the south. It is all good business for dealers who make large profits out of this situation [Agricultural monitor in Guéshémé].

As during the colonial period, the state, through its purchasing agencies (UNCC for peanuts, OPVN for foodstuffs), tries to stabilize the price of millet by prohibiting its export or sale to traders not affiliated with the OPVN, and by fixing prices. But these measures are limited or sporadically applied, as they adversely affect the social strata, which is the principal political support of the government. In addition, its own members and most civil servants profit from this situation. Finally, these attempts to improve the situation prove a total failure. Producers sell to buyers who offer them more than the OPVN, thus giving birth to a black market. An entire chain of petty profiteering grows up around the principal speculators, rapidly spreading to include small and large traders, intermediaries, and transporters.

> Farmers bring millet to the city to a guy and give him 5 F. per bundle. This intermediary receives money from buyers and gives it to peasants. These intermediaries are people with well-situated houses [accessible to trucks]. Peasants sell their millet like that when they are in need. Rich people take their millet to Niamey or directly to traders [Umaru, village of Guéshémé].

Or, again,

> I am the only one in this hamlet who makes sacks from the bundles that I buy. I go to Guéshémé to resell them. I transport them by camel. I give them to a trader who sells them in Niamey. The sack costs 2,500 CFA, 300 CFA for shipping it to Niamey, and they give me 3,500 to 4,000 CFA from the Niamey sale price [Mai Angoal, hamlet of Gérépchi].

These dealers are also farmers, and every farmer, if he has a surplus, is henceforth able to profit from price fluctuations without necessarily being an intermediary.

> I had a harvest of 900 bundles, I sold 13 sacks in Niamey, at 4,000 CFA less 300 CFA for transport, during planting. With that I hired labourers to clear brush land: 3,650 CFA; from the first crop, 40,000 CFA; from the second crop, 20,000 CFA; and from the final harvest 3,000 CFA [Halilu, village of Guéshémé].

Numerous civil servants also participate in this process through toleration of various practices or by actively participating in widespread operations which supplement their salaries.

Such large outflows of millet force peasants to be integrated into the labor market, either by emigrating toward coastal areas or, locally, by working for more wealthy farmers during the farming season.

When peanuts were good, we paid taxes and migrated less, except those who needed money to clothe themselves and their family. Now we pay with millet, and people migrate more [Gona, village of Lokoko].

Here, as in the trade in foodstuffs, employers range from small peasants who hire occasionally, after a good harvest or a profitable migration, to permanent employers of labor. The first case is illustrated by Tankari:

I was a day labourer but stopped when I got a garden. Now sometimes I hire day labourers whom I pay with honest-to-goodness sugar cane. This year I had two labourers who spent a month at 100 F. a day in my garden. For the fields I hire people, but I have to wait until rich people have finished hiring as they offer higher salaries at the start of planting [Tankari, village of Fadama].

The rich have the means to monopolize a maximum number of workers because, on the one hand, they hire every day and thus day laborers do not constantly have to go looking for work and, on the other hand, they go by car to recruit in the poorest regions—in northern Nigeria for the southern Mawri and in villages on the fringe of the arable zone for the northern Mawri. In a different vein:

The chief and his entourage go look for people in Nigeria, but they don't give the sum agreed on at the outset. They tell them: "You get return transportation by car, that's good enough." Once the affair was so serious it could only be regulated by the Sarkin Kabi. It rains later in Nigeria, so they can come, but we don't go to Nigeria; when we want to hire we go to the merchants—they pay better [Chefu, hamlet of Bayawa].

Paid labor is not the only form of labor tapped by the rich, who exploit the dependence relationships offered by the "traditional" system. We have already mentioned those concerning the ruler: *gaya* and *bara,* whose origins should be

recalled here. Before colonization, poor people had the option
of taking refuge with the ruler, who took care of them in
exchange for work. These people were called *bara*. Responsible for the general prosperity and obliged to find remedies for
any failing in the system, the Sarkin Arewa was the only one
who could, and had to, take them in. Disposition of the *bara*,
like the fruits of *gaya* from several villages, is a prerogative
linked to the obligations of the ruler and to the ruler alone. At
another level, each elder had dependents who gave him his
place in the kinship system. Today such traditions still persist,
but are not governed by customary rules. Money has replaced
them, modifying their initial meaning. Now one only has to be
wealthy to have dependents. If the *canton* chief still benefits
from *gaya* and *bara,* so, too, does his entourage, who have no
right to any of the ruler's prerogatives:

> Now Dangaladima,[28] the Deputy, *chefs de secteur,* the chief, all
> demand *gaya.* They pay no one, except for food. Before, with
> Arzika,[29] they gave people beef, a *boubou* to the village chief,
> and paid the *griots.* He didn't ask for as much *gaya.* Now with
> these *chefs de secteur* the canton is in a mess, he lets people with
> money do whatever they want: *"nuce"*[30]—they get their palms
> greased. . . . They bring the chief millet after the harvest. The
> *dogari* go around the villages and demand one bundle per
> family. They requisition camels for transport. It's an obligation
> for us. Garba and Arzika didn't do that. They gave the *talakas*
> gifts. Today I have never seen a chief give anything to a *talaka*[31]
> in trouble. If it's a bad year the chief doesn't even sell within his
> own canton. He only gives to *chefs de secteur* and his own court
> [Yargu, village of Guéshémé].

> The *gaya* for the chief and the Deputy are not *gaya* at all, they
> are obligations. They hardly spend anything. The chief asks
> everybody while the *talaka* asks only his close neighbours for
> *gaya.* People have to drop their work for the chief, even the
> *griots* who aren't paid. But a *talaka* can only ask people when
> they are free. The chief gets a whole village for *gaya,* but there
> are some villages that have never done it. He favours some
> villages [Saru, village of Guéshémé].

Similar stories are also told in the north, but they deal more
with the *chef de canton's* family than with the chief himself,

who follows tradition rather closely. Thus, we find the same abuses with only slight variations and with a slightly lesser degree of coercion, since the aristocracy did not manage to adapt as fast as that in the south. Just as the statutory relationships were redirected, so, in turn, are kinship rules flouted. He who plays the role of elder within a lineage, who keeps his cousins and brothers around him, is no longer the eldest, but the wealthiest. Large family units spring up around the rich, while the poor families break down. There is a new tie that binds: money. To cite just one example, the deputy[32] mentioned above has an estate on which live the family of his brother (who takes care of the fields, hires workers, and so on), cousins of various degrees (both maternal and paternal), four wives, 29 children who all go or will be going to school, and several *bara*. The juxtaposition of lineage and capitalist systems enables those economic "alchemists" who mix them to have an economic reproduction regularly assured by customary obligations. At the same time, they guarantee their descendants access to key positions either through schooling, through the party, or through accumulated property.

When my family[33] came to power I became my own master. When a family controls a chiefship, they gather around (we were separated before) and help each other, organize big projects. Before, chiefs were idiots, they lived like parasites, they didn't work, they did not try to accumulate, but they went around and took things from peasants when they needed them,[34] but in the end they weren't rich. They lost the peasants' respect. If a family gets rich, its members become important through their work, their money, and they will be favourably regarded at election time when poor candidates wouldn't dare challenge a wealthy man. Under the whites, chiefs didn't work their own lands and, despite the prohibition, continued to prey on peasants. *Talaka* families broke up because their fields were so small, whereas my family needs to form big work parties for big projects. For example, everybody rallies around Dangaladima and makes collective decisions. Ties are actually strengthened. For example, when there is a wedding ceremony or a baptism, if there are only three persons present, people will mock, whereas in my family there are always many of us. We bring our friends. It is very important, it proves we are liked, that people are behind us [Suley, village of Guéshémé].

One consequence of monopolizing human energy is a greater access to land. This is what Suley means by "big projects." But this, too, cuts both ways:

> From my business (millet and transport) I first bought two fields which were sold by owners arrested for non-payment of taxes. The next year I bought two others, one was sold to me by a fellow who was getting married and didn't have any money, the other by someone who wanted to buy a camel. Then I bought a fifth one from a Nigerian who was going home [Dogo, village of Korey Mairua].

On the other hand, there are still the traditional means where violence, alienation of land, and customary law go nicely together for the rich. They seek vacant and uncleared land, using the men they can put to work, then using the traditional concept of private property which gives land to whoever works it for ten consecutive years. They keep it. They farm intensively, bringing in fertilizer so that the land will be rejuvenated without rotation. A *chef de secteur* who took a field in his administrative zone, and not in his own village, as was the custom, said:

> Three years ago I took a field in my *secteur,* and I took one for the chief at the same time. It was the chief who asked me, so that the villagers wouldn't have to go all the way to Guéshémé for *gaya.* I take care of the chief's field. They send a vehicle to pick up the sacks [Aska, village of Guéshémé].

One part of Guéshémé's fields are fields that belong to the customary office of chief and not to the person occupying the office. But despite this rule, the chief treats this land as his private property. Usurpations are numerous and vary in technique. Here we will mention only some of the many possible actual cases:

> The chief moved the village of Guéshémé, he took land around the new site which had been farmed by the Fulbe who went into the bush. On top of that he took the fields around the old side, then others that belonged to us. It was our ancestors' land. I myself had five fields taken: three I had inherited and two small ones I had bought. I got others in return, farther away and not as good because I can't get fertilizer from the Fulbe. Under the whites you didn't get expropriated [Sani, village of Guéshémé].

Here is another example: Problems between herdsmen and
farmers are such that the Guéshémé *canton* chief decided to
make an official division into agricultural and grazing zones,
alternating every five years. Each time a zone vacated by the
Fulbe is opened for farming, the peasants are supposed to get
their lands back. However:

> When the bush is opened up the people in charge either get all of
> it, or a large portion. No *talaka* got a field in the first three areas
> of bush left by the Fulbe, even though they had previously
> farmed there. Then they put the Fulbe in other bush areas, and
> after five years those in charge took most of that and left the rest
> for the *talaka*. The *talaka* rushed in and stopped at fields
> belonging to others. You could only have small fields, and not
> your old ones. At the next change they used the same system. In
> the area vacated by the Fulbe you find, side-by-side: Dangala-
> dima with a field bigger than the village; Wakili, the *chef de
> secteur;* Halilu, Dangaladima's courtier; Aska, the other *chef
> de secteur;* all the chief's entourage [Chief of Guéshémé
> village].

In the very process of its formation this class-in-the-making
used its money to invade every sector through the play of
money and its mobility. The creation of market capital
permitted the creation of a labor capital, which made possible
landed capital. This study has not yet brought out the differences between the north and the south of the *dallol* Mawri,
differences to which we shall now turn.

THE NORTH AND THE SOUTH

The processes set in motion are basically the same throughout the rural world, but they take a different form in each of the
dallol's two parts. The north is, and has always been, poorer
than the south: Soils are thinner, water is more difficult to find,
rainfall is lower, and the region was closed longer to outside
influences. The north is a grazing and millet zone; the south, a
peanut zone. The latter thus experienced a more rapid process
of social differentiation which involved the entire society.
Inequalities grew in an unending procession—from petty
trader to big merchant, from small producer to large land-

holder, from camel driver to truck owner—all the while accentuating the disparities among hamlet, village, and town, Through trade the better-off inhabitants of Tibiri and Guéshémé *cantons* quickly progressed to the stage of appropriating the forces and means of production. The land tenure system was undone by the introduction of peanuts; expansion was impossible and all land was rapidly occupied, thereby leading to its privatization while peasant families fell back on small-scale production for the market.

Conversely, the Arewa were able to preserve lineage structures longer, which made the market's penetration more difficult. Credit was not used in the same way as in the south. Interest was frowned upon and was camouflaged behind apparently equal exchanges: A peasant who borrowed a bundle of millet during planting, when it cost 300 CFA, had to repay two bundles at 160 CFA at harvest time. Aside from a few big foreign merchants, trade consisted of numerous small transactions to obtain money, but without any accumulation. Emigration was important, but day laborers were almost all young men working for themselves on their days off.

Land began to be sold around Dogondoutchi, but in the north there was free access to it, since the available acreage greatly exceeded people's needs. Crops spread into the semi-desert zone that was used for grazing in winter. This region's inhabitants could not (and still cannot) imagine how land, property of the ancestors which thus belonged to everyone, could be sold for money. Economic disparities between peasants were slight; on the other hand, a gulf grew between them and their aristocracy, the merchants and traders in the regional administrative center of Dogondoutchi.

The last drought greatly affected the north, shattering social structures. Traditional labor relations, based on lineage principles, broke down and were replaced by wage labor. Elder-junior relationships, *gaya,* and *tanga* all diminished in importance to the point where it was not (and is not) rare to find one brother hiring another, or villages where *gaya* has not been requested or given. This region's impoverishment left no room for exchanges of goods or services, as there was nothing left in the granaries. As mutual assistance was a long-term proposition, no one could wait. Also disappearing were traditional payments within lineage groups which could no longer meet people's needs. The solutions of earlier times—hunting and gathering—were forgotten or were rendered impracticable by the massive reduction in natural resources. A fatalism set in, as those who should have assumed responsibility failed to do so (*yan Kasa,* lineage elders, dignitaries, ruler). Help had to come from elsewhere. Those in charge did nothing, or little; they were preoccupied with problems that scarcely concerned the peasantry. The northern aristocracy had chosen to accumulate and invest outside the region—its capital came from land speculation and from trade in the more prosperous zones and cities. The drought gave it access to labor, which it used on the wet bottomlands for market gardening. But migration made capitalism the principal beneficiary of this labor force. Commercial penetration was not a prerequisite for separating peasants from their land.

The south, on the other hand, was less affected by the drought—or rather, it was affected in a more unequal way. Rainfall, which always varied, continued to change from one season to the next and from one village to another, producing both extremely abundant harvests and serious food shortages. However, the South's food shortages never equaled those in the North. Even though the processes of social differentiation rapidly produced results, the proportion of day laborers and migrants remained smaller here than among the Arewa, even during an economic recession. Conversely, new forms of dependence, stemming from the use of old structures on market bases, were highly developed.

The processes we have just analyzed are neither linear progressions nor quantum leaps, though they may appear to be so. The pauperization process—sale of products, sale of labor, and sale of land—and, conversely, accumulation, is still happening. It is destroying old modes of production and reconstituting new social relationships. This said, each individual's passage to a different phase may take apparently inconsistent directions, with various factors intervening to change the order outlined above. We are trying to describe processes, not present a photograph of society. Concretely, the division of the population into two classes does not exclude the role of chance, choice, and the ability to resist. Many people move between the two poles; at times employees, at times employers, sometimes speculators, sometimes unfortunate sellers. No single factor signals a passage from one stage to another. Someone selling his millet during planting, for example, could be either a poor person forced by debts to do so or a rich person engaging in speculation.[35] The same is true for someone who puts grain aside. He could be either a poor person trying to survive or a rich person stocking up in order to resell or to have several years of security. Similarly, migrations, agricultural day labor, or odd jobs can be undertaken to obtain extras or out of sheer necessity. The breakup of a household can be the result of a conscious decision or the result of an economic breakdown, which exposes its members to instability. It is the combining of all these elements that permits or denies access to a social class.

Outside this mass in midstream, petty production for market makes possible the existence of two extremes rooted in opposing classes. The question is whether petty production for market presently predominant will remain so and can become a permanent phenomenon without breaking down, or if capitalist structures will carry the day. To answer these questions, we must bring out the contradictions within this petty peasant mode of production. The most glaring one is this: Peasants are charged with reproducing the labor force without having the means to do so. Those means are eaten away or absorbed by capitalism. It erodes the kinship structures on which the organization of production was based; it forces the sale of products needed to assure a basic minimum and the sale of labor; nonmarket exchanges diminish or are monetarized; and artisanry disappears, forcing people to buy substitute goods. This precarious equilibrium will be hard pressed to survive.

The contradiction is all the more striking as land—the peasant's last resort—is appropriated. Soon no more arable land will be available and the soil will rapidly be exhausted. Succeeding generations will have scant opportunity to remain in this region. Nonetheless, petty production can delay for a long time yet the final resolution of this contradiction.

Today, we are still in the realm of paradox and disorder. Before, the coherence of value systems and institutions embodying society's search for a stable balance within its natural environment permitted an individual to identify with his group, to partake in the general process of reproducing his world. Ancestor cults were the sign of such continuity. Today, at the height of the phase of de-structuring, this society is witnessing a breakdown of its institutions, groups are without roots, and the depersonalized individual is becoming the only unit possible. Deprived of his ties with the past, and with the future uncertain, only the satisfactions of the present remain. Each concession to the capitalist system—explained by the absence of foresight or of choices, by the need to yield a portion of value produced to protect the essential—engenders permanent, long-term disequilibria. Herein lies the explanation of behavior which, by rational, western reasoning, appears aberrant. For example, peasants will walk for three days to sell an item for a profit of 100 francs because walking *costs* them nothing. Any value realized, however small, is crucial at that moment. Again, take the case of a small producer who hires and is hired during the same season. In the course of a transaction he will make a 500-franc profit. Not knowing how or if to keep it, he will use this sum to hire a day laborer. Returning a month later he finds his granaries empty and is forced in turn to sell his own labor. There is a fascination with money; it burns holes in the pockets of the poor to the point where it is feared and no longer plays its role as a store of value. People who are day laborers by necessity often demand payment in millet and, when there is shortage, this can lead the employer to lower the amount of millet he gives, even though the money price of a day's work remains constant. The circulation of money is a sort of whirlwind that strips the poor as it passes, while giving to the rich in abundance.

> We prefer money to millet. Money gets spent right away; millet is kept and goes into your gullet [Umaru, hamlet of Gérépchi].

The persistence of the "traditional" system, with its gifts and countergifts in kind in the context of kinship relationships, may lessen certain difficulties, but its obligations can also increase them: Bride-price, marriage gifts, and contributions to religious ceremonies linger on, but monetarization turns these "loans" into obligations, forcing peasants to resort to the market.

Economic resistence is not limited to abandoning peanuts or refusing to pay taxes. It seems that despite Islam's efforts, we are witnessing the reappearance of possession cults which are perhaps not unrelated to the need to recreate a community, a force, an identity beyond the reach of those who seek to destroy them. Beyond these hypotheses lurks the clear and stated intention, by both the aristocracy of yesterday and the *colons* of yesterday and today, of crushing the *talaka*. As Chefu says, "They rest in the shade and we farm for them in the sun."

NOTES

1. The *dallol Mawri* is a fossil valley situated 300 kilometers east of Niamey.

2. Yan'Kasa means "sons of the earth." They were priests in charge of ancestor cults.

3. See the map for some of the principalities. After the conquest, the French military attempted to preserve each principality by transforming them into cantons. But the units were too small and they were amalgamated little by little until there were only two cantons in the south, Tibiri and the Guéshémé, and one in the north, whose seat was moved from Matankari to Dogondoutchi in 1905.

4. A peasant who had proved his bravery might be awarded the title of Zasumey (literally, "brave, heroic"), which gave him a considerable role in settling conflicts and in organizing defense. He could become a raid leader, but the Mawri raided infrequently.

5. Peasants owned relatively few slaves. Any slaves they managed to keep ended up being incorporated into the lineage of their masters. By the third generation a slave would have the same rights as a free man. The ruler's slaves retained their slave status, but they, too, were integrated through access to important posts or jobs that they alone could fill, since they were unlikely to usurp the ruler's position.

As far as the Mawri are concerned . . . all retained slaves enter, to varying degrees, a generational cycle of gradual integration leading by the third generation to their holding positions similar to those of "sons of women" at worst, and at best akin to the ruler's privileged agent [Piault, 1975b:339].

6. Regional commander to Resident, Say, November 1, 1899.

7. Political report, second quarter, 1931. Dogondoutchi subdivision.

8. Dyula was originally an ethnic term, but was applied indiscriminately in colonial African French to any small African merchant.

9. Annual General Report, Section IV: Commerce, 1913.

10. Ibid.

11. Quarterly information bulletin. Dogondoutchi subdivision, first quarter, 1948.

12. Political report, second quarter, 1931. Dogondoutchi subdivision.

13. Report of tour, January 12 to February 3, 1934; by clerk of S.C. Cayre, Zabori-Karakara Canton.

14. Report of tour, Adjutant Allier, June 23, 1943.

15. Political report, first quarter, 1947. Dogondoutchi subdivision.

16. Created in 1946, the party had branches in all of the territories of French West Africa.

17. Notably, in plans to export to the Third World industries that would benefit from cheap labor "overseas." Some raw materials would be processed locally and then shipped abroad. On the other hand, food products such as meat (Niger) and vegetables (Senegal) would be imported directly. This obviously would presuppose a changeover to more rational intensive farming and livestock-raising.

18. The following analysis deals with the Diori regime (1960-1974). It must be underlined that the government fell because of its inability to handle the drought. Its indifference to the country's problems was equaled only by its corruption. The Diori regime was replaced after the 1974 coup d'état by a military government that dealt with the immediate problems (feeding the people and fighting corruption). But despite these efforts, the new regime retained intact the society's basic structures, social stratification, and mode of development and exploitation.

19. We can ask why the Arewa did not succeed in extending this mode of production. Gubawa resistence to integration into a hierarchical system, plus the ruler's symbolic but real obligation to assure the prosperity and well-being of the entire society, limited opportunities for exploitation. The Sarkin Arewa ran grave risks of being dethroned by a prince who could obtain the support of competing royal lineages, allied groups, or hostile villages. The Mawri state thus remained embryonic, constantly shaken by internal struggles. Such vulnerability necessitated foreign alliances—constantly broken, patched up, or changed—which created an additional instability, since they were a source of strength. In the nineteenth century, it was tributary to Sokoto.

20. *Griots* are professional musicians who inspire the workers by singing their praises and reciting their genealogies or family mottos.

21. Gao was the second Sarkin Arewa in the north after the arrival of the whites.

22. The capital of Niger was first at Zinder, 1,000 kilometers east of Niamey.

23. Koché was Sarkin Arewa in the North at the time of the conquest.

24. Zaka is a Muslim obligation, a tithe given to the *marabouts*.

25. The *dogari* were the chief's guards.

26. Fields are divided between *gamana* and *gandu*. *Gandu* are collective fields. A *gamana* is a smaller field cultivated by a younger member of a household after he has done his work on the *gandu*. The term *gandu* also refers to the household unit at work. The *gandu's* yield is used to feed the household, while the younger members keep the output of the *gamana* for themselves.

27. A law gives permanent ownership of land to anyone who farms it for ten consecutive years.

28. An important traditional office. In this case, the Dangaladima is the chief's cousin and righthand man, who has a reputation for exactions and injustice.

29. Chief of Guéshémé during the colonial period.

30. Nucé means, literally, to fall in the water—that is, they swallow gifts endlessly and without leaving a trace.

31. *Talaka* traditionally meant a commoner, but today is used to mean the poor.

32. A deputy is a member of the national legislature.

33. The family in question is that of the Guéshémé *chef de canton*.

34. After accompanying officials on tour, I was not convinced that these practices, which our informant considered traditional and different from current ones, had disappeared.

35. A greater or lesser number of transactions of this order at this time of year will remain, however, a particularly important indicator of the stability of social relationships or the development of new relations of production.

REFERENCES

DE LATOUR DEJEAN, E. (1975). "Transformation du système foncier en pays Mawri." In S. Amin (ed.), L'Agriculture Africaine et le capitalisme. Paris: Maspéro.

_____(forthcoming). "La paix destructrice." In E. de Latour Dejean, La Guerre. Paris: Maspéro.

PIAULT, M.H. (1975a). "Le miel et le pouvoir et le couteau du sacrifice." L'Homme, 25:43-61.

_____(1975b). "Captifs du pouvoir et pouvoir des captifs." In C. Meillassoux (ed.), L'esclavage en Afrique précoloniale. Paris: Maspéro.

Baule Peoples

4

AGRICULTURAL PRODUCTION AND SOCIAL FORMATION: The Baule Region of Toumodi-Kokumbo in Historical Perspective

JEAN-PIERRE CHAUVEAU
OSTOM, Paris

The term "peasant society" involves a potential confusion. It can mean a mode of economic organization peculiar to agricultural production in a given place or time; it can equally mean a particular social formation whose principal activities revolve around agriculture.

This confusion is compounded when we consider the relationship between peasant society and the dominant society which imposes on it levies or unequal exchange. Thus, there is a tendency to describe specific structures in terms of their opposition to particular social strata (feudal or urban, for example) or to the mode of production which extracts the agricultural surplus (Asiatic, capitalist, or bureaucratic).[1]

The model of peasant society that we are using involves a particular social formation marked by the predominance of

Editor's Note: This chapter was translated by Robert Barde and Martin Klein.
Author's Note: I would like to thank Pierre Bonnafé for his stimulating comments during the preparation of this chapter.

agricultural activities and divided into similar household units which provide a surplus for a dominant, nonpeasant stratum. There is a structured articulation between the peasant formation and the larger society characterized by a relationship of domination which determines the social division of labor and the extraction of an essentially agricultural surplus. In the context of imperialist rule, rural societies are thus condemned to become peasant societies.

The social system which we are describing is marked by a double division of labor: that which governs agricultural production itself and that which determines the appropriation of agricultural surpluses by dominant, nonagricultural social classes. This scheme resembles the analysis found in typologies based on political and ideological forms of extracting peasant surpluses and in theories about linkages between the capitalist mode of production and peripheral social structures (Post, 1972; Saul and Woods, 1973; Fallers, 1961; Hill, 1970, Amin, 1973; Stavenhagen, 1969). These works, however, give us few details on the social division of labor within specific historical peasant societies on the level of either agricultural activity or its relationship to other activities. One result is a very sketchy treatment of those societies which lack both centralized authority and cohesive dominant social strata. Either the peasant nature of these societies is denied and they are labeled "primitive" or "archaic," or a mode of production is described in which kinship forms the institutional and functional framework—that is, subsistence, domestic, and lineage modes of production (Meillassoux, 1977; Terray, 1977; Godelier, 1977; Rey, 1977).

Agriculture as the dominant activity is insufficient by itself to define particular social relationships (Forde, 1966). The Guinea Coast and its hinterland furnish examples of societies where one can neither see rural communities as producers of surplus for dominant groups nor exclude the importance of sectors other than subsistence agriculture in their economic and social reproduction. Precolonial Baule society presents an interesting case: highly diversified production, pronounced stratification, and the accumulation of a substantial surplus, all without any concomitant centralization of power.

I propose to analyze the historical conditions accompanying the emergence and evolution of this social division of labor. The scope of this chapter and the desire to present sufficiently detailed, concrete information impose certain limitations. With regard to the historical process under study, I will emphasize two essential elements. The first is the reconstruction of precolonial socioeconomic organization. One cannot discuss the evolution of a sociocultural structure by beginning with its confrontation with the colonial system. The second is the mechanics of this confrontation, which led to the establishment of capitalist domination. Any analysis of this domination in the post-1950 era would have to refer to a global system in which the ethnocultural analysis of Baule social structures would no longer be pertinent. It would be, in fact, an entirely different topic.

This essay is subject to another limitation: I will deal only incidentally with organized resistance movements by which Baule peasants, regularly and in varying but characteristic form, fought the gradual loss of their autonomy. This shortcoming is doubly unjust, as it obscures the creative and occasionally determinant character of such protest movements and their ideological bases.

BAULE SOCIETY: AN OVERVIEW[2]

The Baule are located in the Ivory Coast, in the transition zone between the forests and the savanna. They are the westernmost component of the Akan group, found in both present-day Ghana and the Ivory Coast. They are the result of successive Akan migrations from the east that, in the late seventeenth century, expelled or assimilated the original Kru, Mande, Krobu, and Ga inhabitants. The heterogeneity of the settlement might explain the political and economic diversity within the Baule cultural and linguistic complex. Other important factors are the size of the region (more than 30,000 Km^2)

and the local effects of social changes and exchanges that have left their mark on this part of West Africa.

Today, the Baule comprise about 950,000 persons, of which at least one-third have migrated to urban centers as well as the forest plantation area. Rural density (23 persons per km²) is markedly above the national average. On the average, Baule villages number 450 inhabitants. They rarely numbered more than 1,000 inhabitants in the precolonial era. The Kokumbo region has large villages, but rural population density is lower than in Bouaké and the northwest regions. Considered to be very "dynamic," the Baule are the largest ethnic group in the Ivory Coast. Their numbers include the president of the republic, and their representation in the state apparatus is at least proportional to their demographic importance.

It is difficult to isolate any one basic unit of residence, production, and consumption within Baule communities. The "compound" (aulo), the smallest domestic unit, often has meaning only as part of an ensemble, the akpaswa, that comprises a number of compounds under a single head. These are composed of domestic groups bound together by ties of kinship (agnate, uterine, or cognate) and often by captive or client relationships. Villages are composed of a highly variable number of akpaswa. Villages are linked by their association to one of the various traditional "tribes" of the last Akan migration. These tribes were increasingly scattered by various forms of emigration. Local groups maintain reciprocal, privileged relationships, but rarely recognize a common leader. They are rarely united under a dominant village chief. According to the most widespread theory, the Walebo agwa clan at one time had a hegemony over all the Baule groups, but during the nineteenth century its power weakened and became purely symbolic. Prior to the arrival of colonial rule, the Baule were a mosaic of akpaswa-based chieftancies, each of which had control over a village or group of villages.

During the nineteenth century, three events left their mark on Baule social structure: intensified trade with the coast using lagoon peoples as intermediaries, the influx of captives from troubled savanna regions of the Sudan, and occupation and exploitation of gold-producing regions in the south and the east by the central Baule.

The resulting social structure was flexible, integrative, and also very competitive. The kinship system (cognate, with a matrilineal bias) made possible strategies for a kin group to increase the number of its dependents at the expense of the other kin groups belonging to the same complementary kinship system. Similarly, alliance-by-marriage rules were not prescriptive, and were in practice a function of inequalities between two *akpaswa*. The more important or richer *akpaswa* could arrange *ato nvle* marriages: Payment of a substantial bride-price (gold, prestige goods) ensured that the offspring would become part of the groom's family.[3]

There were numerous forms of nonkinship dependence: slaves, individuals pawned for debts or for damages, persons expelled from their groups and taken in, and outsiders living under a villager's sponsorship. Flexibility of kinship and alliance rules and unequal access to captive labor and dependents led to significant disparities between *akpaswa*. Many activities (gold washing and mining, trade, weaving, jewelry-making) created wealth that enriched well-established *akpaswa* or led to breakaway attempts by wealthy individuals and their families.

The Toumodi region was not strictly controlled by the Baule until 1830-1940. It subsequently received many immigrants, largely from the northern groups, who came to exploit gold deposits or to benefit from the trade routes that crisscrossed the Baule south. Kokum Hill is blessed with a gold reef. Kokumbo, the largest village, housed many foreigners; its growth permitted its gradual emancipation from older, neighboring villages. The founder's *akpaswa* extended its authority over nearby villages and agricultural and gold-washing and gold-mining camps. The volume of trade and gold-mining makes this region suitable for an analysis of the historical conditions surrounding the social division of labor.

AGRICULTURAL PRODUCTION, THE SOCIAL DIVISION OF LABOR, AND PRECOLONIAL HISTORY

Baule agriculture was traditionally based on slash and burn. However, it was not shifting cultivation if that term is used to denote substantial, regular moves by the cultivators themselves. Though human settlements moved, this was not essentially due to the conditions of agricultural production, which were technically well adapted to fixed settlement.[4] Yam fields were rotated and cultivated in "mounds." Men cleared and hoed, women burned over the land, cleared weed, planted, and harvested. Women had rights to their own section of the field in which they planted corn, cotton, rice, manioc, taro, bananas, peanuts, vegetables, or various condiments during the second year. The harvested yams were by right the man's, but women (wives, sisters, kin from the *aulo* and *akpaswa*) had access to them. Other crops were the women's. In forest zones like Kokumbo, plantains were more important as a food source, even though the yam had greater cultural prestige.[5] Easier to cultivate, the plantain facilitated the development in these regions of nonagricultural labor—intensive activities such as gold-mining. Aside from hill rice, mainly cultivated by the northern Baule, the principal food crops posed no particular storage or distribution problems. Yams were stocked on storage facilities erected in the fields themselves, and banana production spanned nearly the entire year. The complementarity of crops assured a regular, adequate diet, but at the cost of considerable work by both men and women.[6]

Forms of agricultural cooperation varied according to the size and status of the *aulo* and *akpaswa*. However, even in units having abundant labor in the form of relatives and dependents,[7] the household's work—including that done by allies, clients, and captives—was performed more or less on an individual basis. Each member of the *akpaswa* had access to land-kin, captives, or foreigner-clients. The chief or notables of an *akpaswa* or village regularly received unpaid labor from dependents and from slaves.

The harvest was divided within the *akpaswa* on an individual basis. The actual cultivator kept the right to consume or trade most of his production. Tribute-in-kind was not widespread. There was a sexual division of labor, but the production process was not separated from the distribution process. Men and women were engaged in agriculture, either together or separately. Each sex had its own tasks, as in the case of yam cultivation, and neither had a monopoly over the final product. On the other hand, there was no agricultural division of labor based on status: "Freemen" and slaves undertook the same tasks. Slaves could be obliged to perform tasks generally reserved for women (clearing, carrying), but the Baule were careful to limit the difference between free and captive, for the resultant antagonisms would have destroyed the *akpaswa*. The elders and notables also participated in agricultural activities; however, their official duties (judicial or representative) and private occupations (diviner, herbalist, cult priest, or artisan) often removed them from actual production. Certain important chiefs rarely left their compounds.

The social division of labor was thus supple and diversified. Within an extended family, producers were relatively interchangeable. The *akpaswa* could mobilize a certain amount of surplus[8] without resorting to centralization or redistribution. The actual producer controlled the disposition of his foodstuffs and even traded them on his own account.

Agricultural products were the object of regular exchange. Palm wine was bought with gold dust in "cabarets" along trails or in the villages. Men produced it, but women generally sold it. In the south, yams were sold for gold dust or beads. At certain times, the Baule sold food to their neighbors—for example, in exchange for rubber during the French offensive against the Dida, Guro, and Gba after 1910. Unlike other Akan peoples or the Guro and Bete to the west, the Baule were not greatly involved in the production and exchange of cola nuts. Cola's limited role in the Baule system of production was mostly due to historical circumstances. Cola was not traded to the coast, where the primary export was gold. In the 1890s, rubber was in great demand on the coast: It was produced voluntarily, becoming a compulsory crop only after 1910. However, cola was traditionally grown in the country's southern and eastern forests. Cola production increased with the arrival of Dyula traders after 1900, and then even more with the collapse of the rubber market after 1910.

Weaving and gold-mining were particularly important non-agricultural sectors of production. During the precolonial period, they were the items most regularly exchanged with the outside world. The division of labor in cloth production was the reverse of yam production.

The woman owned the raw cotton; she spun it and gave it to a man (often her own husband) to weave. He took a portion of the woven strips for his services and returned the rest of the finished product to the woman. More specialized artisans, some of whom were itinerants, wove fancy prestige cloths in return for gold dust or other goods. Men's weaving was not subject to any caste specialization.

The exploitation of gold deposits juxtaposed two different production methods: alluvial gold-washing in river beds, singly or by small groups of women; and men mining in pits up to 70 meters deep. In working veins of gold quartz, there were work teams which contained two to eight people. Carrying, crushing, and washing the extracted ore were tasks theoretically reserved for women who kept a portion of the gold dust produced (that obtained from the third washing of the ore, for example). The rest went to the mine operator, who could redistribute a portion to his helpers. The dangerous but lucrative nature of gold-mining explains the importance of slave labor in performing the most arduous tasks. It was probably the sector with the most status discrimination. Many Baule migrants also worked deposits, under local sponsors. Payments were not as institutionalized or as heavy as among the eastern Akan. In Kokumbo the treatment of migrants was especially liberal.[9]

Cloth and gold dust figured prominently in local and foreign trade. Overland and maritime trade in cloth between present-day Ivory Coast and Ghana predated the fifteenth century Portuguese arrival off the Guinea Coast. The Baule continued to supply the "Côte des Qua-qua" throughout the nineteenth century. For the Baule, gold was both the ideal form of wealth and an accepted trade good.[10] As such, it filled the family treasury, discharged fines, and facilitated trade. In certain circumstances such functions were contradictory.

The Baule did not mine iron; this they acquired from the north or from the coast. European bars and Malinke rods were transformed by noncaste blacksmiths. Their occupation was not a low-status one, except in the Baule area, where they were of foreign origin (or perhaps slaves) and more highly specialized. Other artisan activities (jewelry and woodcarving for men, pottery for women) were not exclusive specializations. The goldsmith or metalworker was most often paid with part of the raw material given him.

Thus, productive activity was quite diversified. Not all activities were of equal importance. The larger share of labor was used in agriculture. Other activities were always carried out within the agricultural production unit. The production of gold or artisan goods could tap a source of wealth through trade for both the individual and the "family." Further, agricultural production itself was often oriented toward trade. How were goods put into circulation?

The main trade routes were oriented toward the coastal people to the south (sea salt, iron, guns, powder, beads, various European goods); toward the Malinke, Senufo, and Dyula to the north (iron, slaves, salt, livestock, sudanic manufactured goods); toward the Akan to the east (especially for European guns and goods from the Gold Coast factories); and, finally, toward the western forests (iron and livestock in transit from the Malinke area, slaves and cloth from Guroland).

Foreign trade was conducted in stages. Neither the Baule nor their neighbors went far beyond the bounds of their territory. Even the networks of specialized traders—Dyula in the north, "Asoko" along the southern coast—did not penetrate very far. Baule traders themselves were not very specialized: They went on expeditions, more or less in groups, to obtain products not locally available. Journeys could be long, depending on the destination and nature of the products sought or offered. Itineraries depended on the trader's relationships with groups and villages along the way. There were scarcely any main tracks, but an extremely widespread network of paths gave the traveler a choice of routes. An unwise choice, however, might lead to being captured or held for ransom. Trade between different regions was conducted through trading partners (*sikefwe*) residing in the villages who served as brokers. In the north and south, trade routes led to important centers, linked to the northern market towns or to factories or traders on the coast. In the north, true markets existed for contact with Malinke or even Hausa merchants. In the south, transit villages were common, where brokers put Baule or foreign traders in touch with each other. Traders could leave their goods on consignment, the *sikefwe* taking a commission on any transactions. Although these expeditions sought needed items, the goods exchanged could also generate a profit. Some elders, whose *akpaswa* produced large surplus, could convert it into highly sought-after products (salt, arms, powder, pearls) through traveling intermediaries.[11] These networks of trading partners were often reinforced by marriage alliances. Although commerce was not a specialization, it produced inequalities because it was based on control of a surplus and on interpersonal relations determined by social status. Moreover, trade tended to unite the interests of persons who practiced it regularly and associated with each other in trading caravans.

What stands out in this description of the internal division of labor in the principal productive activities? For any given product, labor specialization was limited and was never exclusive (agricultural production in particular). This was as true for production as it was for processing. If one considers social status (chiefs and elders, youth, descendants of slaves, slaves, and various dependents), no occupation was monopolized by any specific group of individuals. The absence of any central control of the *akpaswa's* production (no centralization-redistribution) and the lack of an institutionalized tribute system blocked the formation of a nonproductive ruling group. Few chiefs or notables were completely involved in their political, religious, or judicial duties. Labor specialization by sex involved division of tasks, but not the monopoly of one sex or the other over a good's total production process. This was especially true for key consumption or trade goods (yams, cotton and cloth, and gold). The customary division of the product, even if unequal, involved a partial appropriation by the actual producer. Thus, the *akpaswa* head was seen not as the richest or the most powerful individual but as the manager of the collective treasury (*adja*), which comprised gold dust, cloths, goldweights, slaves, and the stools of preceding chiefs. The *adja* symbolized the unity of the local group, all of whom shared in its establishment and growth. The elder could use it for himself, but he could convert some of its contents for its further growth. The individualistic nature of production was thus offset by this use of the *adja*. An *akpaswa* chief did not necessarily hold all the wealth; certain *aulobo* (compound) chiefs had their own family treasuries. Men and women kept anything they produced for themselves. The diversity of activities allowed all social groups access to sources of wealth. No one could systematically deprive his dependents of the fruits of their labor.

In practice, however, certain categories of people benefited less than others, especially slaves who had been purchased and were given the most onerous and dangerous tasks (gold-mining and long-distance porterage) without commensurate rewards. But even in their case slaves could, if they showed themselves obedient, work for themselves (agriculture or artisanry) or receive concessions (goldworking or trade). Certain trusted slaves could thus become rich. On their deaths most of their possessions went to the *adja*. Official duties were entrusted to them as well as to their descendants to the degree that having proved their loyalty, their interests were inextricably bound to the group's.

Such a social division of labor had one obvious effect: that of homogenizing an extremely heterogeneous amalgam of dependents (slaves; descendants of slaves; clients; and uterine, agnate, or cognate family dependents) by creating common interests. It actualized the notion of a local group's collective wealth. Potential antagonism among component categories and between the chief and his dependents was dampened by emphasizing rivalries between local groups and dominant and wealthy *akpaswa*.

This rivalry was maintained by the cognate kinship system, which did not guarantee which group the offspring would join. The alliance system, where marriages were loosely sealed by gifts of goods, did more than any specific rules to entrench unequal relationships between *akpaswa*. An *akpaswa's* wealth and power allowed it to augment its dependents. *Ato nvle* marriages and marriages with slaves guaranteed its control of the offspring. There were strategic marriages with distant groups. The *akpaswa* bought slavery, took pawns, and protected clients. Competition between local groups—what one gained, another lost—disrupted the community of interests uniting the "elders" in typical segmentary societies, where the exchange of wives and the allocation of offspring were assured by some unifying principle (bride-price or lineage organization). The social division of labor corresponded to a social structure in which local groups might increase their wealth and power to ensure their stability.

Two elements were particularly important: the possibility of acquiring dependents, especially slaves,[12] and the existence of trade networks where (in contrast to many segmentary societies) strategic goods were neither under the exclusive control of some social stratum nor divided into isolated "spheres of exchange." The division of labor in production involved a continuity between the production and distribution of goods. This continuity enabled a certain number of individuals to increase their wealth and authority, on condition that they "play the game" and identify with the *adja*. But another consequence lay in the ever-possible challenge to the group's stability.

This explains the great susceptibility of Baule society to changing conditions. There was a strong regional diversity with each economic and political configuration linked to a particular economic activity (goldworking in the areas of Kokumbo, Yaule, Dimbokro, Ouellé, and Bocanda; weaving among the Walebo in Sakassou, the Aitu, and the Nanafwe; goldsmithing among the Aitu and the Nzikpli; and long-distance trade in the Bouaké, Tiassalé, and Ahua region).[13] Over time, we note the migrations of small groups devoted to a particular activity, pushing older lineages from the chieftaincy.

Certain developments have had widespread effects. Baule society as described here is probably characteristic of the latter half of the nineteenth century. That period saw the culmination of several developments: an intensification of trade with the coast; an influx of captives due to the upheavals in the Sudan; reorientation of Ashanti economic interests toward trade with the Hausa, freeing the area around the Comoé Valley from Ashanti's inhibiting control; and growing numbers of guns. We cannot pinpoint whether "traditional" sociopolitical structures or long-distance trade were more important in this evolution. Of greater interest is the fact that both were based on a specific social division of labor, yielding a unique articulation between the production process and the utilization of the social wealth produced.[14]

Thus, at the beginning of colonial rule, the region of Kokumbo-Toumodi was a variegated segmentary society in which subsistence agricultural society dominated the entire system of production. A diversified local production system developed in response to each territorial group's specific advantage: goldworking, weaving, goldsmithing, provision of foodstuffs (by certain savanna groups), and control of trade routes toward Tiassalé, Sakassou, Bouaké, and Groumania. Farming hamlets grew up around Kokumbo to supply it and the gold camps. Some individuals and their dependents moved from village to village, group to group, sometimes temporarily, sometimes permanently, to take advantage of political and economic situations controlled by locally dominant *akpaswa* lineages. Territorial or matrimonial alliances were made or broken. Disputes involving varying numbers of villages were settled by important notables, sometimes after armed confrontations. When Tiassalé, in the far south, was occupied by French trops in 1893, a relative prosperity prevailed. Despite the diversity of local interests and rivalries among the most powerful lineages, the common benefits from the exploitation of gold produced a certain solidarity because it was profitable for everyone.

At this point, control of agricultural production was not the locus of internal conflict. Although it mobilized most of the labor power, agriculture was a variable "overdetermined" by the much more complex social division of labor.

What was the impact of colonialism on this coherent and dynamic unity which contained the seeds of deep antagonisms?

COLONIZATION AND THE ESTABLISHMENT OF CAPITALIST DOMINATION

I will not attempt a detailed chronology of events during this period.[15] Instead, I will stress factors having a direct influence on the social division of labor and its metamorphosis. Although there is an element of arbitrariness in the chronology, several distinct phases stand out.

After taking Tiassalé (1893), the French penetrated Baule territory. They had two goals: to attack Samory from the south and to link the Sudan and the coast in order to block British advances from the Gold Coast. After 1895 they ran into fierce armed resistance from the Baule, who forced them to fall back on their military and civilian posts. Until 1898 the Baule remained independent. In addition, an extremely profitable trade with Samory, who were harassed by the French from the Sudan, stimulated the Baule economy. Several features of this period were important.

After open warfare in 1894 and 1895, deserted villages were repopulated. Food production resumed and even took on strategic importance: It could meet the local demands of the colonizers (who were scarcely in a position of strength) but it also increased trade both within—for gold, beads, and coral—and with the exterior. The Baule purchased captives cheaply from Samory, while also capturing refugees fleeing the Almamy's advance. From the north this labor force spread throughout Baule country. In the Toumodi and Kokumbo regions it was complemented by captives transiting through Guro country, where trade was still carried on. This injection of labor enabled agricultural production to meet the needs of trade. It also aided gold production, largely destined for arms purchases,[16] and the first exploitation of rubber and mahogany in the south. Temporary Baule prosperity made French demands for porters even more unbearable. Only groups in direct contact with administrative posts complied with orders to send slaves.

Changes in production were reflected in trade, but with certain modifications. The main trading stations on the southern periphery were short-circuited by the French occupation. The latter's presence and the beginning of rubber production necessitated a restructuring of established trade networks. The Dyula, whose commercial activities as well as craft and foodstuff production were encouraged by the French, became competitors. The *Asoko*, traditional go-betweens in the south, made in-roads in Baule territory. Finally, the growth of trade enabled an increasing number of younger men to trade on their own, especially young men from the north, who profited from slaves, rubber, and ivory sold by Samory.

In expanding, the Baule production and trade system lost its coherence. The new slaves were less easily assimilated than before, given their numbers and their assignment to porterage and unpaid labor for the French. Although the latter did not dare free them, the Baule indirectly encouraged collaboration between colonizers and slaves by using the slaves as straw men. An increasing number of young men and petty chiefs participated in the new trading networks. An additional seed of antagonism between chieftancies developed, those in contact with administrative posts acting as privileged interlocutors with the French. Finally, notables closely tied to trade were tempted to link their interests with the colonizers because the French controlled trade centers on the periphery and the road linking Bouaké and Tiassalé. On the contrary, general dissatisfaction forced chiefs into resistance, which disrupted trade. Nevertheless, the principal concern of chiefs and merchants alike remained the elimination of Dyula traders, who were regularly robbed or massacred. The Baule viewed the French presence as temporary or, at worst, as representing a new element in the local balance of power. On the whole, these changes did not radically alter the precolonial order, but they created an unprecedented level of potential antagonisms. There were unintegrated slaves, "dynamic" young men, private interests; and rivalries among chiefs. We have little information about problems peculiar to women, except that the colonizers took a jaundiced view of women participating in politics. According to Akan tradition, they were always influential in chieftancies and were often accorded formal authority. This explains why, during this period, some French administrators used their concubines in dealing with Baule authorities. It is also possible that men made increased demands on female labor, using agricultural output to purchase captives and arms and to futher monopolize trade during this period of insecurity.

From 1898 to about 1907 the Baule entered a new phase in their confrontation with colonization. The French presence spread and solidified. After suppressing a series of uprisings sparked by the freeing of slaves and the imposition of local taxes, the French administration searched for a *modus vivendi* and pursued a policy of commercial penetration based on collaboration with chiefs. Contradictions that appeared in the preceding phase were accentuated. The colonizers avoided a sudden liberation of slaves—they prefered to use them as a weapon. They correctly saw slaves as the cornerstone of the Baule social system, but were prevented from acting by their fear of a general uprising. Nevertheless, the creation of "villages de liberté" mostly for refugees from the north, the use of former slaves in collaborationist policies, and the increasing number of escaped slaves served to make the Baule elite uneasy, especially when their supply dried up after the capture of Samory in 1898. It became more and more difficult to make the slaves alone bear the burdens imposed by the administration. In Toumodi, escaped or freed captives even purchased the freedom of others from *akpaswa* chiefs who, after 1901, had to pay taxes.

French occupation of the principal gold-mining areas eliminated most Baule goldworking. The French capture of Kokumbo was a harsh blow felt even in the northern savanna regions. At the same time, there was an intensification of local rubber production, with the Baule around Kokumbo also purchasing some from their Guro neighbors. Exports from regions specializing in cloth increased, as did the previously miniscule production of cola nuts. Finally, the administration noticed the dynamism of young Baule men from the north who became traders or salaried porters (paid in gold dust by their Baule employers).

The evolution of trade, begun during the preceding years, continued, notably with the appearance of rubber and ivory caravans trading with the western forests. The Dyula, as traders or collectors of products, replaced the *Asoko* considered by the French to be English agents. They were the object of Baule hostility, but increasingly played the role of intermediaries between the Baule and the French. Another new variable was the creation of food markets around administrative posts and European enterprises such as the company set up in Kokumbo to mine and process gold-bearing ore.

All these changes were not due simply to the need to respond to colonial demands. The strengthening of the French presence did not prevent many areas from remaining hostile. Rather, this period was characterized by the establishment of selective relations between the French commercial apparatus (and its Dyula intermediaries) and the Baule economic system, which developed new activities as substitutes for gold (rubber, kola, pagnes, and food supplies). Trade with the "unpacified" west—across which arms came from Liberia after the French occupation cut off supplies from the east—provided a breathing space for the Baule economic system. It took on a dualistic form: In areas far from French control, its traditional forms were preserved; in other areas, there were selective relations through the Dyula, collaborationist notables, and markets. But this articulation was extremely fragile. There was an increasing emancipation of slaves and young men who enlisted as militiamen, guards, and even as soldiers. There were tensions within chieftancies between factions favoring collaboration or resistance, especially after important chiefs had been imprisoned and massacred by the French. These were accompanied by a monetary crisis characterized by the absence of specialized exchange goods. This crisis was due to a number of factors: the fall in gold production; allocation of gold on hand or in circulation to the purchase of rifles and powder and to the payment of war indemnities; the holding back of French money to pay taxes; and the lack of coins for small transactions. The forms and methods of private accumulation of wealth increasingly deviated from the norm of the collective *adja*. The family treasury was cut off from its main assets (gold and slaves) and had to make certain priority expenditures (arms, fines, taxes).[17]

The following period saw the culmination of these "centrifugal" tendencies. The economic bases of Baule society were definitely destroyed by governor Angoulvant's policy: repression, systematic destruction, and a massive liberation of slaves (at least 6,000 during military operations between 1908 and 1912, mostly in the Baule south). There was also considerable loss of life, a regrouping of villages, imposition of forced labor levies, construction of the railroad and the first private businesses, and, finally, a program of compulsory cultivation and sales.

Control of labor, traditionally assured by the *akpaswa's* social division of labor, was no longer guaranteed. Freed slaves preferred to settle near administrative posts.[18] Forced labor and military recruitment (after 1914) kept many workers from the fields during the farming season. More and more Baule fled toward the coastal regions and the Gold Coast to escape the constraints of colonialism. The need to earn "tax money" accentuated such population movements. From 1913 onward, the French administration noted that women were joining men in leaving for the coastal region. A significant fact is that pawning disappeared with the rupture of bonds of authority and did not reappear until the Depression, when a shortage of money for the payment of taxes led to a recrudescence of pawning in savanna regions.

The productive system was in disarray. Shortages linked to military operations, which were noted during the preceding period, became periodic famines. In addition to the massive destruction of crops and livestock by punitive expeditions, the food-supply system was effected by the shortage of labor. Agricultural production was increasingly oriented toward markets created by the administration. Gold-mining became marginal. Kola nut production was limited to the needs of the Dyula market. Local rubber supplies dwindled as a result of "slaughter-tapping" methods and price-cutting competition from Southeast Asian plantations. There was a sharp decrease in cotton and rice production. Of the major precolonial activities, only weaving remained important, but it, too, faced increasing competition from Dyula and European goods. After an abortive attempt by the French administration to promote a form of private property, Baule were required to plant cash crops on collective fields. Supervision was entrusted to chiefs and local agents. Hostility became widespread among cultivators.

Long-distance trade stagnated, and the Baule abandoned it. Areas along the Bandama River remained the last zones of economic resistance. Baule notables organized trade in foodstuffs (peanuts, maize), salt, and cloth in exchange for kola and rubber from peoples to the west. But the latter capitulated in 1913-1915. The Baule had definitively lost their autonomy. It is instructive to examine the repercussions of this on the circulation of money. Most widely accepted trade goods were scarce (gold, arms, and captives) or controlled by colonial agents (rubber, European money, and iron); only cloth and salt continued to circulate in accordance with their use value. The French tried to impose their currency by restricting the use of indigenous currencies and prohibiting English money. They failed because of this policy's limited diffusion: The Baule refused to accept paper money, although they hoarded coins put into circulation for taxes. The crisis in the money supply, born during the preceding period, deepened. The result was a rise in the price of products sold and a new life for indigenous currencies (including the *sompe*, the Malinke iron bars). Forced use of paper money and the prohibition on the manufacture of indigenous currencies finally broke down all resistance, at the price of an even greater decline in internal trade.

This period thus witnessed the final subordination to colonial power. Formal subordination in an admission of defeat was all the more real because it already involved the destruction of the existing social division of labor, the need to resort to new crops (cocoa) and to new forms of production ("the commandant's fields"); new forms of unequal exchange (compulsory sales, administrative markets), and, finally, compulsory or underpaid labor (forced labor or salaried labor with white settlers). Women completed the process by joining the exodus from Baule country. The colonial system was no longer simply a means of extracting surplus in the form of tribute permitting relatively autonomous production to continue in zones outside the direct control of the administration. But it was not yet, despite the obligatory cultivation imposed by Angoulvant, a terrain ripe for self-sustaining capitalist production. It was the "necessary" stage of "breaking down" the autonomous system of production and trade.

The 1920s were a decade of transition. Individual settlers joined the administration in exploiting the labor force. Their interests were forcefully represented in the colony's administrative council, in the chamber of commerce, and later in the chamber of agriculture. The settlers enjoyed the support of the administration in recruiting and in setting low wages and food prices.[19] Confronted by a double exploitation—by both settlers and the administration—the Baule productive system suffered an unprecedented decline. Bark-cloth replaced cotton cloth. The Dyula and, increasingly, the trading posts monopolized internal trade and later, the collection of kola, rubber, and palm kernels. The exodus to the coastal regions, Anyi country, and the Gold Coast shattered domestic groups. After an initial failure, the administration's efforts made cocoa the best way to pay taxes in the forest zones. It required little work after clearing the land and could be planted along with food crops. Beginning between 1926 and 1928, private cocoa plantations sprang up in the Kokumbo region at the expense of collective plantation.[20] Yam exports to the coast and to the cities increased. Collaborating notables did not view plantations simply as a means of raising tax money; they could build up larger holdings because they were exempt from forced labor. In fact, they received unpaid labor themselves. However, "individualism" in the Baule authority system did not spawn a class of rich planters during this period, as happened in Anyi country. Wealth was tied to personal alliance with the colonial power; it lacked any social basis in the systematic expropriation of labor, which would have been incompatible with the dispersal and demoralization of available labor.

The spread of capitalist exploitation thus depended on organization of the labor force, which in turn forced a Baule response. The French enacted two types of measures. One institutionalized more precise labor obligations to meet European needs. Military reservists were used, a Labour Office was established, and the southern part of Upper Volta was incorporated in the Ivory Coast. But crises such as the Depression and the end of trade during the war, and workers from Upper Volta were unable to resolve the contradiction between a colonial production system, based on an authoritarian control of labor, and the growing number of small- and medium-size indigenous plantations to which were added the large plantations of some chiefs and low-level civil servants—despite the

French administration's desire to keep distinct the interests of local notables and those of native functionnaries, who were forbidden to have agricultural holdings. Economic conditions made cocoa, and then coffee, sources of internal differentiation.[21] A certain amount of "kulak-ization" took place; some notables were able to use paid labor.[22] The administration gradually realized that colonial "development" was based on the mass of the peasants, that this led to an increase in consumption and production, and that it was more advantageous to the metropole in the long run.

Measures were taken to encourage small peasants and free them from administrative restrictions and the heavy influence of large local landholders. They were also given the option of buying exemptions from forced labor. The levying of a "supplementary head tax" permitted the use of paid labor on public works projects. The Labour Office was revamped so it could control the hiring of peasants by the private sector. Credit unions were set up which were forerunners of purchasing and marketing cooperatives.

The promotion of a small peasantry, controlled by a nascent state capitalism, was related to a growing and spontaneous individualism in agricultural production among small farmers. They refused to harvest collective fields. There was a decline in forms of mutual assistance. Patrilineal inheritance was increasingly preferable so as not to discriminate against children contributing to the family's output. Disputes took place over the use of forest reserves. Slaves were given access to land for plantations. Female labor was used in coffee and cocoa production, though the products were appropriated by men, and in yams and food crops, whose sale enabled men to obtain money for the upkeep of plantations.

Nevertheless, these measures were not enough to restore the delicate balance between the area under cultivation where cash crops predominated and the demand for labor. The burden imposed by administrative regulation and the European colonists' lobby now became dysfunctional. It is thus not by chance that under "progressive" Free French Governor

Latrille civil servants and well-to-do planters came together to create the Syndicat Agricole Africain (1944) and then the RDA (1945). These organizations, led by Baule cadres—especially southern Baule from Yamoussokro, Toumodi, and Dimbokro—can best be defined as an alliance of the more privileged groups and the mass of small planters. Among the Anyi, on the other hand, large planters were more frequently traditional chiefs—no less "collaborationist," but whose setting was less directly tied to the colonial development process.

At the end of the war, the main issue was forced labor. The obstinacy of the colonists and the blindness of centrist and socialist governments in France led to violent and bloody conflict. Peasant and RDA actions finally forced the 1946 abolition of forced labor and the Indigénat.[23] The formal freeing of labor allowed colonial development to evolve past this archaic form. After several years of stagnation due to bad faith on the part of the colonists and a faction of the administration, these measures had their effect on the Baule production system and especially on the region under study.

Coffee and cocoa, perennial tree crops, were the crucial element in the system. Other salable products such as kola, cotton, and rubber became insignificant. Food crops were heavily dependent on plantations. During the first years after clearing, when the trees are not bearing fruit, medium and large planters have substantial produce for sale. But afterwards, the upkeep and harvesting of plantations monopolize a significant part of the labor force. If additional areas are not cleared, there is a shortage of food. Such was generally the case for small and medium planters who lacked sufficient family or paid labor or who were obliged to neglect their plantations. Their productivity remains low because their trees do not get enough care. The great beneficiaries of the 1950-1952 coffee boom were large planters whose previous incomes allowed them to plant more of this crop, which requires more labor than cocoa, without cutting back on production of foodstuffs. Foreign agricultural workers or Baule from densely populated savanna areas who constituted a labor reservoir for the forest zones preferred to work for big planters who offered larger monthly salaries or who gave "sharecroppers" a third of the harvest. The population exodus toward the southeast and the Gold Coast diminished in favor of resettlement on the forest fringes. The Toumodi-Kokumbo region received many Baule planters from the northern and southern savannas. Their community of origin permitted progressive integration into the *akpaswa* that granted them land in return for a nominal payment. Dyula and Voltaics—mostly former laborers, workers at the Société Minière de Kokumbo, or kola buyers or middlemen—also settled here, under the Baule landowners, in separate quarters in some villages. Nevertheless, in contrast to the western regions, local Baule remained numerically superior to foreign planters.

At the same time, there was a move to create plantations in Guro and Gban country and, then, in even more distant Guro and Bete areas. European colonists abandoned coffee and cocoa in favor of commerce and more intensive, but also more profitable, crops (bananas, pineapples, palm oil, and rubber). There was a considerable expansion of African plantations, based on the use of agricultural wage labor and massive hirings outside the official framework of the new Syndicat Interprofessional pour l'Acheminement de la Main D'Oeuvre.[24] The most important notables and planters also received, in addition, unpaid labor from villagers and from foreign Baule seeking land. To these activities some added timber exploitation and contracts for the upkeep of important roads.

Internal differentiation among planters increased; this was based more on access to labor than on social status or access to land. Nevertheless, in certain villages where forest reserves were few and dominant traditional lineages had not been splintered by earlier exoduses, there was a correlation between individual status and economic success.[25] The freeing of labor made it the key element in the differentiation process. But one cannot conclude, as have several authors (Stavenhagen, 1969; Amin, 1967) that a capitalist mode of production had developed.

For the small Baule peasant, his use of hired labor flows from a situation that allows him to shift part of the burden imposed by the economic system onto the backs of others less fortunate than himself (farmers from the savanna). Eventually, this "exploitation relationship" became a vital necessity when the terms of trade deteriorated after the temporary rise in prices during the early 1950s; hence, the diversification of forms of wage labor: sharecroppers, jobbers, day, monthly, or yearly laborers experiencing different degrees of exploitation. Only the large planters were in a position to accumulate a surplus by using wage labor and plentiful family labor. But even there the wage relationship was not simply a function of capitalist relationships. The Baule planter remained a direct producer. The *reproduction* of wage labor cannot be guaranteed by the smallholder production system, subjugated as it is to the conjunctures of the world political and economic system. The individual agricultural wage laborer can return to his home community and set himself up as an independent planter (Chauveau and Richard, 1977). Rather than a unilinear tendency to extend the capitalist mode of production, strictly speaking, we are dealing with the creation of specific relations of exploitation in which migratory labor weighs heavily in relations between neighboring social formations. The case of Mossi society in Upper Volta is characteristic in this regard.

The end of forced labor constituted the essential condition for the enlargement of the productive trade system. Hençeforth, the domination of metropolitan capitalist interests was maintained locally by the dependence of food production on perennial tree crops, by the need to earn money to buy necessities, by the need to hire farm labor,[26] and, finally, by the system of debts which tied planters to buyers. Beginning in the mid-1950s, the Baule social formation can no longer be considered in isolation: It was definitively integrated into a plantation economy whose workings were "internalized" by local social reproduction. This transition was reinforced by class alliances. As early as 1947-1948, during the strike on the Abidjan-Niger railway, RDA leaders from coffee and cocoa zones were concerned that planters would be unable to get their crops to market. Beginning in 1951 these same leaders, led by F. Houphouet-Boigny, worked more closely with the administration. The next phase came with self-rule in 1956 and independence in 1960 and the increasing organization of smallholder market production under the aegis of an independent state. The fundamental task was to mold the plantation economy to new constraints: increasing shortages of wage laborers, lack of new land, and the solidification of the state bourgeoisie's economic power base.

CONCLUSION

In this summary and intentionally descriptive review, I have suggested that any analysis of the workings of peasant societies must go beyond the formalims—even reductionism—of theoretical models. "Populist" concepts seem to be common to seemingly opposed interpretations. They tend to describe so-called "peasant" societies as relatively homogeneous; the mechanics of agricultural production are not analyzed as such in relation to other elements of the economic system, but rather as a function of their relationship with an external, nonpeasant social stratum, the state, or a mode of production. Questions such as: Who is a peasant? When is a society a "peasant" one? How is surplus appropriated by dominant groups? tend to disregard internal complexities of these formations, each of which is unique. Models that fit this sort of analysis had, and still have, a heuristic value. But any confrontation with the history of specific formations reveals their limitations. Baule society demonstrates that it is difficult to separate "pre-Colonial" structures from any subsequent evolution and to ignore the specific internal social division of labor and its relationship to previous socioeconomic history.

This criticism is obviously not new (Post, 1972; Rosebury, 1976; Amin, 1973; Olivier, 1975). I must emphasize the necessity, in understanding these formations, of not being limited to the era of world imperialist domination. One must also examine each society's own initiatives, at various times and in various ways, to establish a congruent relationship between its own social dynamic and the global context affecting it. Such initiatives stem from a complex dialectic between "resistance" and "collaboration" that can be understood only through a detailed analysis of the class alliances and contradictions that mark their history. But this presupposes that the terms of reference are not themselves loaded with historically and ideologically based oversimplifications. More concretely, it seems that two perspectives should stand out in light of the material presented. The first questions the extent of the dichotomy between centralized societies and "others," and its economic consequences. The second concerns the complex relationship between the production sector and the sector of circulation and distribution. The uniqueness of the precolonial Baule economic system rested on a specific articulation between the productive system and the system of trade.[27] The impact of colonialism was first felt by the latter; domination by metropolitan capitalism was established only after a "tribute" system of exploitation was abandoned in favor of the development of petty production for the market. Further research and analysis of resistance movements and ideologies, put in historical perspective, will eventually increase our understanding.

NOTES

1. See the typologies elaborated by Kroeber (1963), Redfield (1956), Wolf (1966), and Shanin (1973). All emphasize the characteristics of the larger society surrounding the agricultural one in classifying the resulting whole; but little attention is given to the specific traits of the agrarian societies themselves, other than their relative autonomy vis-à-vis the surrounding society (Mendras, 1976).

2. I have relied in particular on the recent works by Pierre Etienne (1966, 1968, 1975a, 1975b, 1976), Mona Etienne (1977), and Timothy Weiskel (1976a, 1976b). See also Etienne and Etienne (1964, 1968, 1971), Salverte-Marmier (1964), and Chauveau (1972, 1976, 1977a, 1977b, 1979a).

3. Marriage gifts were small and generally composed of everyday goods. The *ato nvle* marriage practice fell into disuse at the end of the nineteenth century, with the influx of captives "produced" by Samory to the north. With the monetarization of the economy, the size of the bride-price tended to increase and take the form of gifts of money and manufactured goods. It remains small in comparison with bride-price

among the Bete, Guro, and Dida to the west. Moreover, the practice of prolonged concubinage is widespread (the woman continues to live with her own parents).

4. For the "traditional" Baule agrarian system, see Etienne and Etienne (1964), P. Etienne (1976), M. Etienne (1977), Miege (1951), and Mazoyer (1975). There is a local breed of cattle and trade in cattle with the north and the Guro which is mostly tied to herding. The Baule do not use animal manure on their fields.

5. There are few agricultural rites. The "yam festival," so important among the eastern Akan, is here more of a family tradition. There exist no special offices such as the earth priest. The head of the village or *akpaswa* contributes to the division of cultivated land—or goldworking sites—and himself makes sacrifices to the land.

6. In many African societies women do most of the agricultural work. Such is the case with the western neighbors of the Baule (Bete, Dida, Guro, Gba, and others).

7. A French agent estimated there to be 300 dependents and relatives present in the *akpaswa* of the king of the Walebo of Sakassou at the beginning of colonial penetration. A notable could easily buy ten slaves. The wealth in gold of the Kokumbo goldworkers was often used to redeem pawns and add them to the goldworker's household.

8. The Baule habitually farmed more than their domestic needs demanded. Famines were rare, according to the early French economic reports.

9. The methods of dividing the extracted gold and the taxes owned on it vary from region to region and even from village to village. A worker's average share might have been one third of the mined but untreated gold ore, which means that the value of the extorted labor was much less in relation to the finished product. Nuggets were in principle reserved for the chiefs of dominant *akpaswa* (but were rare in the Kokumbo region).

10. There was a complex system of brass goldweights. Their function as weights was tied to social and cultural functions. This system also existed among the lagoon peoples and among the eastern Akan.

11. Slaves or social juniors. Women could participate on their own behalf in these expeditions. In certain cases, porters were reimbursed in gold dust or in a share of the profits.

12. Most slaves purchased were kept by the Baule, but a certain number were resold to coastal people and to the Anyi (especially during the influx of slaves and refugees following the campaigns of Samory to the north).

13. However, the same dominant activity produced varying forms of local political domination according to the history of a particular region: liberalism toward the workers in Kokumbo and a more pronounced hierarchy among the Yaule under Walebo control.

14. The spread of this social division of labor would explain the decline of the Walebo kingdom of Sakassou which failed to control gold production and trade at the beginning of the nineteenth century.

15. With regard to colonial penetration, we now have the historical work of Weiskel (1976b), from which I have borrowed a number of interpretations. For transformations under colonialism, see the works of Pierre and Mona (0000), Etienne and Etienne (1964), Miège (1951), Mazoyer (1975), and Benetière and Pezet (1964). For the Kokumbo-Toumodi region, see Blanc-Pamard (1975) and Chauveau (1977a, 1979b).

16. This explains the decrease observed in transactions using gold to procure other products. When the French prohibited the sale of arms at local trading posts, the Baule turned to trade with the Gold Coast.

17. After colonization, the practice of *ato nvle* marriages, through which dominant lineages made payments in gold or prestige goods to assure control of the offspring, disappeared. Etienne and Etienne (1971) attribute this to the spread of marriage with slaves, which also ensured unilateral rights over offspring. Shortage of gold, also a result of colonization, is another explanation.

18. Many slaves remained in the villages. The fate of liberated slaves, directly exploited by the administration when they were not redistributed to collaborating chiefs, was never such as to guarantee their allegiance or that of their descendants to France's "civilizing mission." On the contrary, many slaves took advantage of their collaboration in a basically individualistic way, using a precolonial model of social mobility. Elders in the south reacted to the liberation of slaves, first by creating a local trade, then by buying Guro and Gban children from the Dyula, taking advantage of disruption caused by the French pacification of areas to the west.

19. In the interior, planters settled largely in the Gagnoa-Oumé regions near Kokumbo. Some also settled in the Toumodi region. But above all, Kokumbo was the site of the Société Minière et Foncière du Bandama and its successors, which exploited the gold mines, imposing on the populace a virtual shadow administration and a reign of terror.

20. Likewise, censuses abound and the head tax paid by the head of the family replaced the allocation of tax shares by the village chief. The latter still took a commission, though smaller than before.

21. The Depression and the wartime economy prompted more people to return to the land. Attempts were made to rely on traditional production and trade in the poor zones of the Baule savanna. Plantations were created in the forest zones and increasingly in the coastal region and the southeast. It is significant that Baule weaver-traders brought cocoa seeds back and cultivated them outside the administrative framework. Cotton production declined.

22. While unpaid labor for the administration's chiefs increased, certain chiefs in the Kokumbo region secretly recruited labor for Europeans.

23. The Indigénat was a special law code which gave administrators a great deal of arbitrary authority in dealing with native "subjects." (Editor)

24. The completion of the construction of the port of Abidjan and the policy of keeping urban wages low encouraged the creation of rural wage labor.

25. Baule suspicion of European schools led them to send the children of slaves, instead of the chief's children, to school. One result was that, in the 1950s, many lower-level civil servants were the descendants of slaves.

26. The monetarization of labor relationships concerned not only wage labor, but also family labor. Starting with women, dependents demanded adequate remuneration for agricultural labor in the absence of which they looked elsewhere for better pay (plantations, rural labor migration, or migration to the cities). Although the men were the first to migrate, such migrations developed a stronger appeal for women. Female migration was marked by longer stays and these women became more urban-oriented.

27. The failure to consider the role of circulation in the Baule agricultural system keeps Mazoyer (1975) from grasping the radical differences between precolonial and postcolonial Baule agriculture.

REFERENCES

AMIN, S. (1967). Le développement du capitalisme en Côte d'Ivoire. Paris: Les Editions de Minuit.

_____(1973). Le développement inégal. Essai sur les formations sociales du capitalisme périphérique. Paris: Les Editions de Minuit.

BENETIÈRE, J. J. and PEZET, P. (1964). "Histoire de l'agriculture en zone Baoulé." Etude régionale de Bouaké, document no. 2. Abidjan: République de Côte d'Ivoire, Ministère du Plan.

BLANC-PAMARD, C. (1975). "Un jeu écologique différentiel: Les communautés rurales du contact forêt-savane au fond du 'V' Baoulè, Cô d'Ivoire". Thése de 3ème cycle. Paris: Ecole des Hautes Etudes en Sciences Sociales, Université de Paris I—Sorbonne.

CHAUVEAU, J. P. (1972). "Bibliographie sur la société Baoulé (Histoire, anthropologie)." In V. Guerry, La vie quotidienne dans un village Baoulé. Abidjan: INADES.

_____(1976). "Notes sur les échanges dans le Baule précolonial." Cahiers d'Etudes Africaines, 63-64:567-602.

_____(1977a). Réussite économique et statut social en milieu de plantations villageoises. Résultats d'enquête sur huit villages Baoulé de la sous-préfecture de Toumodi. Abidjan: ORSTOM. (mimeo)

_____(1977b). "Société baule précoloniale et modèle segmentaire. Le cas de la région de Kokumbo." Cahiers d'Etudes Africaines, 68:417-434.

_____(1978b). "Contribution à la géographie historique de l'or en pays baule (Côte d'Ivoire)." Journal des Africanistes, 48:15-69.

_____(1979a). "Notes sur l'histoire économique et sociale de la région de Kokumbo (Baoulé-sud, Côte d'Ivoire)." Travaux et documents de l'ORSTOM no. 104. Paris: Office de la Recherche Scientifique et Technique Outre-Mer.

_____(1979b). "Economie de plantation et 'nouveaux milieux sociaux': Essai d'analyse comparative et historique à partir d'observations en pays Gban et Baoulé. Côte d'Ivoire." Cahiers ORSTOM, série Sciences Humaines (à paraître).

_____and RICHARD, J. (1977). "Une 'périphérie recentrée': à propos d'un système local d'économie de plantation en Côte d'Ivoire." Cahiers d'Etudes Africaines, 68:485-524.

Dialectiques (1977). Anthropologie tous terrains, 21 (automne).

ETIENNE, M. (1977). "Women and men, cloth and colonization: The transformation of production-distribution relations among the Baule (Ivory Coast)." Cahiers d'Etudes Africaines, 65:41-64.

ETIENNE, P. (1966). "Phénomènes religieux et facteurs socio-économiques dans un village de la région de Bouaké (Côte d'Ivoire)." Cahiers d'Etudes Africaines, 23:367-401.

_____(1968). "Les aspects ostentatoires du système économique baoulé." Economies et sociétés, 2:793-817.

_____(1975a). "Essais de sociologie baoulé." Thèse de 3ème cycle. Paris, Université de Paris I—Sorbonne, "Introduction." (mimeo)

_____(1975b). "Les interdictions de mariage chez les Baoulé." L'Homme, 25:5-29.

_____(1976). "Le fait villageois baoulé." In Communautés rurales et paysanneries tropicales, Travaux et Documents de l'ORSTOM, no. 53. Paris: Office de la Recherche Scientifique et Technique Outre-Mer.

_____and ETIENNE, M. (1964). "L'organisation sociale des Baoulé." In Etude Régionale de Bouaké. I: Le peuplement. Abidjan: République de Côte d'Ivoire, Ministère du Plan.

_____(1968). "L'émigration baoulé actuelle." Les Cahiers d'Outre-Mer, 21:155-195.

_____(1971). "A qui mieux-mieux, ou le mariage chez les Baoulé." Cahiers ORSTOM, série Sciences Humaines, 8:165-186.

FALLERS, L. (1961). "Are African cultivators to be called 'peasants'?" Current Anthropology, 2:108-110.

FORDE, C. D. (1966). Habitat, economy and society. London: University Paperbacks, Methuen.

GODELIER, M. (1977). "Infrastructures, sociétés, histoire." Dialectiques, 21:41-53.

HILL, P. (1970). Studies in rural capitalism in West Africa. Cambridge: Cambridge University Press.

KROEBER, A. L. (1963). Anthropology: Culture patterns and processes. New York and Burlingame: Harbinger.

MAZOYER, L. (1975). "Développement de la production agricole marchande et transformation d'une formation agraire en Côte d'Ivoire." In S. Amin (ed.), L'agriculture africaine et le capitalisme. Paris: Anthropos.

MEILLASSOUX, C. (1977). Femmes, greniers et capitaux. Paris: Maspéro.

MENDRAS, H. (1976). "Un schéma d'analyse de la paysannerie occidentale." In Communautés rurales et paysanneries tropicales, Travaux et Documents de l'ORSTOM no. 53. Paris: Office de la Recherche Scientifique et Technique Outre-Mer.

MIEGE, J. (1951). "L'agriculture baoulé." In Compte-rendu de la première Conférence internationale des Africanistes de l'Ouest, tome II. Dakar: Institut Français d'Afrique Noire.

OLIVIER, J. P. (1975). "Afrique: Qui exploite qui?" Les Temps Modernes, 346:1505-1551; 347:1744-1775.

POST, K. (1972). "Peasantization and rural political movements in Western Africa." Archives Européennes de Sociologie 13:223-254.

REDFIELD, R. (1956). Peasant society and culture. Chicago: University of Chicago Press.

REY, P. P. (1977). "Contradictions de classe dans les sociétés lignagères." Dialectiques, 21:116-133.

ROSEBURRY, W. (1976). "Rent, differentiation and the development of capitalism among peasants." American Anthropologist, 78:45-58.

SALVERTE-MARMIER, Ph. et M.A. de (1964). "Les étapes du peuplement." In Etude Régionale de Bouaké. I: Le peuplement. Abidjan: République de Côte d'Ivoire, Ministère du Plan.

SAHLINS, M. D. (1968). Tribesmen. Englewood Cliffs, N.J.: Prentice-Hall.

SAUL, S. and WOODS, R. (1973). "African peasantries." In T. Shanin (ed.), Peasants and peasant societies. Aylesbury: Penguin.

SHANIN, T. (1973). "Peasantry as a political factor." In T. Shanin (ed.), Peasants and peasant societies. Aylesbury: Penguin.

STAVENHAGEN, R. (1969). Les classes sociales dans les sociétés agraires. Paris: Anthropos.

———(1975). Social class in agrarian societies (J.A. Hellman, trans.). Garden City, NY: Anchor.

TERRAY, E. (1977). "De l'exploitation. Eléments d'un bilan autocritique." Dialectiques, 21:134-143.

WOLF, E. (1966) Peasants. Englewood Cliffs, NJ: Prentice-Hall.

WEISKEL, T. C. (1973). "L'écologie dans la pensée africaine traditionnelle." Cultures, 1:129-151.

———(1976a). "L'histoire socio-économique des peuples baule." Cahiers d'Etudes Africaines, 61-62:355-395.

———(1976b). "French colonial rule and the Baule peoples: Resistance and collaboration, 1889-1911." Ph.D. thesis, Balliol College, Oxford.

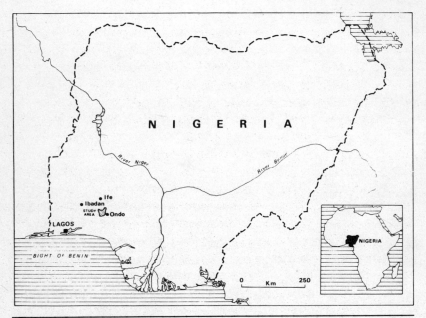

Location of the Okeigbo and Ifetedo Area in Nigeria

5

PEASANTIZATION AND LANDHOLDING: A Nigerian Case Study

JULIAN CLARKE
University of Liverpool

INTRODUCTION

The designations "tribal cultivator" and "capitalist farmer" are generally considered inadequate for certain categories of agriculturalists whose existence, exact nature, and relation to the various sets of conditions in which they have emerged and in which they are reproduced are therefore serious problems for a wide range of disciplines and methodologies.

On the African continent the transitions which have occurred since the establishment of the colonial states, are generally seen to have been from tribal to peasant or quasi-peasant forms of agriculture. Post (1972) identifies for West Africa what he calls a process of "peasantisation." This process is one

AUTHOR'S NOTE: This article is based on material collected during 1973 and 1974. Fieldwork was financed by a postgraduate grant from the Social Science Research Council. I would like to thank Phil Burnham, Barry Hindess, Elizabeth Kingdom, John Peel, and Pepe Roberts, who have read and commented on the whole paper or various parts of it. I am grateful to them for the many improvements that they suggested. Responsibility for the final form of the study rests entirely with me.

through which cultivators who had primarily produced agricultural goods for their own use on communally possessed land were either compelled to produce or were drawn into the production of agricultural commodities which they did not consume themselves.

Within the process of peasantization as conceived by Post, various features of the transition from tribal cultivation to peasant farming (such as the transformation of modes of possession and distribution of land) are seen as a direct effect of incorporation into a world commodity economy. The components of the transition which Post outlines are relatively familiar:

(1) A shift from a division of labor based on kinship to a division of labor with some other basis.
(2) A shift from "premarket" forms of distribution and exchange to the operation of the market principle.
(3) A shift from communal land ownership, with group or individual use, to individual ownership.

Post implicitly adheres to a notion of economic type and to the idea that economic transitions are to be conceived of as transitions from one discrete type to another. Nowhere does he argue that these discrete types appear "concretely" but implies that particular changes are to be understood in terms of a transition from one type to another. At its most general level the notion of economic type implies that a series of elements defined as economic (production processes, modes of possession of means of production, modes of appropriation of product, and so on) can be characterized or defined in relation to a single term, principle, or set of principles. Post's conception of peasantization—the process of transition from non-peasant to peasant economy—has much in common with substantivist notions of "mechanisms of integration" and with some notions of "precapitalist modes of production" which have been developed recently.[1]

The object of this chapter is neither to engage in a general debate on the validity of concepts, such as mode of production, nor to engage in a major criticism of the ideas of Post on the basis of such schematic work as his peasantization article. Rather, it is to show that, suggestive as Post's work is, he makes an unannounced shift from description to explanation which is not justifiable.

Post may be right in saying that, throughout West Africa, the three categories of change occurred roughly simultaneously. But there is also the implication that it is possible to conceive of the process of peasantization as providing the principle which both unifies its constitutive elements and dictates the point at which one element is replaced by another. This implication must be challenged. There may indeed be definite relations among changes in divisions of labor, forms of distribution and exchange of product, and modes of possession and distribution of land; however, to analyze those changes in terms of their being "part of the process of peasantization" is to provide an essentialist analysis which cannot conceptualize the specific nature of these changes. It provides no more definite explanation of how these changes are linked than that provided, for example, by the notion of modernization. Again, it is not my concern to argue against Post in detail; it is, rather, to make an initial general point that a shift from communal possession to individual ownership has to be examined in terms of its own particular determinants. These determinants may be changes in divisions of labor and distributions of product, but the connections must be made, insofar as it is possible, in a specific manner.

This chapter explores the concrete conditions in which there was a shift from communal possession of land to private ownership in a specific community in the Yoruba-speaking area of Nigeria between about 1900 and 1960.[2]

The first section deals briefly with the concepts of possession and ownership of agricultural land. The second and third sections, respectively, look at existing work on land possession and ownership in the Yoruba-speaking area, and situate the community studied within this area. The fourth section analyzes the transition within the community from definite conditions of communal possession to a definite form of

private property. This transition is related to the development
and rapid expansion of cocoa cultivation and to the appearance of a category of migrant, rent-paying tenant farmers.

Concepts of Possession and Ownership

The conditions under which the primary means of production—land—is distributed to and among producers is of
central importance to any kind of agricultural production. The
way in which land is distributed to producers and the propor-
tions in which it is distributed among producers can be
connected in many ways to the way in which agricultural
production is organized. The concepts of possession and
distribution refer to the conditions under which producers gain
access to land for cultivation, the conditions under which they
use it, and the means by which such access and use are
regulated.

The phrase "communal possession" applies when a community effectively occupies a tract of land. The occupation by
a community is effective as long as it can regulate the distribution of land both to and among its members and restrict
the access of nonmembers. The use of notions of communal
ownership and tenure have been criticized by writers such as
the Bohannans (1968). They argue that communal ownership,
or any other form of ownership, can only exist in conditions in
which there is a definite title to definite tracts of land, and that
to speak of communal ownership or tenure is to distort the
description of tribal society (Bohannan and Bohannan, 1968:
87-88). This criticism is justified. But, the notion of communal
possession is not intended here to suggest that a community
has title to land. Rather, the notions of communal possession
and distribution of land are used here to refer to the conditions
under which members of a community gain access to land. The
notions are applicable whether the community has purchased
the land and has legal title to it (in conditions where legal title
exists) or whether the land is occupied because the community
defends it militarily. The Tiv may not make land maps or have
land titles, but, as the Bohannans show, the conditions under

which the cultivating group has access to land include the existence of a specific community.

The ways in which communities regulate access to land vary immensely. The variation may relate to the size of the community, whether it holds a fixed territory or not, and the nature of its internal divisions. However, access to land is dependent on the relationship between the community as a whole and the land occupied by its members; whether this is fixed, expanding with population, or contracting.

It is possible to argue that land was communally possessed in precolonial West Africa. It is, however, particular forms of communal possession and the way in which they were reconstituted within colonial states that were of prime importance in determining the form in which the private ownership of land developed.

Within the colonial states the private property rights of individuals and corporate groups were established and maintained in specific conditions and by specific legal and political institutions. The mechanisms by which titles in land are acquired and distributed are completely different from those relating to communal possession, and in many cases they are incompatible with them. Incompatibility, however, is a logical notion and does not explain why one form of possession should replace another.

Given prevalent notions about the destructive effects of capitalism, it is paradoxical that the British colonial states of West Africa expended considerable time and resources in investigating and attempting to preserve certain aspects of communal possession.[3] In some Yoruba-speaking areas colonial authorities tried to prevent people from alienating communal property. The authorities reconstructed political systems (which regulated the distribution of land) and gave these reconstructed polities property rights which now became geographically fixed in a way they had not been in the precolonial period.

Despite the complexity which was injected into the distribution of land, there was a discernible shift from communal forms of possession to private ownership. This change has been attributed in a general way to the effects of incorporation into a world market, to the needs of expanding capitalism[4] and more specifically, to the entry of West African cultivators into export crop production and the resulting land scarcity.[5] Here I want to examine the argument that commodity production as such brings about the development of private ownership. To do this it is necessary to take a step back and look at how production can be organized in a situation of communal land tenure.

It was noted earlier that the modes of control of land and control over the organization of production processes may be linked in particular ways. More specifically, it can be argued that control over means of production is only effective insofar as the access of agents involved in production is controlled. In fact, the mode of control of agents involved in production constitutes the mode of control over means of production. If the mode of control over agents entering production processes varies, so does the way in which means of production are controlled and so will the way in which the product is distributed.

Where land is possessed communally, production agents cannot be said to possess land, but only to have access to it under definite conditions. Access to land and control over production processes will be linked in a specific manner because only those production agents to whom the community mechanism of allocation actually allocates land will be able to organize production processes. This may, in fact, be equivalent to the allocation of land to those social agents who control labor. Production agents only get access to land as independent producers under conditions defined by the rules of communal possession.

Communal possession does not imply communal use or communal organization of production. It is possible, however, that production could be organized communally: In this case, land may not be distributed among separate production units because the effective labor unit is the whole community. On the other hand, land may be allocated to separate production units which are organized in a specific manner—perhaps in relation to households or families, and in this case it is the socially defined organizers of production who will gain access to land. When the phrase "allocation of land" is used, it may mean nothing more than that it is possible for a production organizer to farm on a piece of land which is not already in use and that no other production agent has claims on the production organizer's labor power.

It is crucial, then, in the above context to understand how particular categories of production agents enter production—that is, how their access to use of land is defined and regulated. An independent organizer of production may be defined as an adult male of certain age, as the head of a household, or even the household considered as a single social agent. It is important to note that it is the socially recognized organizer of production to which land is allocated and that there may be a variety of means of preventing unrecognized social agents from organizing production. The socially recognized organizer of production has rights to use only, and to use only under conditions of communal allocation.

Under certain conditions, a socially recognized organizer of production in a situation of communal possession and distribution of land may be constituted as a farming enterprise in relation to one or more commodity markets. The only market which is incompatible with communal distribution of land is a market in land. It is also possible, however, that communal possession of land can persist if communally defined organizers of production purchase land, as long as this land is not part of the community territory. There is, therefore, no general sense in which communal possession of land is incompatible with the production and sale of commodities for one or more markets. There is also no general reason why entry into market relations should affect socially recognized modes of the control of labor and organization of production. Farming enterprises which produce food and market agricultural commodities can, therefore, do this using communal land, with no supposition that communal possession will be dissolved (except in definite conditions); and using labor forms previously associated with nonmarket production, with no supposition that these will break down. It should be noted at this point that communal possession may not be compatible with all forms of commodity production.

In the community which is the object of this study, however, communal possession of land has been replaced by private ownership of land; this has taken place in conjunction with the development of commodity production and the breakdown of traditional labor patterns. It has been argued that there is no general explanation for the occurrence of this conjunction; however, it can be shown that the development of a specific form of private property in land has its roots in the development of commodity production. In addition, it can be shown that the development of property relations alters the way in which production agents gain access to land. Land is no longer allocated to producers because they are the socially recognized organizers of production; land is distributed by those agents who have property in land. They may not be organizers of production. This means that agents who were previously defined as production organizers under conditions of communal possession may have no access to land (because they are not necessarily property owners). Nonowners may, however, gain access to land by entering into market relations with owners. These nonowners may or may not be production organizers in the sense specified under communal conditions of possession.

We now return to the problem of finding out how and why land which was communally possessed comes to be constituted as individual private property. Before this problem can be approached, we must look at the literature on the Yoruba-speaking area.

Landholding in Yorubaland

There is a wide literature on Yoruba land tenure. Much of the work deals with legal aspects of tenure and does not attempt to account for specific forms of possession and distribution within definite politicohistorical contexts.[6] There are, however, some notable exceptions: Lloyd's (1962) classic work on Yoruba land law is one of these. This study discusses specific legal aspects of land tenure within the context of definite political units, and is based on a study of four Yoruba kingdoms which were incorporated into the Nigerian colonial state (with all the modifications that such incorporation implied) as administrative divisions.

Lloyd's argument is that farmland in Yoruba communities is divided up among corporate descent groups (Lloyd, 1962, 1966). These groups are recognized as the exclusive corporate owners of specific tracts of land, and may dispose of the land as they see fit. The land is usually allocated among the members as farm land, but may be alienated subject to the conditions of communal ownership.

Lloyd implicitly raises an important point: that property titles in land develop in forms which depend on the conditions in which these property titles come to be constituted. Lloyd tends to assume, however, that lineage property developed in some Yoruba kingdoms because lineages were the precolonial possessors of the specific land tracts in which they now have private property rights. Where Lloyd recognizes that descent group ownership of land is a recent development, he pays insufficient attention to the importance of the introduction of cocoa. It seems doubtful that descent groups had exclusive rights over land in the nineteenth century in the way that they do today. Very little direct evidence is provided for nineteenth-century land ownership by descent groups. Although Lloyd's documentation of existing land rights is impressive, he pays little attention to the effects which the development of cocoa production and changing political conditions have had on the development of the forms of possession and distribution of land.

One of Lloyd's most serious omissions is a failure to account for the emergence of a category of rent-paying tenants in many cocoa-growing areas. This is surprising, because in an earlier article (Lloyd, 1953) he deals with the problem of tenancy. He identifies several historical tendencies in relation to land tenure, and sees a tendency toward the closer geographical demarcation of lineage land holdings beginning with the period of military chaos in nineteenth-century Yorubaland. This tendency is implicitly connected to population pressure. The other major tendency is for political and economic ties, particularly with respect to land, to become detached from one another, and for tenancy and rent to replace allegiance and tribute.

While it is likely that concentrations of population in certain areas led to stricter regulation of access to land and to attempts to control access to portions of community territory, Lloyd does not indicate how this might have changed the fundamental tie between land use and political allegiance. For instance, he designates some nineteenth-century migrants to the large town of Iwo as "tenants." In describing how they obtained land, however, he shows that it was not possible to hold land within that community without definite political ties. He states that the descendents of these immigrants either founded their own lineages or were incorporated into already established ones, and that their land rights became no different from those of other members of the community. The notion that the difference between these nineteenth-century migrants and twentieth-century rent-paying tenants is one of degree is misleading—it is a difference in kind.

In arguing that the development of tenancy is the continuation of nineteenth-century tendencies, Lloyd is ignoring real discontinuities brought about by the development of the colonial state and commodity production. Nineteenth-century migrants from one community to another suffered none of the disabilities of today's tenants. In seeking the origins of current land possession patterns—including the development of tenancy—in the nineteenth century, Lloyd confuses the closer demarcation of landholding within a community with the development of property rights. The latter may imply the former, but the reverse is not the case. For Lloyd these tendencies become explicit with the development of cash cropping. However, it is clear from his examples that the tendencies he observes within nineteenth-century Yoruba communities were reorganizations within those communities and were not related to a complete change in forms of possession.

Lloyd's contribution to the study of Yoruba land tenure is impressive. It is unfortunate, however, that he pays insufficient attention to real alterations in the forms of landholding and the conditions in which these alterations came about.

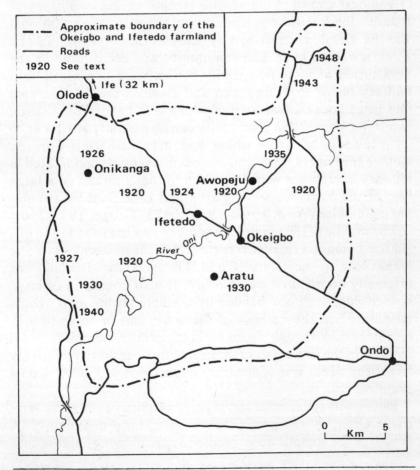

FIGURE 1   The Expansion of Cultivation from the Okeigbo and Ifetedo Area, 1920-1950

Okeigbo and Ifetedo: A Historical Summary

The history of the Yoruba-speaking area in the nineteenth century has been described in the literature as a period of chaos and disruption followed by a period of political transformation and reconstruction. An old and stable order dominated by the Oyo empire was destroyed both from within and from outside in the early part of the century. It was replaced by new and volatile social forms whose development was arrested only by the colonial invasion in the 1890s.[7]

The best known of the new nineteenth-century polities was Ibadan. Ibadan did not have the structure of the traditional Yoruba kingdom described by Lloyd (Lloyd, 1968, 1971): First, it had no king. The community was constituted by the association of large households which were organized on a military basis. Both free men and slaves were incorporated into large households, each of which was headed by a single man. The form of this community can be partially attributed to its origins in an army which had detached itself from its mother settlement.[8] The constituent households cooperated in military campaigns which resulted in the conquest of a large part of the Yoruba-speaking area and established a tribute-paying empire (Awe, 1964, 1965, 1973; Oroge, 1971:210).

The middle of the nineteenth century saw the foundation of a similar but much smaller community in the eastern part of the area, close to the city of Ondo. Okeigbo, like Ibadan, was originally constituted by an army. It also consisted of large households, each one headed by a single strong man, which cooperated in the defense of the town and in slave-raiding campaigns. Although Okeigbo conquered no empire, it did control, in the latter part of the nineteenth century, a relatively large area which was of strategic importance to Ibadan and its enemies.[9]

Despite its reliance on slaving and its ability to exact tolls on trade, Okeigbo was primarily an agricultural community. A British peace commissioner recorded the following impressions:

> The road by which we travelled during the day lay through farms and I was surprised to see the extent of land under

cultivation. It is a curious fact that while the Okeigbo people go in so extensively for farming, the Ode Ondo [the city of Ondo] people do very little in that way, and are almost entirely dependent on Okeigbo for supplies of corn and yams [IUP, 1973:375].

How, then, was this production organized? How was land allocated and how was access to land controlled?

Okeigbo was established as a community in the early 1850s. By the 1880s, when the peace commissioner visited it, it had a population of perhaps 5000 people.[10] The present town occupies a site close to the Oni River approximately 10 miles from Ondo and 30 miles from Ife. The army in which the community probably had its origins came from Ife and was involved in an internal dispute within Ondo. A combination of circumstances led to the sacking of Ondo and the establishment of Okeigbo on its present site, which had probably been a base camp for the Ife army. During this period, cultivation probably extended no more than six to nine miles from Ife or Ondo.[11] Okeigbo dominated a territory far larger than the cultivated area.

Okeigbo cultivators practiced a combination of slash and burn and bush/fallow cultivation, primarily of yams and maize.[12] Production was carried out under the umbrella of the large military households, but it seems that production was effectively organized by smaller groupings within the household. The degree of direct control exercised by the head of the household over the amounts of land to be cleared and the combinations of crops planted seem to have been limited; such production decisions were probably made by others. Small domestic units coexisted with quite large agricultural production units. For instance, in the most important household in the town, that of the famous Aderin Ologbenla, the household head's male children and his slaves worked side by side under the supervision of a senior slave.[13] The literature on Ibadan shows that those who were technically slaves (individuals incorporated into the community through capture) could acquire power and prestige through military exploits (Awe, 1973:67).

More generally, it appears that people cleared farmland out into the forest on the side of the town where they lived. For reasons of security, the areas cleared in the period before the establishment of colonial rule probably did not extend more than two or three miles from the town.

The farmland allocated to a particular production unit was not a definite tract which was owned by that unit. Production units moved on from year to year and the amount of land that they cleared varied with the size of the labor force.[14] One informant told me that the members of a household farmed in areas which they were committed to defend on behalf of the community. He also made the following comment, which was echoed by many other community members:

> Okeigbo was a small place surrounded by forest. Not until after the wars had ended would anyone dare to sleep out on the farms. In my grandfather's time people were farming yearly. When they met someone else's land [that is, land actually in use], they moved to another place. Now people are settled. In my grandfather's time there was no settled property.

The next section describes how precolonial modes of regulating access to land were transformed. Before undertaking this, however, we must outline the way in which Okeigbo was incorporated into the colonial state and the way this provided definite conditions for the alteration of land distribution modes and patterns.

The first 15 years of this century saw the development of what is popularly known as indirect rule. In the Yoruba-speaking area;

> The essential attribute of this concept of government was that there should be found a native agency on whom could be devolved in a real sense the burden of local government [Ikime, 1968:434].

This involved the creation of native authorities responsible for administering customary courts and collecting revenue. Indirect rule consisted of formalizing what were considered to be the "traditional" political structures and using these as the basis of day-to-day administration. The native authorities were based on Yoruba kingdoms and the "traditional domains" of respective Yoruba *obas* (kings) were made subordinate to these authorities. The two authorities of concern here are those of the Ife and Ondo administrative division, which incorporated the kingdoms of the *oba* of Ondo and the *oba* of Ife.

Okeigbo was placed in Ondo Division because the colonial authorities believed the claim of the *oba* of Ondo that Okeigbo was a town which belonged to his kingdom.[15] This claim, in fact, had no historical foundation. During the early years of this century the *oba* of Ondo tried to get the people of Okeigbo to recognize his authority and was resisted. It is also significant that much of the Okeigbo territory was incorporated into Ife Division, where the Okeigbo people were defined as "strangers."

The development of cocoa production, particularly a massive expansion in the area cultivated between 1920 and 1930, saw Okeigbo farmers move into Ife Division. They regarded this land as part of their own territory, despite the existence of an administrative boundary; but, as they were officially strangers, they were compelled to pay a tax to the Ife native authority on the cocoa trees they planted.[16] This was resented since a majority of Okeigbo people could trace their descent from mid-nineteenth-century migrants from Ife. This shows how indirect rule, which was supposed to reproduce the traditional, completely changed it. The change did not relate simply to the subordination of Okeigbo to a political center (Ondo) with which it had no political ties: The fundamental change lay in the fact that Okeigbo was subordinated by the colonial state to another political center through definite political and legal mechanisms. It would have been just as much a change for Okeigbo had it been subordinated to Ife with which it has "traditional" political ties. The regulation of access to land during the expansion of cocoa cultivation thus lay effectively in the hands of those who controlled the political centers, and, in the case of the Okeigbo, was complicated by the fact that the land they came to farm during the first 30 years of this century fell under two separate native authorities.

Until 1931 the Okeigbo people farming in Ife Division regarded their stranger status as an imposition. In 1930 a new *oba* was installed in Ife. In 1931, in an act of generosity or of complex political manipulation, he decided to refund half of the cocoa tree tax to Okeigbo farmers on the grounds that they were of Ife descent. The money was transferred via the Ondo native authority. Subsequent to the transfer, a charge was brought by members of the Okeigbo community that an Ondo official had embezzled a part of the money. An enquiry by the district officer determined that the accusation was groundless. Following this finding, four Okeigbo men were tried for sedition in Ondo, and one was sentenced to a short prison term.

The following night a large proportion of the Okeigbo population (some say the whole population) crossed the divisional boundary and camped in Ife Division. A complex political wrangle followed this; the upshot was that a new settlement, called Ifetedo, was established about two miles from Okeigbo but on the Ife side of the divisional boundary. Approximately half the population of Okeigbo either remained in or returned to Okeigbo. Broadly speaking, those with farms in Ife Division stayed in Ifetedo and those with farms in Ondo Division remained in Okeigbo. Ifetedo became subordinate to the Ife native authority.

Following the end of World War II, large numbers of migrants came from the savannah Yoruba towns seeking land on which they could plant cocoa. The influx of migrants continued steadily from 1948 until the mid-1960s, when the difficulty of finding land in the Okeigbo and Ifetedo areas caused migrants to seek land elsewhere. The migrants did not settle in either Okeigbo or Ifetedo, but lived in farm villages close to the land which they had been allocated. They did not become politically incorporated into the community as had the precolonial migrants. The most striking feature of their establishment as cocoa farmers is that they did so as rent-paying tenants *and* they became the tenants of individual Okeigbo and Ifetedo farmers. This, as will be seen, was a crucial factor in the development of property rights in land.

In 1973-1974 the two towns, Okeigbo and Ifetedo, were still located in different administrative divisions.[17] For many purposes they could be regarded as separate communities, subject to separate sets of administrative constraints and thus focused on different political and economic arenas. With respect to land, however, there is an important sense in which they still constitute a single community. People from Okeigbo own land in Ife Division and Ifetedo people own land in Ondo Division. This fact is of considerable importance in under-standing the development of forms of land ownership. One of the principal means of establishing ownership of land is through reference to descent from the original occupiers of the land, to the supposed internal organization of precolonial Okeigbo, and to the area which it controlled in the nineteenth century. The area which may currently be called Okeigbo and Ifetedo territory by virtue of its occupation by farmers from the two towns and those that rent land from them has been defined in relation to the precolonial political unit. This unit and its territory only continues to exist insofar as claims to ownership of land are based on actual or supposed descent from members of the precolonial community.

The next section shows how a continued community of interests in land is of central importance in accounting for the way in which property in land developed.

The Development of Private Property in Land

This section documents the development of private property in land. It does not attempt to provide an explanation of this development in the sense that the factors adduced to account for the emergence of private property in land are seen to exist at a level different from the development itself. For example, the development of private property cannot be explained as the effect of "general processes" or "hidden structures" which have an ontological status distinct from the development and its demonstrable conditions. This type of explanation was criticized above. In the case described in this chapter the problem of explanation is posed in a different way. Explaining a development is seen as documenting its sufficient conditions. I do not pretend to have fully achieved this type of explanation here, if only because conditions themselves always have conditions. There are some points where it is obvious that I have not been able to arrive at final and definite or even relatively complete accounts of certain occurrences or sets of occurrences. Any attempt to fill these gaps by reference to general processes or hidden structures would only give spurious definition to what are problematic points of description.

The emergence of cocoa cultivation as a principal activity of Okeigbo farmers took place between 1900 and 1915. The constitution of the colonial state brought about disintegration of the large military households.[18] The large households were replaced by households of a smaller size with few or no slaves and dependents who were mostly close kin.[19] These smaller households coincided much more closely with agricultural production units than had the military households. Production units based on these households expanded cocoa cultivation.[20] I am not going to try to describe the conditions in which Okeigbo farmers took up cocoa cultivation; that would be beyond the scope of this chapter. However, an attempt will be made to show how cocoa cultivation affected the distribution of land.[21]

Cocoa cultivation, although it probably began around 1900 in Okeigbo, did not develop rapidly until after 1915. Up to that time maize and yams were the principal crops, and cocoa, it seems, was being grown experimentally alongside other cash crops such as cotton. However, between 1915 and 1920 there was an upswing in the overall rate of planting which placed hitherto unprecedented demands on both land and labor.

Patterns of cultivation in the early 1900s were fairly standard. Males performed the initial labor of felling, clearing, burning, heaping, and planting, and women shared in the labor of weeding and harvesting. A labor group might have consisted of a male household head, his wives, perhaps four or five sons or other dependent male kin, perhaps the wives of one or more sons, and the unmarried daughters of the head. According to older informants, such a labor group would have cleared between one-half and one acre of primary or secondary forest per adult male per year.[22] The actual amount cleared depended on the size and age composition of the unit. Newly cleared land was planted with yams; sometimes it was interplanted with cowpeas. In the following year the land was planted with maize and supplementary vegetables. Thus, the amount of land "occupied in use" by a production unit was about double what it could clear in one year. Land was occupied for two years—at the outside, three—and then abandoned. The tendency, again according to older informants, was to clear bush in an area which bordered on existing farms, but this depended on estimates of fertility and the proximity of other cultivators.[23]

A labor group consisting of five adult males would clear between two and five acres each year and be in occupation of a similar amount from the previous year. It seems that there was no attempt to establish rights of return to land which had been cultivated and abandoned; informants were insistent on this.

The adult male population of Okeigbo was about 1200 in 1931. It is likely that in 1900 the adult male population of Okeigbo was between 700 and 1000.[24] Informants stated that before the colonial invasion cultivation did not extend beyond a three- or four-mile radius form the town. If 75 percent cultivable land is assumed, a figure of between 13 and 24 acres per adult male is obtained (working on the higher figure of 1000 adult males). If it is further assumed that one and a half acres per man was always in use, this means that land would have to be recultivated at periods of between eight and sixteen years at a constant adult male population of 1000.

Although informants maintained that some primary forest was cleared each year by all production units, this seems unlikely if the farmers were operating within a three- or four-mile radius of the town. It must be remembered, however, that by 1900 Okeigbo cultivators would not have been through two 24-year cycles and that in the early 1850s, when the town was founded, the adult male population was certainly not at its 1900 level.

The important consideration here is whether the pattern of cultivation described above was compatible with communal possession in a very direct sense. For instance, sixteen-year-old secondary forest is usually much easier to reclear than primary forest. It would be reasonable to assume that some attempt would be made to retain production unit rights in specific plots of land. In addition, in a situation where production units have to recultivate land after a well-defined period, it is reasonable to assume that production units would want to retain rights in land which they had cultivated previously. In short, it might reasonably be assumed that production units would attempt to claim some kind of exclusive rights of use in particular plots of land.

Although it might be reasonable to assume these things, there is no evidence to suggest that rights in fallow were retained by Okeigbo farmers. For a production unit of five adult males, this would mean retaining rights over 65 to 120 acres of land for between eight and sixteen years, while cultivating between five and ten acres yearly. Although this point was pursued with older informants, they remained adamant: both de facto and de jure exclusive rights in land was something which developed with cocoa production. It might be argued that informants were just wrong or were covering things up for reasons relating to current disputes. The latter seems hardly likely in a situation where private property has subsequently developed. It may seem strange that there was no attempt to retain rights in land, but there was no necessity for this. Providing that cultivators did not recultivate land too quickly, there is no reason why a production unit should return to the specific plot it had cultivated previously, especially if primary forest was being cleared continuously between the early 1850s and 1900.

The approximate calculations made above relate to the period immediately prior to the colonial invasion, when cultivation extended into an area that was easily walked on a daily basis. After the establishment of the Pax Britannic security constraints no longer applied, but it does not appear that cultivation extended much beyond a four-mile radius until after 1915.[25]

The expansion of cocoa cultivation after 1915 entailed an expansion in the total land area occupied by Okeigbo cultivators. Cocoa is a permanent tree crop which bears a harvestable crop from about its seventh to its fortieth year.[26] Cocoa altered the nature of occupation in use by cultivators: Land was no longer used for two or three years before being abandoned; but was occupied on a permanent basis. Just as it was possible for adult males to clear up to an acre of land and plant up to two acres with food crops, so was it possible for them to plant a part of this acreage with cocoa. Even at the rate of a quarter of an acre a year, 1000 adult males will permanently occupy 250 acres each year. In practice it seems that before 1915 labor groups expanded cocoa cultivation at a rate which did not interfere with existing patterns of foodcrop production. The amount planted each year by particular labor groups was thus likely to be roughly proportional to the number of adult males in the group.[27]

The fixing of land in use by the planting of cocoa did not initially represent a major departure from the existing mode of access to land, which was governed by the ability to organize a labor unit. But because cocoa trees, like food crops, were regarded as the property of the producer, planting trees on a particular plot of land effectively gave the planter exclusive rights over the land. Thus, while there was no formal change in the allocation of land and rights in land, the mode of distribution of land was being altered.

Okeigbo, as has been stated, is situated between Ife in the northwest and Ondo in the southeast; the major city of Ilesa is situated about 30 miles due north. At the turn of the century Ondo cultivation extended to within about five miles of Okeigbo.[28] There seems to have been a mutually agreed-upon boundary area, and as Ondo farmers were expanding in other directions from Ondo there was very little dispute in the area. To the north and west of Okeigbo there was uncultivated land. The land to the north was in Ondo Division and Okeigbo farmers could expand in that direction as "native occupiers" of the soil.[29] To the west the land was also uncultivated, but it was in Ife Division. In the 1920s Okeigbo farmers opened up new farming areas moving out in both directions from the town. These new areas were situated between four and seven miles from Okeigbo. This roughly doubled the land area available to Okeigbo farmers. Cultivation did not extend on a steady front as land supplies close to the town ran out. In fact, islands of cultivation were created in places considered suitable for cocoa and the areas between these islands and the town were sometimes not cultivated until the 1930s.[30]

Expansion continued in both directions in the 1930s. It was, however, checked in Ife Division by the Ife native authority on an eight-mile radius from Okeigbo by the expansion of Ife farmers. The Ooni of Ife himself established farms in the mid- and late 1930s, which effectively blocked any further expansion by Ifetedo farmers. Expansion to the north continued until 1948 when an area ten miles from Okeigbo was opened. The occupation of land in this area is interesting because it shows that Okeigbo and Ifetedo still operated as a community as far as land was concerned: Land was cultivated by farmers from both towns and the farm villages on the area are peopled by farmers from both towns.[31] Expansion in this direction was blocked by the southward expansion of farmers from Ilesa.

The year 1948 also marked the arrival of the first migrants from the northern Yoruba towns. Given the fact that expansion had been blocked, in that very year it may seem strange that the Okeigbo and Ifetedo area was able to accommodate extra cultivators. It must be remembered, however, that cultivation was not continuous from the two towns to the boundaries of expansion. There were large tracts of uncultivated land which could be and were allocated to tenants between 1948 and the end of the 1960s. In 1931 the joint population of Okeigbo and Ifetedo was about 6000 and by 1974 this had risen to about 18,000 by natural increase. In addition, there were in excess of 20,000 migrants living in farm villages scattered throughout the area.

Individual private property in land developed in two phases. The first involved the attempt by cultivators to retain or gain exclusive rights of access to and use of particular plots of land. Such attempts were made both for land which the claiming individual had previously cultivated but was vacant and for land which had not been cultivated by the claiming individual. The second phase involved the allocation of plots of land by community members to migrant nonmembers from whom they received a cash rent.

Three interrelated questions are raised by the nature of these developments. Why did cultivators attempt to establish exclusive rights of access to particular plots of land? How were these claims established? Why and how was land allocated to migrants?

It has been shown in what agricultural context cocoa was adopted. Cocoa fixed land in occupation and this process led to the expansion of the area in which community members established farms. Cocoa farms were established by household-based production units of limited size.[32]

Cocoa trees were the property of the individual who organized the production unit, usually a household head. The organizer controlled access to the trees produced under his supervision, appropriated the product, and controlled the distribution of returns from its sale. In this formal sense cocoa was no different from food crops, but the fact that it was always sold and never consumed by the producing unit gave rise to different problems of internal distribution of the product.[33]

As was seen, before cocoa production developed, one adult male might productively occupy about one acre per year. In 1974 the average size of a farmer's holdings was in excess of ten acres for community-member farmers and about three acres for migrant tenants. Seventy percent of this land was exclusively planted with cocoa.

From approximately the mid-1930s, the organizers of labor groups faced a particular problem in the future expansion of their cocoa plantations. They also faced the problem of providing their sons with land to cultivate.[34] In the 1920s this was no problem because the new areas of cultivation were both sufficiently far from Okeigbo and Ifetedo and sufficiently sparsely occupied for cultivators to expand their cocoa without problems. As more land came under cultivation, however, its extension became problematic because neighboring farmers wanted to expand onto the same land.[35] Farmers began to attempt to secure exclusive access to land which bounded their existing cultivation. Where farmers had established cocoa in more than one location, they attempted to gain rights in several places. The process was complicated later by the inheritance of cocoa plantations as property and claims for rights of inheritance in uncultivated land.

What form did this process take? It is very difficult to ascertain in what way disputes over particular plots of land emerged, and it cannot be assumed that claims for exclusive access to land were uniformly met by opposition from other interested parties. Older community members said that they and their fathers had begun the custom of marking out their land with a small red shrub (*igi ala*). A majority of farm boundaries are marked in this way today. One farmer who had done this work on his father's land said that his father "could foresee the future" when land would not be open to any community member to cultivate if he could.

Why should these claims for exclusive access have been successful, and on what basis were they made? In the records of the customary courts relatively detailed information can be found about how land relations developed. These records also played an important part in determining that exclusive rights of access should also be legal property rights.

It must be assumed that few disputes over rights of exclusion ever reached the courts and that many claims were either never disputed or settled by the chiefs outside the courtroom. Details of this kind of dispute settlement were very hard to come by and often confused. The examination of court cases, as already suggested, performs a double function: The records reflect the changing nature of claims over land and, in addition, they are a primary condition for the constitution of exclusive rights as formal legal property rights.

It is possible that if there had been no colonial invasion, cocoa or other cash cropping would have developed on a similar scale and that some form of exclusive rights over land might have been claimed and established. Such a development would have occurred within the politico-legal context of a Yoruba community and the pattern of relations between different Yoruba communities.[36] There is, however, no reason to expect that rights of exclusive access would have been equivalent to individual private property rights as established by court decisions. There is no reason to suppose that these rights would have extended to the sale or renting of land on an individual basis to migrant farmers.

The customary courts were supposed to give judgments in accordance with "native law and custom." Although in some sense they did this, they were linked to a complex colonial legal apparatus which differed from the precolonial legal structure, if only in that it transcended the boundaries of the previous political and legal units. The courts gave formal legal status to attempts to establish exclusive access rights to plots of land and, in doing so, created the form in which those rights were and are held.[37]

Before examining several court cases, it is necessary to note that that form in which private property developed—that is, as the property of individual cultivators—was dependent on the manner in which claims to exclusive rights were made. In the Okeigbo and Ifetedo areas claims were not made by lineages or other corporate groups, but by individual cultivators. Land was not distributed to production units by virtue of lineage land-possession: It was the production unit which was the key unit, and land was distributed among these units by occupation in use. The fact that units tended to farm in the same locations as close kin does not alter this fact. The heads of households *qua* organizers of production attempted to reserve land against future use and they (and their sons) fought court cases.

Prior to 1948 almost all court cases which involved land were concerned with the ownership and inheritance of cocoa trees. However, after this date (and it must be remembered that this coincides with the arrival of the first northern Yoruba migrants) cases concerning uncultivated land began to appear in the records. For instance, in 1953 an Ifetedo man laid claim to "title of his father's land." Two years later a case appeared in which a farmer laid claim to title in his father's "uncultivated bush." The claimant said that the defendant had been clearing bush which the claimant's father had "staked out more than thirty years ago." The claimant won this case, but the defendant was not ordered to quit the land because, as the court said, at no time had the claimant ordered the defendant not to plant "memorable crops" (cocoa). The claimant was awarded possession of that part of the land not already cultivated by the defendant; the defendant was ordered not to extend his cultivation.[38] The court here recognized two things: First, a claim for exclusive rights in land could be based on the fact that the claimant's father had staked out the land at some prior date (in this case, in the mid-1920s); and, second, actual occupation in use of a plot of land was seen equally to establish rights in land.

Cases such as this rest on the conversion, through court proceedings, of one kind of relationship into another. The father of the claimant had been involved in the outward expansion from Okeigbo in the 1920s: He had cleared bush in a particular location with friends and relations and had some influence over who joined the group cultivating land in a particular location. The defendant was the son of one of the other members of that group, and considered that he had an equal right to cultivate bush in that location. What had been a vague political function relating to the distribution of land for cultivation in a particular location in the 1920s was used in the 1950s as the basis for a claim of ownership of uncultivated bush.

This type of case became more frequent in the 1960s, as did another similar kind of dispute which arose out of competing claims to the right to clear the same piece of bush. These disputes usually took the form of contesting the position of a boundary; each claimant saying that the "real" boundary between the two farms was in such and such a place and that this entitled him to cultivate the land. These disputes also came to involve the right to place migrants as tenants on particular plots of land and to claim rent from them.

By the mid-1960s claims to title in land (where they were upheld) finally displaced claims based on the investment of labor and occupation in use. Farmers who lost cases of this kind were ordered by the court to harvest foodcrops and quit or, if they planted cocoa trees, to uproot them. The basis for property claims and the disputes concerning these claims have been variable, but they usually centered (after 1970) on the claim of prior occupation or intention to occupy the land in question by an ancestor. Sometimes claims would be based on the fact that the land in question was the hunting territory of the claimant's grandfather. Although hunting rights were traditionally granted by *obas* to hunters, the allocation of such rights traditionally conferred no rights over the land to the descendents of the hunter in question.[39] More often, claims were of the kind which appeared in the court cases cited above.

It might be thought, given the foregoing description of the development of private property rights, that the allocation of land to migrants as rent-paying tenants can be explained fairly easily. But, as has been pointed out, the development of private property even in a formal legal sense does not imply that commercial relations will develop in respect of land. With regard to the emergence of a category of rent-paying tenants, the development of commercial relations of a particular kind are to be accounted for.

The courts invested individuals not only with exclusive access to particular plots of land, but also formal property rights. The granting of property rights to individuals by the courts did not include the injunction to dispose of the land outside the community, but it did create the possibility that such disposal could occur. The granting of exclusive rights of access to particular portions of a community territory may be compatible with a definite form of communal possession. (The giving of exclusive rights may be regarded as one form of distribution of a communal territory among members of the community.) The existence of individual private property rights only creates some of the conditions for the dissolution of the communal territory from within. However, the actual disposal of land to nonmembers may take other forms than sale or renting. The right to dispose of land does not create a market in land, although it is an essential condition for the creation of such a market.

At this point we must recall the circumstances in which rights of exclusion were claimed—that is, with regard to the extension of cocoa farms. The rate of extension of cocoa farms was limited by the size of the labor group and the way efforts were distributed between cocoa and foodcrops. The increasing importance of education after World War II meant that many young men either were unwilling to engage in dependent agricultural labor or were actually withdrawn from it by their fathers. Education created a double problem: it diminished the size of labor groups and increased the cash expenditure of the household head/production organizer. The first problem could be remedied by the employment of wage labor, but the second problem could only be solved by the extension of cultivation and the raising of production levels. It might have been possible to attract more wage labor from outside the community with higher wage rates, but this would have created immense problems of organization for farmers and also the forward commitment of a relatively large proportion of their cash returns.

The migrants who arrived in 1948 did not come looking for wage labor opportunities; the postwar rise in the cocoa price made them come seeking land on which they could work independently. There was, however, no question of outright purchase: They did not have the cash resources to buy land, and even if they had, it is not certain that individual landowners would have been prepared to make an outright sale. Even today, sales of uncultivated land are extremely rare, although cocoa farms are bought and sold quite frequently.

The first migrants to arrive approached individuals who were said to control uncultivated bush. These individuals allocated plots of land to migrants which were, in 1948 and 1949, relatively large and ill-defined for an initial payment of between £3 and £5. The plots of land allocated to the first tenants were effectively limited by placing additional tenants in the same location, and boundaries were worked out—not without considerable dispute—as new migrants arrived. Although the tenants were well organized and often quite militant in 1974, in 1948 they were relatively few and insecure and tended to accept the decisions of their new landlords about the placement of new tenants.

In the circumstances which have been described, the disposal of land to migrants under tenancy arrangements appears as a compromise which suited all parties. Farmers could not extend production without the employment of considerable numbers of wage laborers who were either not available or were too expensive.[40] Tenants would expand cultivation at no cost and no risk to community-member farmers and would then pay rent. The arrangement suited the migrants who could not buy land but who wished to cultivate land on an independent basis.[41]

A feature that marks off tenants from community members is that they have been incorporated into the community in a novel way. Tenants live semipermanently in farm villages close to their farms and retain community ties with their towns of origin from which they marry and in which they build their town (as opposed to farm) houses. Thus, their urban lives are conducted at a distance and sporadically because their agricultural commitments only permit them to return to their home towns for about a month every year. Ifetedo and Okeigbo farmers often live in the farm villages surrounding the two towns for most of the year, but they usually return to the central settlements every two weeks.

These farm villages appeared with the Pax Britannica and the extension of cultivation from the towns to a distance which was not easily walked on a daily basis. Community members, however, only consider that the farm villages provide temporary accommodation. Tenant farmers feel much the same way, but their conditions are different. In the precolonial period such partial migration would not have been possible. Migrants to a community would have been incorporated into the central settlement through attachment to a specific compound or household. They would also have obtained farmland under much the same conditions as native-born community members and would have been able to enter into the political life of the community. Although there are political connections between the migrants and community members, collective action, when it is undertaken by migrants, is always directly related to matters concerning the regulation of landlord-tenant relations.

Landholding and the Distribution of Land

The previous section showed how both individual private property in land and tenant landholding developed. This final section will describe the consequences of these two developments as they were apparent in 1974 with regard to the distribution of land among farmers and the implications of this distribution for the structure of agricultural production.[42]

There are, broadly speaking, two major categories of land users in the Okeigbo and Ifetedo areas: community member owners of land and migrant tenants. These categories are almost exclusive because private ownership of land has almost invariably been obtained through personal claims, such as those discussed in the previous section, or inheritance. The only way a migrant could gain private property rights was through purchase. Although such purchases of uncultivated land are extremely rare, a small, though not insignificant, number of migrants have been able to purchase mature cocoa farms from community members and thus have acquired property rights in land.[43]

Apart from private property in land and tenancy in hitherto uncultivated land, there are two other forms of tenure, which, although not of the same significance as private property and tenancy, are important: a sharecropping relation and what may be designated "temporary loan." The sharecropping relation holds when one farmer makes an agreement to take over the mature cocoa belonging to a second farmer for a period of an agricultural year. The first farmer works the hired farm as if it were his own, taking responsibility for all labor and inputs. After the cocoa harvest he pays the owner of the cocoa trees half the value of the cocoa harvested in that year. If both parties are satisfied with the outcome for one year, the arrangement may continue indefinitely.[44] Within this relationship it was actually possible for a community-member landlord to hire cocoa from one of his tenants, pay him the value of half of the cocoa harvest, and then receive rent in return. Although I never encountered a case like this, there were several cases of community-member farmers whose cocoa had not fared well who had hired cocoa from the tenants of other community members.

Under the "temporary loan" form of tenure, a loan of a definite plot of land is made, usually by a community member to a kinsman, friend, or "boundaryman."[45] Loans are sometimes made to migrant tenants. Such loans have helped to fill an important and increasing gap in the land needs of those farmers who have planted all their land with permanent tree crops and have no land on which to plant food crops. It is clear that this form of tenure could not have come into existence if land which was not planted with tree crops was available to whoever wanted to cultivate it. The understanding behind a loan is that the individual to whom the land is lent will not attempt to plant cocoa or other permanent tree crops and will grow food crops primarily for his own consumption. No rent or tribute is demanded, but occasional gifts of small amounts of produce are common. It seems that this form of tenure only emerged in the 1960s in relation to a conjunction of the establishment of private property in uncultivated land and the continued extension of cocoa cultivation within the area possessed as private property.

Although this type of tenure is not significant in terms either of numbers of farmers holding land in this way or area of land held, its existence throws light on the categories of individual ownership and tenancy. The temporary loan does not make sense except in relation to the two major categories. Unless uncultivated land is private property, the notion of a short-term loan, made under quite stringent conditions, would have no place in the allocation and distribution of land. The fact that land is lent for food crop production with no expectation of rent or other return to the owner shows that not all land rights are marketable. While all land may be individually owned, the relations between an owner and a nonowner user do not always involve a monetary transaction. This may be due to the fact that, although food crops grown on land acquired in this way may be sold, they are not usually grown specifically for sale, but primarily to provide nonmonetary means of staple consumption. This shows that fixed private property in uncultivated land does not entail that all rights in land are marketable, and confirms comments made in the first section about the variety of possibilities which can emerge from a situation where property rights in land are being established.

Although the most apparent and the most significant divisions among landholders are those between community member private owners and migrant tenants, both categories are subdivided in ways which are significant for the construction of categories of farmers—from the point of view primarily of cash income size. The following tables show how much land a sample of 49 community-member farmers held, under what form of tenure they held it, and—in the case of plots held as private property—the source of the land.

TABLE 1   Landholdings: Community Members

Number of Plots	Number of Farmers	Average Total Holdings (Acres)
1	15	20
2	14	10.19
3	12	19.67
4	5	9.47
More than 4	3	21.55

NOTE: Estimates of plot size are based partly on measurements and partly on farmers' estimates.

TABLE 2   Landholdings: Type of Tenure for
114 Plots

Type of Tenure	Number of Plots
Individual Property	101
Tenancy (previously uncultivated land)	1
Sharecropping	10
Temporary Loan	2
TOTAL	114

TABLE 3   Landholdings: Source of Land Held
as Private Property

Source	Number of Plots
Father	81
Mother's Family	7
Father-in-law	1
Own Claim	5
Purchase	7

The total number of plots held by the 49 farmers was 114; the average size was 6.9 acres. The average total holding per farmer was 16.18 acres.

There was considerable inequality among farmers in terms of total holdings of all kinds. Out of the 49 community-member farmers surveyed, 21 held a total of less than 7 acres, 13 held between 8 and 14 acres, and 15 farmers held over 15 acres; many of them held in excess of 20 acres. The importance of these differentials for agricultural production will be commented on shortly. First, however, it is worth commenting on the evaluation made by farmers of these differentials.

When a sample of farmers were asked why some farmers had more or larger plots of land, they tended to answer in terms of the conditions under which a man might take on extra land to expand his holdings of cocoa. That is, a farmer would take on more land if he could find the resources to extend cultivation. When the question was repeated and a request for a judgment on the fairness of the inequalities was made, farmers again tended to offer explanations of the inequalities rather than reflect on their injustice. Even those farmers with under 7 acres of land did not see the uneven distribution of land as being unfair in any general way. The most frequently offered explanation was that a particular farmer owned above the average amount of land because either he or his father had the foresight to claim more land than was immediately needed at the time when it was possible to claim free land. This was, in turn, related to the amount of labor which particular farmers or their fathers had had at their disposal when land was free for the taking.

A further form of differentiation among community-member farmers concerned the possession of tenancies. Only a third of the farmers surveyed received any benefit from tenancies (17 out of 49). Of these, 11 had placed tenants on land which they owned themselves and 6 had inherited tenancies from their fathers, these being held jointly with other heirs. The average number of tenancies held was 3.65, there being a range of 1 to 12 for particular cases. This means that with regard to the whole sample, 62 tenancies were distributed among 49 community-member farmers. The effects of the unequal distribution of tenancies among community-member farmers on income distribution is of some importance, but is beyond the scope of this study.

A similar sample survey covered 41 migrant tenants, selected from 6 villages in the Okeigbo-Ifetedo area. Despite the fact that there were considerable differences among tenants in terms of land area held, patterns of tenure among migrant tenants were much simpler than those for community members.

Over 75 percent of the tenants surveyed had only one plot of land; less than 5 percent had three or more plots. The average size of tenant land holdings was much smaller than for community members. Those tenants who had acquired land before 1955 had holdings which averaged five to six acres, whereas those arriving after 1960 held land averaging only just over three acres.

Migrants who arrived between 1948 and approximately 1955 had to make an initial payment to their landlord (*onile*) of between £3 and £5. This rose to between £10 and £15 in the mid-1960s for, as noted above, a smaller plot of land.[46] Following the initial payment, tenants could cultivate the land allocated to them and were expected to start paying a cash sum to the landlord when the cocoa first produced a harvestable crop (5 to 7 years). Prior to the payment of a cash rent, tenants were expected to give the landlord a nominal rent in kind, usually five or ten "big yams" each year.

In the early 1950s when the first cash rents fell due, they were usually set at the value of 56 pounds weight of cocoa (2 quarters weight); after 1955 the rents were set at the value of 112 pounds weight (one hundredweight). It can thus be seen that the actual money rent varies with the price of cocoa[47] and that the proportional importance of the rent to the tenant decreases as his output rises. This means that in the early rent-paying years of a tenancy—for example, the seventh to the thirteenth years—the rent is much more of a burden than in the years which follow—that is, of course, until yields begin to fall with the increasing age of the cocoa tree. It follows that an increasing cocoa price is of interest to community members and tenants alike because even though for tenants it means a higher cash rent has to be paid, it also means that for a given output the absolute net income for the tenant will also be higher. The characteristics of rent may go some way to explaining the unity felt among farmers with respect to the government which, as it set the price of cocoa, was responsible for the fortunes of all.[48]

In all but a few cases where disputes which had arisen between tenants and landlord has been prolonged, tenants characterized their relations with their landlords as being good.[49] The question about whether it was fair that they should have to pay rent on crops which they had produced with their own labor was answered uniformly. All tenants thought that it was a fair arrangement and all gave the same reason: The land they were occupying had not belonged to their fathers, but to the fathers of the present landlords. The major complaint among tenants was that their cocoa was not yielding well enough for them to be able to pay the stipulated rents and that the cocoa price was not high enough.[50]

One reason for a lack of serious disputes between landlords and tenants was the flexibility in the amounts of rent paid in a given year. In some villages there had been an agreed-upon reduction of rent from the one hundredweight level because of consistently poor yields which were attributable to low-quality land. In 1974 in one village where land was exceptionally poor, tenants were paying a fixed yearly rent of N10, while the cocoa price increased from N20 to N27 in the same period.[51]

Finally, it is necessary to make some brief comments about the implications of landholding differentials for agricultural production. All cocoa farmers were restricted with regard to their possibilities for expansion of holdings and the degree to which they could make production more capital-intensive. The only major technical innovation that has been made is the introduction of chemical pesticides and fungicides and associated hand-operated spraying equipment. Farmers with larger incomes (over N300 in 1974) could invest more in paid labor and chemical coverage, but the production techniques employed by farmers with large cash incomes were not qualitatively different from those farmers with incomes of under N300. Although income size was not uniformly correlated with landholdings, it was found that community-member farmers with cash incomes above N300 held on average 13.87 acres and those with cash incomes below N300 held 8.37 acres. The small number of tenants with incomes above N300 held an average of 4 acres, and low-income tenants held an average of 2.9 acres. Low-income tenants had, on average, much lower incomes than low-income community members.

Survey results showed that high-income farmers holding higher-than-average land areas tended to get a better return per day of labor (paid or family); whereas lower-income, lower-land farmers got a poorer return per day of labor, but a much better return per acre. Low-income farmers also invested a higher proportion of their gross cash income in production (primarily in chemicals) and this appeared to be a condition for their getting a higher return per acre. Why, it may be asked, were high-income farmers not spending more and getting higher returns per acre? The answer seems to lie in the prohibitive costs. For the farmer with larger acreage to achieve the same per-acre output as the small acreage farmer, he would have to employ more wage labor and the proportion of wage labor to family labor would rise. This would raise costs to a point where the strategy would be self-defeating. Large acreage, large income farmers obtained their results through a relatively low investment strategy; their higher incomes came from a low output at low cash cost on a higher acreage. Small acreage farmers were forced to go for a high output, high cost strategy on a small land area in order to keep up absolute income levels.

It was estimated that the optimum farm size from the point of view of a costs/productivity balance, under current conditions of production, was between six and ten acres. As the majority of farmers either fell below this figure (virtually all the tenants), or had more than ten acres, it can be argued that existing distributions of land, quite apart from consigning many farmers permanently to a low income category and a poor standard of living, contribute to a low efficiency agriculture, especially in current conditions of low levels of capital investment in improved agricultural techniques.

SUMMARY AND CONCLUSION

This chapter sets out to show that the development of private property in land and the development of a particular kind of market in land rights was the result of quite specific historical processes. These specific processes, it was argued, cannot be explained as the effects of some more general process of peasantization, commoditization, or modernization.

The emergence of a specific form of private property in land is related to the conjunction of the development of cocoa production and specific legal and political conditions. The development of a specific kind of market in land rights—namely tenant holding—is analyzed in relation to the characteristics of the development of cocoa production and to the conditions in which cocoa production expanded after World War II.

Developments in the forms of landholding are examined in terms of the consequences which they have had for the distributions of land among different categories of small-scale, commodity-producing enterprises. In turn, the effects of these land distributions on the productive capacity of farming enterprises is briefly investigated.

It may seem, in the light of recent radical developments in the study of peasants, that this chapter represents a step backwards. There is only a passing mention of forms of exploitation or modes of production. Certainly, the flight from structural-functionalism and neoclassical economics and the search for radical political relevance represents a positive advance in Third World studies. The espousal of various forms of structural Marxism, however, has had very mixed effects for the study of Third World societies. On the one hand, developments such as the reexamination of the position of women in tribal and peasant sectors of specific social formations are extremely important and in some respects point the way for other areas of study. On the other hand, the development of a particular kind of formalism, perhaps best exemplified in the phrase, "the articulation of modes of production," has been largely negative. Fortunately, this latter tendency, which added spurious suggestions of necessity to what were shown to be no more than contingent relationships, seems to be on the decline.

The limited scope of the study might legitimately require justification on the grounds that a study with wider reference (for example, the whole of the Yoruba-speaking area) would necessitate a more general conceptual framework. However, the criticism of the notion of a general process which was used in the early part of the chapter holds *a fortiori* for larger scale studies. It is not the scale of the study which is of primary importance; it is the way that the elements of the situation are identified and are linked which is crucial. Even of more importance, perhaps, is an awareness that the links which have been constructed among the elements of the situation are only as good as the next examination which is made of them.

NOTES

1. The "substantivist" conception of economy has been subject to criticism for many years. The most recent systematic critique is by Jenkins (1977). For a summary of the modes of production debate, see Foster-Carter (1978); for a critique of the concept mode of production, see Hindess and Hirst (1977).

2. A definition of this area in ethnic terms can be found in Fadipe (1970:29). In very approximate terms, Yoruba-speaking groups dominate in the southwestern states (Oyo, Ogun, Ondo, Lagos) of Nigeria and also parts of Kwara state. In addition, there are Yoruba-speaking groups in the western part of the Republic of Benin.

3. This is reflected in the work of the West African Lands Committee (Colonial Office, 1916).

4. For a criticism of this type of view, see Clarke (1977).

5. A fuller criticism of this view can be found in Clarke (1978:chap. 5).

6. A complete list of works on Yoruba landholding can be found in Baldwin and Baldwin (1976).

7. There are many accounts of this period: See, for example, Johnson (1921: 178-271), Akinjogbin (1966), Morton-Williams (1964), and Law (1971).

8. For an account of this process, see Mabogunje and Cooper (1971).

9. For a detailed account of the foundation of Okeigbo, see Clarke (1978:chap. 2). Assessments of the strategic importance of Okeigbo are given by Johnson (1921:45).

10. This is a retrospective estimate based on figures which appear in the colonial records for 1931: Nigerian National Archives, Ibadan. See Oyo Prof 1/644.

11. This does not include the areas cultivated by certain towns subordinate to Ife and Ondo.

12. See Awe (1973) for an account of agriculture in Ibadan.

13. This information was provided by E. A. Aderin, the late Oluoke (oba) of Okeigbo. He was the last surviving son of Aderin Ologbenla.

14. This varied between one-half and one acre per man per year depending on the condition of the forest. Wilks (1977) has made calculations for this type of agriculture in the Akan-speaking part of Ghana. Although all his assumptions do not apply to the case being examined here, his comments provide a useful framework for reconstructing the details of this type of cultivation.

15. A more detailed account can be found in Clarke (1978:chap. 2).

16. The Yoruba term for stranger is alejo. At its most general, the term refers to an individual who is not fully incorporated into a particular community but is resident in it. When the administrative divisions of the colonial state were set up, migrants from one division to another were designated as alejo, although the disabilities that they suffered were not the same as the precolonial alejo (see note 29).

17. In 1978 the two towns are actually situated in different states of the Federal Republic of Nigeria: Ifetedo in Oyo State and Okeigbo in Ondo State.

18. The conditions for the reproduction of the military household were removed by the colonial state. These conditions included slave raiding and the importation of military materials.

19. The smaller units usually included wives of the household head, his unmarried sons and sometimes his married sons and their wives, and his unmarried daughters and sometimes the children of his full and half-siblings. Although slavery had effectively disappeared before 1915, some households contained pawns (*iwofa*). For accounts of *iwofa*, see Johnson (1921:126-130) and Fadipe (1970:189-193).

20. By an agricultural production unit I mean a unit which performs an agricultural production process or part of one. It is a unit for which agricultural production decisions are taken (perhaps by the members of the unit and perhaps not) and within which they are activated.

21. I have tried to explain the development of cocoa production elsewhere (Clarke 1978:chap. 3). Many of the elements of my explanation were derived from a prior work (Berry,1975).

22. In terms of the reckoning of older informants this corresponds to the space occupied between 1500 and 3000 yam heaps (*ebe isu*). An adult male in this context was, roughly speaking, any male over the age of 16.

23. One of my informants maintained that his father (c. 1870-1936), who had been a hunter and a soldier, could tell from the wild plants growing in a particular spot whether it was suitable for food crops.

24. See note 10.

25. Older informants recall the 1920s as the period when Okeigbo farmers moved out into areas which were seven or eight miles from the town. Although it is not certain, farmers seem not to have gone much beyond the four-mile radius before 1915.

26. These comments apply to the Amelonado variety of cocoa. This is the original variety of cocoa planted in the Okeigbo and Ifetedo area, and is now being replaced by faster maturing hybrid varieties supplied by government agencies.

27. In the 1960s an individual farmer working alongside a wage laborer could plant at the rate of an acre a year. It should be noted here that between 1920 and 1960 cocoa cultivation completely altered patterns of foodcrop production. Yams were replaced by cassava, the latter having much lower labor and land requirements for a given weight of output. The effective agricultural labor supply relative to population declined because of the increasing importance of education, although the supply was augmented to some extent by migrant labor. It does seem, however, that the bulk of the labor for the expansion of cocoa cultivation was provided by the local population. This was partly achieved by the induction of women into more stages of more agricultural production processes than had hitherto been the case.

28. This boundary was established by effective occupation.

29. The provincial divisional structure imposed by the colonial state was supposed, in some measure, to correspond to traditional political divisions. One of the consequences of this, in the Yoruba-speaking area at least, was to give native-born status to all individuals in relation to a particular native authority. In the case discussed here the relevant native authorities were the Ooni of Ife and the Osemowe of Ondo whose domains were, respectively, Ife Division and Ondo Division (see note 16).

30. On the notion of suitability, see note 23.

31. The new farming areas were based around secondary farm villages (*aba*). These *aba* are collections of roughly built houses located usually not more than a mile

from the farms of the individuals who reside in them. Community-member farmers who all have rights of residence in more substantial dwellings in Okeigbo or Ifetedo do not usually live in their farm houses for more than two weeks continuously, except during the cocoa harvest. Migrant tenants spend at least ten months of the year living in a farm village.

32. It is important not to confuse the notion of a household-*based* production unit (that is, a production unit which has as a condition of its existence the existence of a household which provides some farm labor and domestic services but which is not coterminous with this household) with a household production unit. In the latter case it is implied that the household is coterminous with the production unit in the sense that all members of the household participate in all agricultural production processes under the supervision of the household head. When paid labor is employed, the household and the production unit are not coterminous (unless, of course, the wage laborer is fully incorporated into the household).

33. For instance, wives were reluctant to work on the farms unless they received a cash "gift" after the cocoa harvest. The size of the "gift" was always open to negotiation and dispute.

34. In the 1930s and 1940s the importance of education grew. In addition, wage laboring opportunities opened up during the same period and attracted young men from Okeigbo and Ifetedo to the larger population centers. In these circumstances it became progressively more difficult for farmers to retain their dependent labor. One method adopted by farmers to retain their dependents was to allow them to plant their own cocoa as well as working as dependent laborers.

35. It must be emphasized that the expansion of cocoa cultivation refers in this instance to the unbroken extension of an existing holding. Even during this period many farmers had planted cocoa in more than one place, usually moving to a second location further from one of the towns because they thought the land was better there (it was certainly less likely to have been cultivated during the precolonial period). The problem was aggravated by the fact that many farmers were allowing their sons to cultivate their own plots of cocoa in the same location as the fathers' cocoa farms. While the son was still dependent on his father, the father was responsible for finding him land to cultivate.

36. Cash crop production in the forest section of the Yoruba-speaking area neither developed primarily as the result of the imposition of colonial production quotas *nor* as the result of the imposition of a head tax.

37. The customary courts exist in essentially the same form in Nigeria today.

38. See Okeigbo civil court cases 10/56 (University of Ife Library).

39. A group of Ifetedo farmers were involved in a dispute with an Ife chief over land in the Ifetedo area. The claim of the chief was based on the allocation of hunting rights to one of his distant and probably mythical ancestors. The Ifetedo farmers did not dispute the truth of the story, but argued that the allocation of hunting rights to an individual conferred no rights of any kind on his descendents.

40. In conditions where tools and basic production techniques have barely changed since 1900, increases in productivity (per acre or per man/day) are not possible, except through working longer hours or, of course, investing money in new production techniques.

41. Adegboye (1966) describes (for other parts of the Yoruba-speaking area) a situation where migrants arrive in a community and work for a number of years before

trying to obtain land as tenant farmers. This happens in the Okeigbo and Ifetedo areas, but it has not been the dominant practice. Migrants who came in the late 1950s and 1960s usually stayed with relatives or people from their home towns (and worked for them) while they looked for their own land. The explanation of the development of this form of tenancy is based on discussions with older informants and is not based on detailed knowledge of enterprise income allocations in the late 1940s. That information was simply not available.

42. It is not really possible to refer to the state of landholding as it exists in 1980 using material collected in 1974. A Federal Government Nationalisation Decree (1978) has potentially altered land ownership conditions in a radical way.

43. Sale of cocoa farms only takes place in extreme circumstances, such as debt incurred through illness or isolated old age. The purchase of a cocoa farm carried with it the right to replant trees on the same land.

44. As should be obvious, the arrangement is fraught with difficulties and potential sources of conflict. Although some sharecropping arrangements persisted for as long as five years, the majority only lasted for one cocoa season.

45. A boundaryman (*alala*) is simply any other farmer whose farm is separated from another's by a common boundary.

46. For a full description of the phenomenon of rising payments and the decrease in size of land allocations, see Clarke (1978:chap. 5). Very little land was given out to tenants after 1968; by that time there was very little uncultivated land left in the area. Community-member farmers decided to hold onto what little uncultivated land they had left because in the late 1960s and early 1970s tenancy did not seem to represent the same optimal solution to the labor shortage problem as it had done in 1948.

47. Since 1947 successive marketing boards have gazetted a minimum producer price at the beginning of each cocoa season. In 1973-1974 this was N20 per hundredweight (112 lbs).

48. In 1973-1974 the Cocoa Marketing Board was directly controlled by the federal government.

49. This may have changed in 1980. See note 42.

50. Yields and incomes had fallen in the three or four years prior to the 1973-1974 season despite increases in the producer price. Many tenants had been able to negotiate a reduction in rent because of poor yields.

51. In 1973 the Nigerian unit of currency was changed from the Nigerian Pound (£) to the Naira (N). The new unit of currency was set at half the value of the old (£ = N2).

REFERENCES

ADEGBOYE, R. (1966). "Farm tenancy in Western Nigeria." Nigerian Journal of Economic and Social Studies, 8:441-453.

AKINJOGBIN, I. (1966). "The Oyo Empire in the eighteenth century: A reassessment." Journal of the Historical Society of Nigeria, 3:449-460.

AWE, B. (1964). "The Ajele System" (A study of Ibadan imperialism in the nineteenth century). Journal of the Historical Society of Nigeria, 3:47-71.

(1965). "The end of an experiment, the collapse of the Ibadan Empire, 1877-1893." Journal of the Historical Society of Nigeria, 3:221-230.

_____(1973). "Militarism and economic development in nineteenth century Yoruba Country: The Ibadan example." Journal of African History, 14:65-77.
BALDWIN, D., and BALDWIN, C. (1976). The Yoruba of South-western Nigeria: An indexed bibliography. Boston: Hall.
BERRY, S. (1975). Cocoa, custom and socio-economic change in rural Western Nigeria. Oxford: Clarendon.
BOHANNAN, P., and BOHANNAN, L. (1968). Tiv economy London: Longmans.
CLARKE, J. (1977). "Some problems in the conceptualisation of non-capitalist relations of production." Critique of Anthropology 2:59-66.
_____(1978). "Agricultural production in a rural Yoruba community." Phd. thesis, London University.
Colonial Office (1916). West African Lands Committee, Committee on the tenure of land in the West African Colonies and protectorates. Draft report minutes of evidence and correspondence.
FADIPE, N. (1970). The sociology of the Yoruba. Ibadan, Nigeria: Ibadan University Press.
FOSTER-CARTER, A. (1978). "The modes of production controversy." New Left Review, 107:47-77.
HINDESS, B. (1977). Sociological theories of the economy. London: Harvester.
HINDESS, B., and HIRST, P. (1977). Mode of production and social formation. London: Macmillan.
IKIME, O. (1968). "Reconsidering indirect rule: The Nigerian example." Journal of the Historical Society of Nigeria, 4:421-438.
Irish University Press [ed.] (1973). Parliamentary Papers, Vol. 63.
JENKINS, A. (1977). "Substantivism as a theory of comparative economic forms." In B. Hindess The sociological theories of the economy. London: Harvester.
JOHNSON, S. (1921). The history of the Yorubas. Lager: CSS.
LAW, R. (1971). "The Oyo Empire: The history of a Yoruba state." Phd. thesis, Birmingham University. (unpublished)
LLOYD, P. (1953). "Some problems of tenancy in Yoruba land tenure." African Studies, 12:93-103.
_____(1962). Yoruba land law. Oxford: Oxford University Press.
_____(1966). "Agnatic and cognatic descent among the Yoruba." Man, 1:484-500.
_____(1968). "Conflict theory and Yoruba kingdoms." In I. M. Lewis (ed.), History and social anthropology. London: Tavistock.
_____(1971). The political development of Yoruba kingdoms in the eighteenth and nineteenth centuries. London: Royal Anthropological Institute.
MABOGUNJE, A., and COOPER, R. (1971). Owu in Yoruba History. Ibadan, Nigeria: Ibadan University Press.
MORTON-WILLIAMS, P. (1964). "The Oyo Yoruba and the Atlantic slave trade, 1670-1830." Journal of the Historical Society of Nigeria, 3:24-45.
OROGE, E. (1971). "The institution of slavery in Yorubaland." Phd. thesis, Birmingham University. (unpublished)
POST (1972). " 'Peasantization' and rural political movements in Western Africa." European Journal of Sociology, 13:223-254.
WILKS, I. (1977). "Land, labour, capital and the forest kingdom of Asante: A model of early change." In J. Friedman and M. Rowlands (eds.), The evolution of social systems. London: Duckworth.

6

EXPORT CROPS AND PEASANTIZATION: The Bakosi of Cameroun

MICHAEL D. LEVIN
University of Toronto,
Toronto, Canada

Coffee and cocoa are among the classic commodities in the world market. As such, they are some of the substance of the relationship of trade and dependency which begins with peasant producers and ends with consumers in capitalist countries. As examples of economic links between the developed and underdeveloped world, coffee and cocoa are little different from other commodities in terms of marketing and distribution. Prices are determined in speculative markets and distribution is powerfully controlled by large corporations, leaving little freedom for the operation of consumer sovereignty. The uniformity of this industrial picture, however, is not found on the production side. Smallholder production is the source of the major part of the crop in many parts of the world. The production of such crops is an example on the supply side of a pure type of dependency—production of a product that has no

AUTHOR'S NOTE: Field research on which this chapter is based was supported by the Foreign Area Fellowship Program.

or insignificant local use. Does such production make its producers peasants? What is the extent of the dependency? How are peasant social structure and economic dependency related as structural conditions? Is the social structure of such communities an underdeveloped one or a result of a process of underdevelopment? Is a peasant structure transitional in a process of underdevelopment?

Peasants and Underdevelopment

One view of underdevelopment, with which this author does not agree, is that exchange between two sets of actors determines the social system of the weaker set of actors. In this view a contemporary peasantry is either (a) totally or partly derivative from capitalism or (b) a capitalist structure and characterized by capitalist relationships. Underdevelopment, in this view, precludes the possibility of the relationship through exchange of two different modes of production which may modify social relationships internal to the system, but does not generate an identity of social structures. Local social structures are seen as open, passive, and impotent in the face of external forces, their form unilaterally determined by the relationship generated by the metropolitan center. Resistance is temporary and merely an obstacle, sure to disappear in the path of inevitable and unidirectional change. Such a view does not allow an adequate understanding of social change except on a purely abstract and ahistorical level; it blinds us theoretically to the strength and continuity of indigenous and traditional structures as well as to local solutions to problems of change; and, finally, it does not require any sort of inquiry into the effect of capitalist intrusions into other sectors of the world economy.

The recognition of such dependency and the capitalist character of the marketing networks of the products, however, should not lead us to assume that the producer's orientation is capitalist, though production is definitely for sale and responsive to price. Nor can we assume that producers are adopting methods, orientations, or structures that are necessarily capitalist. The possibility of survival of a strong or adaptive indigenous social structure with some meaningful relationship of continuity with traditional forms and developing indigenous solutions must be considered. One cannot assume that the structure of the periphery is determined by the structure and the needs of the center; that capitalist forms are the only forms of structure that can coexist, or between which trade can be conducted.

The autonomy of interacting economies, including the possibility of distinct class and social structures and independent adaptations to political and economic circumstance, is a more realistic assumption for the explanation of under-development (Laclau, 1971; Brenner, 1977). The view taken here is that the development of peasantries from other types of societies must be seen in the context of indigenous social structure—in particular, concepts of ownership and relationships of inequality. The form of national social and economic structures, whether of colonial or independent states, must also be taken into account.

This chapter will attempt to answer these questions about the relationship of peasant structures and dependency by reference to a particular case—the situation of baKosi cocoa and coffee smallholders in Cameroun. The baKosi case will be used to illustrate the effect of traditional social structure and contemporary perceptions in mediating the capitalist relations inherent in commodity production. It will also show how traditional concepts, rooted in specific situations, obscured important changes in the mode of production. The review has two main parts: The baKosi peasantry and peasantry and dependence.

THE BAKOSI PEASANTRY

The key to understanding present-day baKosi social structure is the interaction of local structures within the changing economic and political environment. The story of the expansion of cocoa and coffee farming in West Africa is well known, and the baKosi experience does not appreciably alter our understanding of the forms of organizational change that accompany these forms of commodity production. The changes in economic organization, and the forms of ownership, labor recruitment, and capital formation have been described and analyzed in detail (Berry, 1975; Hill, 1963). Little that is new about these aspects of the impact of permanent cash crop production can be learned from the examination of the baKosi case. The unique characteristics of the baKosi case are two: (1) it was a "tribal" movement led by a "tribal" chief, and (2) it evolved into a sort of transhumant pattern of seasonal production based on two crops. These factors, however, are not of major interest here. What is of interest is the effect of cash crop involvement on the social structure—that is, the effect of the rearrangement of productive activities and resources on other aspects of the social system. The links between traditional forms and economic change have been discussed in some detail (Hill, 1963; Douglas, 1969). Of particular interest in the baKosi case is the unbalanced integration of the baKosi economy into the national economy, the impact of relatively rapid increases in rural incomes, and the evolving relationship between city and country in the Cameroun state.

Bakosi Political Economy

The traditional[1] baKosi political economy was land-based and organized in terms of kinship units of a segmentary system. The goals of production were subsistence consumption, limited exchange for prestige and ceremonial purposes, and narrowly restricted trade. The introduction of permanent tree crops—cocoa and coffee—was seen initially as a progressive change, because the potential for disruption was not as perceptible as were the obvious advantages. The obvious advantages of such innovations were the cash incomes that such crops gave and the goods that such incomes could buy. The level of income was far above that possible from trade which had limited possibilities and, in particular, restricted access. The early period, moreover, allowed the baKosi to organize the production of these crops on a plantation model, following the German example. The initial inducements were great. The long-term changes, even if this was as short as 40 years, could not have been evident.[2] A combination of political and economic forces was weakening the traditional structure and bringing it into conflict with its ecological, economic, and political limits; and this was not evident until many years after the introduction of cocoa. Only in very recent years have the consequences of these agricultural changes become clear and attempts made to contain them.

The discussion of this transformation of the baKosi political economy in this section is divided into four parts. The first is a brief description of the traditional system of political economy. The second presents a history of the innovation of cocoa and coffee production. The third is an analysis of the way new techniques, both of technology and organization, required by cocoa and coffee production, transformed the political economy of the baKosi. The fourth is a discussion of present-day trends and potential.

Traditional system of political economy. The segmentary lineage system of baKosi society was the basis of organization of political and economic activities. Membership and status were based on the criteria of descent; inequality derived from descent. The main expressions of inequality were in the sphere of political activity, and in particular in the disabilities of slavery. In the economic sphere, the main area of differentiation of access to resources was in the control of trade; trade was the monopoly of adult free men, and in effect ultimately the members of the ruling secret society, *Ahon*. As Coquery-Vidrovitch (1969) and Hymer (1970) have pointed out, rules against the concentration of land sustained the egalitarianism of these societies. Rules alone did not prevent accumulation; ecological relationships, the agricultural system, and the environment precluded accumulation. At no point in the system was accumulation favored. Land, population, and technology did not allow for accumulation; no locally produced goods were a store of wealth; and demographic and political limits constrained the growth of lineages. Thus, a relatively stable system characterized by equality of wealth was sustained.

Agricultural production was labor-intensive, not demanding of land, and limited in crops. The main crops were cocoyams and plantains, planted in a system of shifting cultivation. The extremely fertile soils of volcanic ash allowed three years of cultivation in a single plot. The cocoyams could be continually replanted during this period, after which the plot reverted to fallow for seven to ten years. The perceptions of baKosi farmers were that land has always been plentiful and that food is abundant. Land was never reported in short supply or unavailable. Access to land was through membership in a lineage or through acceptance of the residence of a person or family in a village. Land to be brought under cultivation was usually allocated by a lineage or village head and cultivated by the women in individual but adjacent plots. Further evidence of the relative abundance of land was the openness of discussion of migration of lineages and of the process of absorption into the village. Products of agricultural labor were the exclusive property of the cultivator. Women produced cocoyams; men grew plaintains and kept livestock—dwarf cows, goats, sheep, and chickens.

Food was perceived to be in abundance. No hungry period was reported. Nevertheless, the shortage and almost total lack of some commodities such as salt were noted. A major innovation in food production was the introduction in the nineteenth century of a new type of cocoyam (*Xanthasoma* Spp.) which required less intensive preparation of plots and allowed continuous cultivation. Productivity is also said to have increased markedly. Trade was the source of salt, iron bars, brass rods, and, later, manufactured trade goods.

In this system and with these resources, intensification of production was simply not possible. Labor was the major variable of input. Most goods could not be hoarded, speculated in, or even stored. Even had there been a form of currency or a type of good that could function as a store of wealth, accumulation of wealth had no purpose and conferred little advantage. The only paths of investment were ceremonial display and a single payment of fees to join the secret society, *Ahon*, or other men's societies. Even the accumulation of trade goods could only benefit a man in these areas of spending. Ownership of slaves brought wealth only in the direct sense of an increase in the number of one's followers. The unit of consumption was a household with a clear division of labor between husband and wife or wives. Cooperation of brothers and co-wives was valued and in certain circumstances necessary, but could not be enforced.

Labor within the lineage—to the benefit of another member —as an act of reciprocity or collective effort was approved, as was service to an in-law or other relative. Labor for anyone outside of such lines of relationship was interpreted as servitude, and negative connotations of such work are still prevalent. Collective action was possible, however, at several levels of solidarity, and compensation was limited. These occasions were usually single tasks such as clearing land or building a house. Reward was food and drink and took a relatively modest, though special, form. The ultimate form of solidarity was defense, but it had limited economic significance.

The introduction of cocoa in baKosi. Compared with Western Nigeria (Berry, 1975) and Ghana (Hill, 1963) the baKosi cocoa enterprise was limited in scale and minor in migration. This indigenous economic expansion also began much later, beginning in the 1920s, because of German colonial policy which restricted production and purchasing of export crops to commercial plantations. The main interest in the baKosi case lies in the social and political aspects. The economic transformation, while having similar economic impact to that experienced in Western Nigeria and Ghana, barely altered kinship and micropolitical relationships. Economic change took place within the limits of understood structures, and the main political impact was seen as a strengthening of ethnic boundaries and political unity in face of the colonial regime.

During the German colonial period (1894-1916) the development of commercial or cash crop agriculture was confined to colonial plantations. Cameroonians were involved only as labor. After the conquest of German Kamerun and its partition under League of Nations mandate by the British and the French, the baKosi area came under British jurisdiction. A period of indecisiveness on the part of British officials about the disposition of plantations which had been seized as assets of enemy aliens allowed a baKosi initiative. Under the leadership of the Paramount Chief[3] and with his active encouragement and example, individuals took over an area of land reserved for plantations, cleared it, and began the cultivation of cocoa. The process of economic expansion and transformation took place in the context of indigenous political form, and found legitimacy in the traditional rituals and forms of negotiation and allocation of land.

The effect of this pattern of development was to create smallholder farms and settlements grouped together in broadly defined genealogical sets. Farms were individually held and worked, but the farmers of one village, or larger genealogical segment, would find themselves together. Adjacent to them would be their clan brothers of another village, and so on. Although general principles of genealogical organization were the basis of allocation of land, the land-genealogical identity was quite loose. The effect, however, was to sustain the genealogical model as the conscious model of social organization. The identity of the baKosi as a people with a particular area of land—a territory—was also enhanced.

The pattern and structure of smallholding is similar to that found elsewhere in West Africa. Labor was the basis of, and main constraint on, expansion. New farms were created initially by clearing forest either individually or with cooperative labor, and the extent of the farms was limited only by the energy of the farmer and the resources at his disposal to mobilize labor. Late-comers to cocoa growing were often former plantation workers who, with their savings and their experience, would establish holdings in excess of the ability of one man to maintain. The employment of labor where kinsmen were not available then became necessary. Most often, this labor came from the northern parts of West Cameroon. Within a few years of the establishment of the smallholder cocoa farms, coffee was introduced. The planting of coffee was a significant innovation for economic development, as it could grow at higher altitudes and lower temperatures than cocoa, and therefore permanent cash crop farming could penetrate to every village in baKosi. It was first adopted in the upland villages and spread throughout them. Ultimately, as cocoa trees aged and became unproductive, coffee was planted to replace them. The lower labor requirements and relatively higher prices also made coffee more attractive than cocoa. The major implication of coffee growing was to create a year-round cycle of production. A pattern of transhumant cash crop farming developed with farmers moving between upland coffee farms which were harvested in the dry season (October to March) and lowland cocoa farms in the rainy season (April to September).

Thus, the broad lines of unity, the symbolic importance of the Paramount Chief, and the extension of "tribal" power complemented the economic expansion that cocoa and coffee production created. Furthermore, the initial delay in integrating the traditional villages into the system of permanent tree crop cultivation softened the resistance to change. The implications for social structure at this stage were latent, hidden by the circumstances, but they were to become far-reaching.

Transformation of baKosi political economy. Production for exchange was not uniquely created by the growing of cocoa and coffee. Kola nut, livestock, and other goods which were also locally consumed had been used in trade to the coast over a long period of time prior to the introduction of cocoa. Trade, in these goods and slaves, for some time had been part of baKosi economic life; production of goods that had no local use was, however, a significant change. The flow of income into baKosi generated by cash crop production far exceeded the ability of the baKosi to usefully consume or invest for some time. A major reason for this weak side of the baKosi economy was the isolation of baKosi from centers of administration and trade. The 1920s were years of expansion, but the development that might have followed was cut off by the economic depression of the 1930s. Until after World War II production was the more active side of the local economy. The immediate postwar period was characterized by high prices and a boom. It was not until the 1960s, however, that the poor seasonal roads of the area were improved to all-weather quality. Before this, crops went out to the marketing boards in West Cameroon or by smuggling across the border into East Cameroon, but goods did not come into the area in sufficient quantity to meet demand. Developments begun in the 1945-1960 period accelerated after independence and reunification; the southern edge of the baKosi area became one of the main routes connecting the eastern and western parts of Cameroun. In this period private buyers, the cooperatives associated with the marketing boards, and private produce companies bought the crops.

These phases mark changes in the intensity of communications with the central government, and the degree of integration with national institutions as developments in transportation were paralleled by other aspects of colonial and national development. The general trend, although not uniform in all institutional aspects, was continuing penetration of the state into local affairs. The transformation and integration of the baKosi communities cannot, however, be seen as a smooth development, nor as a dramatic fall into a state of dependency. The initial adoption of cash crop production had little apparent impact on traditional structures. Indeed, the one factor that might have been thought to be disruptive—the new locations for the permanent cash crop farms—softened its effect by reducing the pressure on land and avoiding the new choice of land allocation within the boundaries of traditional groups. The value of innovation was established before it was absorbed in the villages, where its future impact on land use and the cycle of rotation was overshadowed by the more immediate prosperity it offered.

Production levels and world prices were such during these early decades that consumption simply could not keep pace. In the 1920s cocoa made a few people wealthy, but accumulation and investment depended on the ability to recruit labor to carry goods to the villages. A few—not more than six—substantial houses of cement and sawed lumber date from this period. Subsistence farming or food production was still the main source of livelihood. Cash crop incomes were being absorbed in minor changes in consumption of what must still, in this period, be referred to as trade goods and prestige expenditures, a phenomenon noted elsewhere (Balandier, 1970:178-183). The opportunities for education were severely limited; until the late 1950s there were no secondary schools in West Cameroon. Investment in housing was possible, but materials for improvement—in particular, cement—were not readily available. Bust and boom cycles are recalled, but the period must vividly remembered is the postwar period of high cocoa prices and nothing to spend the money on. People recollect buying cases of smuggled Spanish gin and brandy and consuming it in long and extended drinking bouts. Shouting and singing echoed through the cocoa farms throughout the night; pits were dug to bury the empty bottles. No farmer had to work. For one-third of the crop, a sharecropper would tend the farm and harvest and process the cocoa beans for sale. An owner might assist in the 24- to 36-hour drying process that could not be interrupted. By the 1960s those who recalled the lazy days of the past were doing all the labor on their farms and engaging in reciprocal exchanges of labor during tasks of peak demand, such as harvesting and drying.

The retrospective view of this period is one of regret and realism. No forms of reasonable investment were accessible. Expansion even where land was available made little sense; today, in the full-scale market economy such lack of effort seems more costly. Today, the money seems to have been ill-used despite the realistic recognition that at the time it was spent in an economic vacuum. In later decades, prices fluctuated and generally declined, and the share given to hired labor was forced upward from one-third to one-half. The large incomes of the 1940s—some above £400 per farmer—where they existed were absorbed by increasing costs, a higher standard of living, and opportunities to invest in housing and education. The integration of the rural economy was continuing apace in both physical and institutional aspects.

By the 1960s two major changes affected baKosi: roads opened the area to relatively easy movement of people and goods, and educational institutions were being built in many parts of the country. Investment in housing and education became the major outlets for any excess wealth from sales of cash crops. The mid-1960s were marked by declines in prices, which put a further squeeze on incomes and caused tenants and sharecroppers to demand better terms. Many of those baKosi smallholders who had used outside labor were compelled to do all the farm work themselves. In this period, involvement in the national economy, the supply of goods, and occupational opportunities all increased. The main economic link with the national economy was through the export crops of cocoa and coffee, but a secondary relationship developed that was created by, and dependent on, the development of roads. This new market was for food stuffs, plantain, and cocoyams, which were bought by traders-transporters who created markets where the roads gave them access.

The institutional structures of which the local economy was a part were battered by the negative consequences of the process of integration, against which it had few defenses. The political and military functions and institutions had been destroyed early by the colonial governments. Economic integration was limited by isolation, which further protected traditional institutions of ownership and control of land in particular, which in turn sustained the collective unity of village communities. The new crops, however, threatened the concepts of property and the structural controls; limits on the use of resources became increasingly inappropriate and feeble in the face of these social and technical changes. The agricultural system and the concepts of ownership lent themselves to easy change of crops but ultimately allowed the limits on accumulation to be undermined. Two concepts—"farm" and "land"—as they were understood to be related to labor and ownership, took on new economic aspects of meaning with the introduction of permanent tree crops. The "farm" was the creation of labor regardless of whether it was an annual crop, such as cocoyams, or a permanent one, such as cocoa; the land in use was the main criterion. The "land," on the other hand, was not owned except in the sense that any member of the community had a right to access, a right to use it for purposes of cultivation or building a house. This right was the main form of property in regard to land. Under cocoyam cultivation, land reverted to fallow and the user far outlived his farm; under cocoa the farms outlived the user and, in effect, though not in principle, the land was out of rotation and therefore out of the collective pool. The collective aspect of the system had not needed explicit controls, as the inherent limits of the agricultural system and of the crops fit a collective control of land and egalitarian rules. Neither selling a farm nor accumulating land made sense.

After the introduction of cocoa, the difference between "land" and "farm" became meaningful in terms of ownership. The ambiguity of definition allowed the sale of the "farm" and allowed avoidance of the issue of the sale of the "land." It was always claimed that the land was separate and distinct from the farm; in effect, the distinction often could not be enforced.

The present-day conflicts and weaknesses arise out of the limits on economic relationships among or between "brothers," whether immediate kinsmen or simply co-baKosi. As such, kinship and ethnic relationships are seen as opposed to maximization of gain and price. The economic advantages that are possible in dealing with "strangers"—non-baKosi—are not considered possible for transactions between fellow baKosi. Exchanges between kinsmen are limited by tradition; indebtedness is expected and accepted within the relationship; hard bargaining and demands for payment and written contracts with precise obligations are not. Dealing with kin on economic matters such as "pledging" a farm is not advantageous. Price alone is not the only drawback; ownership and control can easily become confused in the absence of such technicalities of transfer of rights as are found in a contract. The closer the relationship, the more likely conflicting claims will arise. Because of these limits on economic specificity in dealing with kinsmen, pledging tends to be a transaction between baKosi and non-baKosi. The rational or maximization aspects of the transaction, however, do not eliminate disputes.

Despite these perceived advantages in pledging to non-baKosi, the right of redemption was often submerged in disputes about value and investment. Pledges were for a specified period, or might have required refund of the original sum of money. In the latter case, the tenant often tries to increase the amount owed by paying more until the sum becomes very difficult to raise. In the former case, the period simply runs out, although a tenant may improve the farm and claim compensation for his efforts. If he has the farm on an indefinite basis, the baKosi owner will claim that it must be allowed to decline and then the land reverts to him; the tenant, on the other hand, can renew the farm and extend his life and attempt to extend his period of occupancy. The pressures inherent in this changing situation are toward individual or small family control and away from any form of collective solidarity; they further weaken village- and ethnic-based institutions. These transactions work against the marginal smallholders in particular and often lead to their losing land permanently. In contrast to Mayan peasant communities (Cancian, 1965), there are no institutions that compel solidarity through religious or economic commitments.

Trends and potential. During the fieldwork period in 1968, trends of change were becoming clear. Larger families, most importantly those with one adult male member in a salaried occupation and a second adult male managing the family farms, were the most successful in sustaining their rural resources and using them as a base for mobility into the national occupational structure. Families with marginal farms too small to provide needed income and enough work were the most likely to pledge and risk losing their farms. At times this was a device used by a father's brother to reap maximum benefits from his custodianship of the nephew's inheritance. This sign of economic differentiation may be the beginning of concentration of landholding and the creation of a landless class. The labor-intensive nature of cocoa and coffee cultivation makes this unlikely, as does the flexibility of inheritance rules, which allow those staying in the villages to cultivate the farms.

The economy of baKosi was firmly within the national and international system. Consumption was seen as potentially unlimited and income was now severely limited. Those who expanded their farms despite the apparent pointlessness in the 1930s were now seen as wise. After ordinary consumption goods, the possibility of improved housing, and education were the main uses for income. Educational costs for secondary school fees were high enough to be seen as the major restraint on discretionary spending. In a general evaluation the economy is seen as having declined; the pressure of scarcity is much greater; but conditions have improved. The trend toward social mobility through education was well understood; the consequence, that agriculture would come to be seen as the work of failures, those who did not succeed at school, and therefore a second-class occupation, was not. Most of this difference was seen as a broad trend of progressive social change; and in terms of individuals, a generational difference between older people who had no access to education and younger ones who had access. At that moment, the lines of mobility were open through education, but rural-urban links may in the future be weakened or broken. Two factors work against this: the urban dweller's conception of the village as home and the place to build his house and of ultimate retirement; and his sense of responsibility to sponsor youth from home. Although these links are cultivated by some, they are not enforceable and they are, therefore, weak guarantees of continuing association.

In the rural sector production was oriented toward the market, but the line between the cash crops and food crops was no longer clear. The improvement of road access allowed buyers to create markets for plantains and cocoyams on an occasional basis in most villages. These markets, while again offering the producer the weak side of the transaction, protected him through diversifying his sources of income. In the longer term, as the proportion of urban population grows, the demand for food crops can be expected to expand to the benefit of the producer.

PEASANTRY AND DEPENDENCE

To answer the questions posed at the beginning of the chapter requires confronting the problem of the place of a peasant structure in the relationship of dependency of the peripheral rural sector to the metropolitan center (see Levin and Derman, 1977). That the peasant community is within a larger society is a matter of definition. Peasant structures, societies, or communities are by definition "part-societies, with part-cultures" (Kroeber, 1948:284), and explicitly they are oriented economically at least in part to an external market (Wolf, 1966). The relationship with the institutions of the larger society is the matter in question. This relationship is described variously as resistance to the state, solidarity and identification with the community in the face of external pressures, unresponsiveness, inward orientation, exploitation, and penetration by capital and the state.

These symptoms of the state of dependency of the peasantry are usually described, but the condition of dependency itself is usually implicit in the literature; these forms of reaction are indications of the degree of dependency and its degree of intensity. In anthropology, in its struggle to escape particularistic dead ends, the differences in national social structures are sometimes ignored in the search for generality. The cost is a great loss in the understanding of the variations within similar commodity production systems (Stavenhagen, 1975). In particular, in regard to peasantry, models developed for the study of Latin American social structures have been exported to Africa where the national systems, the history, and the present social structures do not support the analysis.

Two recent contributions are concerned with the concept of peasantry and the problem of locating peasants in a larger social system. In a general sense this chapter supports their views: there is no essential peasantry. In a specific sense it disputes them; the problems of rural social structure and history cannot be generalized or deduced from the broad concept of the state and national economy.

The position of Bernstein in a recent article (1977) is that "peasants have to be located in their relations with capital and state, in other words, within *capitalist relations of production*." He argues further that there is no single or essential peasantry, nor can there be a "uniform 'model' of class action by peasants" (1977:73). The major line of argument, however, assumes that the basic element of peasant social structure is an atomized household, with neither social relationships nor institutions that affect or mediate capitalist relations of production. Thus, the initial problem seems unresolved. Roseberry (1978) considers whether peasants should be studied and considered as proletarians; and he argues that the difficult problem of articulation of modes of production can be resolved by beginning the study of commodity production from an understanding of the total society. He concludes that anthropologists should "add 'peasants' to our list of traditional categories" (1978:16) rather than continue to strive for a generalized definition.

In the baKosi case described here kinship relations affect the economic relationship with the capitalist market; the mode of production established has both traditional and collective aspects which do not fit the conception suggested by these authors at the level of peasant social structure, or petty commodity producers. That this structure cannot be understood except in its relationship with the state, however, is clear. The general point of this review is also in agreement that there is no single model of peasantry; peasant models, however, well represent much of the empirical evidence.

The baKosi cocoa and coffee farmers are clearly in a relationship of interdependency with world markets and a national system. They view this process of integration as progressive, but also negative in many aspects. Their production of these crops for an external market clearly marks them as peasants (Wolf, 1966), as does their allocation to the market of some food or subsistence crops. Production of a commodity for world markets does not alone make its producers peasants, as the work of Northrup (1978) on the palm oil trade in southeastern Nigeria in the nineteenth century shows. To assess the extent of dependency and the extent of integration implies a prior assessment of self-sufficiency. For the baKosi, self-sufficiency is a potential state, but at a reduced level of consumption and involving a regression in economic development. In this general sense, a peasantry is in a state of dependency, and peasant social structure and dependency are related conditions. In another sense the extent of dependency is great and increasing. Options such as moving into food production would take considerable time and labor and would meet structural opposition, as food crops are the products of women's work. Such change, however, is certainly possible, and the number of crops marketed gives more flexibility than a monoculture; dependency continues as a concomitant of market orientation. Both peasant social structure and dependency are relationships of a part, with the center, of a larger socioeconomic system. Peasant societies are characterized by resistance and involvement with the city, or center. Where, as in this case, the rural sector was politically and culturally autonomous, the degree of economic dependency may be limited and the opposition characteristic of peasant societies may express itself in other ways—for example, in organizing to educate the young in anticipation of their careers in government service, which are expected to have direct and indirect benefits for their families and communities. The community is being drawn more and more into the larger system that is the state; the autonomous hunting and agricultural and trading baKosi are becoming the rural baKosi.

The questions about the historical aspects of these changes are more difficult to answer. Stavenhagen (1975) sees African peasantries in a transitional stage. His perspective assumes an inevitable course of change. The potential for collective action is neglected and the openness and mobility in rural-urban relationships that now exist are ignored; yet these aspects of social structure are likely to continue in such settings. The nature of underdevelopment from the perspective of this type of rural economy is also difficult to assess. The economy has grown; this change is perceived as progressive—a good thing—but it has become dependent; and this is regretted. The processes are sometimes associated. These changes are the result of a historical process, not simply of underdevelopment or trade (Northrup, 1978), but also of incorporation into a state. The periphery is dependent on the center for markets and on the government for pricing of export crops, and is the weaker partner in the transaction. However, the condition of dependency is universal in the agricultural sector, not only that of African peasantries.

The structure of such rural communities might have changed differently. In this case the indigenous expansion has been stimulated but not directed or manipulated from abroad, although the modern state has lately intervened to control marketing and the surplus profits of cocoa and coffee production by establishing marketing boards, setting prices, and levying export taxes. The terms "underdeveloped" and "underdevelopment" may be applied in an evaluative sense. The direction of the process of change allows for several alternatives, the likelihood of which depends on one's evaluation of the oppressiveness of government policy, the strength of local organization, and other aspects of political and economic change.

THE FUTURE

The position of the rural community is not a stable one, nor can it be described definitely in class terms (Stavenhagen,

1975). Class distinctions, in the broad sense of socioeconomic differences, are growing, but are tempered by kinship and ethnic ties. Rights to use of land are respected and, to the present, honored. The possibility of a rural proletariat developing as a result of land pressure or pledging away of land exists, but ethnic differences are likely to be the most striking differences between the landed and the landless. The distinction will be obscured by the lack of traditional claims of non-baKosi; landless baKosi are likely to migrate; rural urban migration is not always social mobility. The pressure on the peasant producer will continue through pricing and marketing mechanisms, but ownership and control are securely within his hands. Local control through awareness of ethnicity may be strengthened despite the lack of cohesive village institutions. Integration into the national system will continue, and penetration of the state will deepen; local control will be the essential element in the stability of the village. There is sadness at the loss of traditional unity and institutions, but the benefits of a more open structure are perceived and welcome. Furthermore, individual control of farms is likely to lead to more dynamic growth and independence of production than that achieved through lineage or village control The loss of traditional institutions may be compensated for by the openness of the new structures.

NOTES

1. "Traditional" structure or system is defined here as the structure or system that existed prior to the colonial period. The reality of the system or structure as described cannot be confirmed, but it is a likely system or structure—that is, one that could evolve to the present-day system and that is in accord with cross-cultural data.

2. The editor, discussing this chapter with me, wondered "why the baKosi went into cash crops in the first place." The "obvious advantages" alluded to here are simply the benefits of cash incomes and relatively high ones at that. Some farmers during the cocoa boom of the late 1940s had incomes in excess of £400. In 1977 the per capita income in Cameroun was estimated at only about $300.

3. It must be noted that the traditional political system did not allow for a single predominant leader or office. Closest to this was *Ahon*. The Paramount Chieftaincy was the creation of the colonial authorities—for the British, in the form of the native

authority. The baKosi situation was one where their creature soon showed his independence and "nationalism" and by the same token displeased his colonial rulers.

REFERENCES

BALANDIER, G. (1970). The sociology of black Africa. London: Andre Deutsch.

BERNSTEIN, H. (1977). "Notes on capital and peasantry." Review of African Political Economy, 10:60-73.

BERRY, S. S. (1975). Cocoa, custom and socio-economic change in Western Nigeria. Oxford: Oxford University Press.

BRENNER, R. (1977). "The origins of capitalistic development: A critique of Neo-Smithian Marxism." New Left Review, 104:25-93.

CANCIAN, F. (1965). Economics and prestige in a Maya community: The religious cargo system in Zinacantan. Stanford: Stanford University Press.

COQUERY-VIDROVITCH, C. (1969). "Research on an African mode of production." In M. A. Klein and G. W. Johnson (eds.), Perspectives on the African past. Boston: Little, Brown.

_____(1976). "The political economy of the African peasantry and modes of production." In P.C.W. Gutkind and I. Wallerstein (eds.), The political economy of contemporary Africa. Beverly Hills, CA: Sage.

DOUGLAS, M. (1969). "Is matriliny doomed in Africa?" In M. Douglas and P. M. Kaberry (eds.), Man in Africa. London: Tavistock.

HILL, P. (1963). Migrant cocoa farmers of southern Ghana. Cambridge: Cambridge University Press.

HYMER, S. (1970). "Economic forms in pre-colonial Ghana." Journal of Economic History, 20:33-50.

KROEBER, A. L. (1948). Anthropology. New York: Harcourt Brace.

LACLAU, E. (1971). "Feudalism and capitalism in Latin America." New Left Review, 67:14-38.

LEVIN, M. and DERMAN, B. (1977). "Peasants, propaganda, economics and exploitation." American Anthropologist, 79:119-125.

NORTHRUP, D. (1978). Trade without rulers: pre-colonial economic development in South-Eastern Nigeria. Oxford: Oxford University Press.

ROSEBERRY, W. (1978). "Peasants as proletarians." Critique of Anthropology, 11:3-18.

STAVENHAGEN, R. (1975). Social classes in agrarian societies. New York: Doubleday.

WOLF, E. R. (1966). Peasants. Englewood Cliffs, NJ: Prentice-Hall.

7

REGIONAL AND SOCIAL DIFFERENTIATION IN BROKEN HILL RURAL DISTRICT, NORTHERN RHODESIA, 1930-1964

MAUD SHIMWAAYI MUNTEMBA
University of Zambia

INTRODUCTION

The twentieth century witnessed the forward thrust of capitalism and the incorporation of Zambia into the world system. While incorporation has been achieved, capitalist relations of production have not developed in all sectors of the economy. While the industrial, manufacturing, largely urban sectors are capitalist, the agricultural sector remains predominantly peasant. An African rural bourgeoisie comprising active or retired politicians, technocrats, and professional people has been slowly emerging since independence in 1964. This class did not exist before 1964; until then the African agricultural sector was totally peasant.

In this chapter I examine differentiation within the peasantry by looking at one district, Broken Hill Rural. Until 1953 Broken Hill Rural was part of Broken Hill District. However, in that year the district was divided in two: Broken Hill Urban

District to deal with Broken Hill town, white settler, and Indian communities; and Broken Hill Rural District to administer Africans in the reserves. Since 1967 the district has been known as Kabwe Rural District and the town of Broken Hill as Kabwe. With independence in 1964 Northern Rhodesia became Zambia. In this chapter I use the colonial names, since I deal only with the period before 1964.

The study covers the years 1930-1964. This period witnessed greater opportunities for improving the productive forces for some peasants and intensified handicaps for doing so for others. However, I give a pre-1930 background, which I have divided into two parts: the precolonial, to 1899, and the early colonial, 1899-1929. There were regional differences, but not differentiation in precolonial times. Social differentiation existed, although this was later transformed by the capitalist relations of production. I use "differences" to refer to natural dissimilarity and "differentiation" to refer to the social structure in which one group is structurally and rigidly set apart from another as a result of what takes place in the sphere of production. The 1899-1929 period shows a preliminary stage of regional and social differentiation.

ECOLOGY AND SOCIAL COMPOSITION

There are three main ecosystems in the district, which I shall refer to as Ecosystems 1, 2, and 3. Ecosystem 1 comprises 2000 square miles of swamps, and fishing has been the main occupation. Ecosystem 2, which covers the largest portion of the district, is identified by lateritic and light sandveldt soils (Trapnell and Clothier in Northern Rhodesia government, 1937a:5, 11). The soil's productivity is low and cannot be cropped continuously for more than three to five years without fertilizers. Lateritic soils produce millet only; sandveldt soils are best suited for sorghum production and for certain varieties of tobacco. Without the use of fertilizers, they are very poor maize soils (1937a:5-6). Some parts of the ecosystem are free from the tsetse fly, and producers have kept cattle. Red and brown loams, sandy in poorer parts and a heavier texture in others, characterize Ecosystem 3. These soils have a higher inherent productivity than those of Ecosystem 2. Sandier soils produce sorghum and tobacco; the heavier textured soils provide excellent maize and grazing foods. The latter are also good for cotton production (1937a:7, 13). Regions in this ecosystem have been free from the tsetse fly for a considerable time, and cattle have been reared. Many rivers and streams, some of them perennial, traverse some of the regions in Ecosystem 3.

The Lenje are the dominant ethnic group. Until 1899 the area was known as *Bulenje*, but others, such as the Swaka, Lima, and Twa, have also lived here for a long time. The Twa were fishermen who lived in the swamps until 1928 when, to facilitate tax collection, the government moved them to the mainland. In the twentieth century, particularly after World War II, individuals from other parts of the country migrated to this district. Some immigrants came from outside Northern Rhodesia. The largest single migrant group was that of the Shona and Ndebele from Southern Rhodesia. By 1964 the district was heterogeneous. However, from the seventeenth or early eighteenth century the area gradually came under the Mukuni chiefs. On local issues the district is still under those chiefs today (Muntemba, 1973, 1977).

The district is composed of one class: the peasantry. Class refers to the people's relation to the means of production—in this case, land. Except for bonded slaves in precolonial times, all adults have for a considerable time owned or had access to land. But by 1964 regional and social differentiation was marked. This resulted from the producers' capacity to increase labor's productiveness. In precolonial days this largely depended on the soil's inherent productivity and the efficient control and organization of exploitable labor. With the penetration of the money economy, labor's productiveness became highly dependent on capital formation. To accomplish this, producers required more efficient tools and methods of production, in addition to adequate labor supplies and good soils;

they needed markets with favorable marketing conditions and additional cash resources from the government. Government resources were important because many producers were not able to create sufficient capital independently.

Since the turn of this century, at different times and in varying degrees, producers have sold their food surpluses and other products within and outside their regions. Capitalist penetration, which came with colonial rule, opened markets in urban centers and white settler farms. After 1930, local mining and metropolitan demands for agricultural produce grew. The market expanded accordingly. To maximize production, the government provided cash and technical resources. However, this developed against a background of destructive measures for most peasants: removal of Africans into the reserves with poorer soils and farther from the markets; disproportionately controlled financial and technical resources; and unfavorable marketing conditions.

From precolonial times, the ability to increase productivity stratified society. After 1930, greater opportunities for capital formation accelerated differentiation in the district. By 1964, three strata within the peasantry had emerged: rich, "progressive" peasants who had improved their productive forces, sold to the market regularly, and had lifestyles distinctly better than the others'; middle peasants with varying productive capacities, who met their subsistence requirements and sold to the market when there were surpluses; and the poor, whose subsistence had become precarious primarily because the soils they cultivated were poor and because they lacked exploitable labor.

Differentiation within the district was developing simultaneously between regions and within regions, and the process itself was interconnected. However, I shall analyze regional differentiation and social differentiation within regions separately. (I shall do this both to demonstrate the structural differentiation more clearly and to facilitate the task for myself.) Regions with unfavorable conditions comprised largely the poor peasants and a very few middle peasants. Other regions were marked by a social stratification comprising a few rich, a large middle, and some poor. A few of the poor in these regions were in the process of losing their land to rich peasants.

THE PRE-1930 BACKGROUND

Precolonial

Regional differentiation did not emerge in the precolonial period. Regional differences, determined by ecological factors, were the basis of interregional trade in which both sides benefited. However, social stratification existed even in this period.

Social values and indicators of differentiation vary from society to society. Nevertheless, differentiation is connected with access to and control over the productive forces. A low technology characterized precolonial economies. Access to land and the ability or opportunity to control exploitable labor and labor's produce influenced differentiation.

Cattle ownership was the most important basis of wealth and social prestige in *Bulenje*: "What was a person without cattle?" An individual's esteem shot up if, in addition to cattle, he also owned slaves. Slaves enabled owners to create surpluses with which they bought cattle. The ability to entertain generously and distribute use items particularly to needy relatives also earned the esteem of others. Luxury items were rare, but where they existed they accentuated an individual's economic and social standing (Muntemba, 1977:I).

There were four identifiable groups: chiefs and their families who controlled exploitable labor and the produce of others; members of nonchiefly families who, through efficient organization and control over exploitable labor, created surpluses to invest in more labor and indicators of prestige; the majority of the people who only subsisted; and, finally, slaves formed the last and most distinctive group.

Chiefs controlled the labor of those under them in two ways. First, they directly controlled exploitable labor. Some young men and girls resided at the courts and produced for the chiefs and their families. Other labor was sent in from the nearby villages when there was a need. Through fines and capture, the chiefs also procured slaves. Such control enabled them to create surpluses which they used to enhance their political hold through entertainment and distribution, the purchase of use items, and investment in cattle. Second, through the tributary system, chiefs extracted the products of other people's labor. These were agricultural products—destined for their own consumption and for distribution, iron products to increase production and to trade, ivory to exchange for luxury items, and cloth. Cotton was not extensively cultivated; thus, cloth was in short supply. The chiefs did not allow their subjects, including the producers, to wear this rare item. Chiefs and their families, then, were differentiated from the rest of the people by their ability to distribute and entertain generously, by possession of the rare luxury items, and by ownership of cattle.

Initially, the second group sold surpluses for use items. Later, producers channeled some surpluses into trading for slaves. This was particularly the case among maize and tobacco growers. Slaves enabled them to create more surpluses with which they bought cattle and fulfilled other prestigious functions. The majority, the third group, engaged in trade to get use items for subsistence. That they rarely had surpluses is evidenced by the fact that they sometimes sold food which they needed later in the year. When this happened, they were saved from starvation by their more productive leaders and relatives. They also gathered food from the forests.

Slaves fell into two categories: those with access to land which they cultivated after fulfilling their obligations to the owners, and bonded slaves who were denied access to land. The master/mistress had exclusive right over bonded slave labor. As the slave trade intensified after about 1850, the line of demarcation between the two categories became thinner. Previously, nonbonded slaves could marry free persons and their children could be free. They could also be freed as a reward for good services. They were sometimes freed because of marrying free persons, especially if the spouse was from the master's or mistress' family. After 1850, chances of freedom diminished. Free persons avoided marrying slaves lest they too became slaves through association. Both groups lost control over their own labor power; they became a despised group to be sold off when the need arose: "A slave was a slave."

1899-1929

Colonial rule and capitalist penetration transformed pre-colonial social stratification. The colonial and capitalist systems changed relations to the means of production, and altered labor relations. The administration and capitalist companies held the mineral and land rights, while the tributary and slave systems were abolished. Capitalists gradually controlled labor. The money economy was introduced and steadily dominated transactions. New social values and alien indicators of wealth and social prestige emerged. The importance of cattle persisted, but birthright alone was not enough to sustain the chiefs' distinct positions. Stratification also found expression in western lifestyles: houses, clothing, and food. To attain these, people needed money which was dependent on labor's productiveness.

Between 1899 and 1902 some mines were opened in or near *Bulenje*, and the companies started small-scale mining. In 1906 the railway line from the south reached Broken Hill and influenced the growth of the mine there. Mining remained marginal throughout the country until after 1926; however, the companies required labor even for their limited production. Labor demands increased after Southern Rhodesia and Katanga started recruiting labor from these parts of Northern Rhodesia in 1907 and 1911, respectively. In 1926 the mines entered the construction period and required more labor than previously. Alongside these demands were labor requirements for white farmers who settled in the railway region between Livingstone and Broken Hill. By use of government force, by the tax mechanism, and by land alienation, pressures on Africans to sell their labor mounted (Muntemba, 1977:III).

Ironically, however, by labor force, the administration and capitalists provided markets for Africans. This was because initially there were very few white settlers. Then, after 1910, settlers found a more profitable market in Katanga, where the labor force was larger than in Northern Rhodesia. Third, throughout the period settlers where undercapitalized, while some did not have the necessary expertise to enable them to increase their production. One of the ways they increased their marketable produce was by trading with Africans. Although most farmers did not pay in cash, a few did. In the 1920s some started trading ploughs for grain.

The availability of a market encouraged Africans to increase their surpluses and, thus, to avoid wage labor. As labor pressures mounted, it became difficult to evade wage employment completely. Therefore, producers devised methods of organizing their labor. They went into wage employment at those times when their labor was least required in their agricultural and fishing cycles. In addition to a more efficient organization of labor for their purposes, some bought cattle for prestige but also to use as draft animals. These were the farmers who either bought ox-drawn ploughs or hoped to do so. A few bought bicycles to facilitate transportation of merchandise to the markets. Some of the producers worked on settler farms to pick up new techniques—specifically, the use of the ox-drawn plough—while others learned more productive methods from mission schools.

In varying degrees all regions participated in the trade, although those closer to the markets did so more than the others. Except for children, most sections of the community took part, the younger ones by taking the produce themselves, and older ones and women from farther distances by prevailing on the services of others. These opportunities notwithstanding, the trade was limited, and yielded marginal profits. As a result, capital formation was slight. To be sure, a few producers bought ploughs and bicycles; but this occurred toward the end

TABLE 1   Land Division in Broken Hill District

Area	Land in sq. mile	Population
Broken Hill District	9,842	35,981
Alienated to Europeans	422	not available
Crown lands	1,088	
Lenje Native Reserve No. VI	6,700	not available
Swamps in Reserve No. VI	2,000	
LuanoLala Reserve No. V (portion in B.H. District)	632	3,302

a. Crown lands did not include land which had already been alienated, but into account future alienations.
SOURCE: Northern Rhodesia Government, 1946:39

of the period. This, then, was a transitional stage, a time of adjustment from old to new social formations; a time when seeds of differentiation were sown. Producers closer to the markets, those who grew crops required by the capitalists and who had learned new techniques from settlers and missions, were in the process of building their financial resources to enable them to improve productive forces.

While these processes were shaping in the late 1920s, the mining industry in Northern Rhodesia started to expand. White settlers saw a cheaper internal market. Both industries required more labor. Settlers also feared competition from African producers, who had started to expand their own production in response to the growing market. For these reasons, the mining companies and settlers successfully pressed the government to divide the land into Crown Lands for non-Africans' mining purposes, and towns and native reserves for Africans. In 1928 the government established the desired division. Broken Hill District was divided in the manner shown in Table 1. These divisions greatly influenced regional differentiation after 1930.

1930-1964

Ecological and geographical factors continued to influence regional and social differentiation. The internal and external markets expanded. Regions capable of producing the required crops—maize, tobacco, and cotton—benefited. In addition, places closer to the lines of communication and the urban markets were advantaged above the others. Government policies played a significant role in the process of differentiation. Ecological constraints on productivity were accentuated by the land policy, which moved many producers from regions suitable for market production. The government attempted to increase peasant production by giving loans and bonuses and by disseminating technical information. Even this was restricted to market-producing regions closer to the urban centers, and in these regions help was confined to a few members of agricultural schemes.

General Developments

The first major development during this period was the removal of Africans from Crown lands into reserves. In the absence of statistical data it is difficult to estimate the numbers affected by this transfer. Elsewhere I have argued that the south-central parts of the district, most of which now fell within Crown Lands, had been more populously settled. This was because good soils, the presence of perennial rivers, and the absence of the tsetse fly, which allowed the people to keep cattle (Muntemba, 1977:I). Administrative correspondence between 1931 and 1936 also indicates that a large proportion of the district's population was moved (District and Provincial Commissioners' Correspondence, 1931-1936; National Archives of Zambia, Sec/SL/107).

Table 1 shows that land in the reserves was more plentiful than in Crown lands. However, reserves were created both to control labor and to curtail African competition in agriculture. Therefore, the soils in most of the reserves were poor, barely supporting crops for subsistence and hardly capable of producing marketable ones. The Ecological Survey of 1935 found that less than 40 percent of the land in the two reserves was cultivable (Northern Rhodesia Government, 1946:38). Much of the soil was "rock and rubble," swampy or light in texture, and susceptible to erosion. It was poor for grazing purposes, while those limited parts composed of good soils lacked water.

Africans from the northeastern parts of the district were moved into "rock and rubble" areas where the fly was advancing; those from around and near Broken Hill went to the swampy areas; while others searching for better soils and perennial rivers went to already densely populated parts of the district,

> and this augmented population has increased the duty on light soils and the available water holes to such an extent that water for stock is almost unobtainable in the dry months. . . . [T]hese people own fairly large amounts of cattle [District Commissioner to Provincial Commissioner, 4.4.36; National Archives of Zambia, Sec/SL/107].

Of Africans living to the immediate west of the railway line between Chisamba and Broken Hill, the same officer wrote: "The whole area which was formerly occupied by Liteta is on Crown Land. The general direction of Liteta's people is westward across the Great North Road into the waterless region" (District Commissioner to Provincial Commissioner, Feb. 10, 1931; National Archives of Zambia, Sec/SL/107). Six years later he admitted that the government had not fulfilled one of the prerequisites for moving people into the reserves, namely to provide wells and dams for domestic use and for stock (District Commissioner to Senior Provincial Commissioner, July 4, 1937; National Archives of Zambia, Sec/SL/107). The waterless region comprised part of Ecosystem 3 capable of supporting sufficient food and cash crops. Most of the newly arrived settled by the edges of the swamps, along nonperennial rivers, or in already heavily populated areas. Africans from around Lusaka moved westward into sandveldt soils liable to erosion and where there was insufficient water.

There was another disadvantage connected with the land division: Settlers did not wish Africans to pass through their lands, which were up to 20 miles on either side of the railway line, to get to the urban centers and markets. The government had allowed one corridor 15 miles wide north of Lusaka for African use. Only a few Africans close to the corridor could effectively utilize it.

The major effects of land division, then, were twofold. First, many Africans who had started growing for the market were reduced to cultivating for subsistence only. Subsistence cultivation could not lead to increased production. In addition, many could not grow the crops they had been cultivating. Further, subsistence agriculture is precarious, as it is not easy to measure exactly how much food to cultivate. Second, the need to follow water, away from fertile regions, and constraints in access to markets frustrated even those producers in Ecosystem 3 whose soils could support the crops required by capitalists and who were closer to the lines of communication and urban markets.

Soon a contradiction appeared. From the late 1920s the labor force in the country started to expand. There was a disruption caused by the depression. After 1933, however, the force rose steadily as the mines recovered. World War II demands led to further expansion, while the methods of production required by base metals resulted in moves to stabilize labor. After the war, the increase in mineral production led to the expansion of other industries and to urbanization. Thus, an urban community was created which was dependent on others for its food requirements.

White settlers whose responsibility in the colonial economy was to provide food requirements did not adequately do so. They did not grow legumes and nuts which the mine employers needed for their African workers. From 1926 and after 1933 settlers did not supply enough beef (Agricultural Advisory Board, 1936:2); after 1938 maize supplies lagged behind consumption levels (Colonial Office Reports on Northern Rhodesia, 1938-1952). Whenever there was a conflict of interests between the mining companies and settlers, the government sided with the companies because they provided more revenue for the country. The companies were also politically stronger than the settlers. They did not actively participate in Northern Rhodesian politics, but their superiors in London and British investors had influence with the Colonial Office and used it whenever their interests were threatened.

After the war other cash crops were added to food requirements to bolster the British economy, which the war had left in
a weak state. Nationalism was also rising in Northern Rhodesia. In the rural areas agricultural grievances started to form
the backbone and rallying point for nationalism. It was
necessary to blunt and sublimate political consciousness. The
government encouraged African production to raise enough
food for the labor force, to maximize Northern Rhodesia's
agricultural raw materials for the metropolitan economy, and
to blunt African political consciousness.

Three factors influenced the government's approach to African agriculture: concern not to damage labor flows to capitalist
sectors; financial constraints; and settler influence. The district was not a major source of mining labor after 1930, but
settler farmers continued to experience chronic labor shortages.
This was exacerbated by the fact that settlers preferred labor
from the agriculturally producing areas of the southern and
central provinces. This labor, they argued, was more conver-
sant with their agricultural patterns (Memorandum by Cart-
land, 1945, Public Record Office, C.O. 795/128). The second
factor was more important up to 1945; after that period the
government was richer and the Colonial Office encouraged the
administration to make more money available to Africans to
maximize production.

Settler influence remained strong throughout the period.
Within the schema of a colonial economy, settler interests
prevailed over those of Africans:

> Were the Government to encourage native grown production
> (for example by organising the marketing of maize) most
> Europeans would be ousted within a few years. . . . Thus it is
> contended that in the interests of the territory as a whole while
> no artificial obstacles to the entry of the native into the maize
> market should be imposed, no direct encouragement in this
> should be given [Memorandum by the Department of Agricul-
> ture, 1937; National Archives of Zambia, ZP 11/1].

From 1924 settlers sat on the Legislative Council, where
agricultural policies and finances were discussed and approved. From the 1930s they sat on advisory and other boards

connected with agriculture: on the Land Settlement Board and the Agricultural Advisory Board, for example. They had influence on the country's higher Executive Council. It was through their influence that measures were passed, such as maize control dividing the market 75 percent for settlers and 25 percent for Africans. Through their influence the Agricultural Advisory Board established the African Improvement Fund by which Africans did not receive the full price for their produce. Settler control over finances restricted government financial and technical help to African producers when these became available. White farmers monopolized infrastructural improvements, so that before 1964 only a few roads connected African areas to the markets (Hellen, 1968:114).

Constraints brought about by the above factors were responsible for the "reinforcement of success" approach which the government adopted toward African agriculture. The government singled out regions closer to the existing lines of communication and urban centers for market production. A fortunate coincidence was that these regions were capable of producing the required crops—maize, cotton, tobacco, nuts, and legumes—and of attracting educated Africans who were actually or were feared to be the political organizers. At the same time, these Africans had a higher capacity for independent capital formation and had acquired some technical knowledge from schools. In Broken Hill District less than one-third of the African areas were selected for improvement.

From the late 1930s the government voted some funds to be expended on digging dams and wells in fertile but waterless parts so that these could become settled. The administration opened another corridor south of Broken Hill for African use, thus allowing them another passage to the railway line through settler lands. The Maize Control Board, sole buyer after 1936, operated in the selected parts, extending its activities to other regions in the district only at such periods as it became necessary to "skim off the surplus foodstuffs."

In 1951 the government established an agricultural station at Keembe, the heart of the market-producing regions. Assistants traveled from here to the villages to disseminate technical knowledge. The Department of Agriculture introduced the "Peasant" and "Improved" Farmers' Schemes. Blocks of land were set aside for "peasant" farmers, who were given initial loans of more efficient instruments of production, such as furrow and ridging ploughs, cultivators, planters, and harrows. The department also created a Revolving Fund from which producers could get loans to meet their agricultural requirements. "Improved" farmers could borrow money from the Department of Agriculture (out of the money accrued from the African Farming Improvement Fund), provided they put a 50 percent down payment on the loan. They received a bonus for each acre cultivated according to the department's instructions. The bonuses ranged from 8sh. to 15sh. in 1948-1949 to 15sh. to 27sh. in 1953-1954 (Rees and Howard in Northern Rhodesia Government, 1955:3). However, because of limited funds affecting the numbers of "peasant" blocks to be established and the activities of the agricultural assistants; owing to the "reinforcement of success" approach; and the regimental nature of disseminating knowledge, only a few peasants in the favored regions benefited from the schemes.

The above measures were aimed at (1) increasing rural productivity to supplement settler agriculture and (2) creating a group of producers through which the government could demonstrate its concern for rural betterment and defend itself against rural discontent. But the measures also reinforced the geographical and ecological influences on regional and social differentiation which had emerged by 1964.

Regional Differentiation

Ecological factors, distances from the urban markets, and government policies were responsible for regional differentiation. Many Africans who moved out of Crown lands in the wake of the land division went into lands falling within Ecosystem 2. Some of these settled in areas of lateritic soils, where they found they could not grow some food crops which they were used to eating. In the words of a local chief:

The greatest suffering was connected with soils. We used to have good soils there. What do I have here? Swamps, swamps, swamps. Not even sorghum can hold well; not even sweet potatoes can grow. How can we grow maize for sale? [Chipepo, 1975].

In dealing with these soils former producers of sorghum had to adjust to millet as a staple grain and the lack of other food crops. Producers who used to sell maize to farmer-traders and who used to travel to Broken Hill—sometimes two times in a day to sell fresh maize, cucurbits, and poultry—could not do so now. Both their diet and money resources were upset. In 1975-1976, when I did fieldwork, old women passionately remembered this loss of economic opportunities and their reduction to a life of dependency on male wage workers.

Other producers moved into areas with light sandveldt soils—good sorghum soils—where they continued to grow their staple grain. They grew other crops, such as cucurbits. Nevertheless, opportunities for getting cash through sorghum did not exist for the greater part of the period. Capitalists fed their labor on maize meal. Only when the government was pressed for grain in 1941-1942 did it buy sorghum from the regions in Ecosystem 2. The soils could support maize, cotton, and some varieties of African tobacco; however, the latter was not bought. In any case, the productivity of Ecosystem 2 soils is low and their yield poor in quality and quantity unless fertilizers are used. Local methods of fertilizing involved chopping and burning trees, which, in the long run, meant that areas thus fertilized were always small. In addition, as the lack of economic opportunities became evident or diminished, many young men left the regions for the better-placed regions or towns. There was not enough labor left to undertake the task. Modern artificial fertilizers depended on the Department of Agriculture making them available to producers and on cash to buy them.

To these disadvantages were added those of distances from the main lines of communication and towns: Producers could not go to the towns to sell produce like poultry, cucurbits, vegetables, and milk.

The major crop was not required by capitalists; the distances could have involved the government in greater expenses. These considerations influenced the government in selecting those regions falling in Ecosystem 3 which were closer to the main lines of communication and urban centers. Between 1936 and 1959 the Maize Control Board bought produce from African producers; it did not buy from more distant regions. The board traded with the latter only when the country was under pressure to increase foodstuffs, as occurred during World War II and between 1950 and 1952 following immense food shortfalls of the 1948-1949 agricultural seasons. The Grain Marketing Board took over from the Maize Control Board in 1959. By 1960 political developments in the country were such that the government extended agricultural activities to parts of the country considered economic burdens (Northern Rhodesia Government, 1961). The board bought surpluses from hitherto neglected regions in Broken Hill Rural District. Lacking technical and financial resources, only a few producers created surpluses.

As I have mentioned, the government confined technical and financial help to selected regions, neglecting other regions until after 1960. Producers, then, did not have the necessary technical knowledge to improve their agricultural methods. A few who picked up techniques such as the use of modern fertilizers did so from friends and relatives in favored regions. They did not have the cash to buy inputs and more efficient implements. The hoe remained the major tool.

The physical infrastructure remained undeveloped. The only roads were those paved by the native authority to important chiefs or by the government to major mission stations and the few primary schools that also included clinics. There were four such roads. The few roads built after 1960 were confined to the selected regions. Many producers did not live near the existing roads along which depots were occasionally situated.

Ecosystem 1 is fish-producing. In 1928 fishermen living in the swamps—except those on Chilwa Island, which was accessible—were moved to the mainland into Ecosystem 2. They soon became agriculturalists, periodically living in the swamps during their fishing activities. Some mainland people, including those who moved there after 1930, became both cultivators and fishermen. Both groups fished for subsistence, but also to raise cash to buy necessary commodities. Others hoped to create capital to invest in better instruments of production for fishing and agriculture. Three major factors militated against the fishing industry: distances, government policy, and loss of exploitable labor.

There were three main points of entry to the swamps. One was to the eastern parts of the swamps located about 40 miles from Broken Hill, which was not utilized during this period. Producers from near Broken Hill who could have exploited it had been moved. There was no road connecting it to the town, while passage to town through settler lands had been sealed off to Africans. A second point of entry was to the southwest in Chiyuni Muundu region, of which more will be said below. Some of the former swamp residents had been moved to this location, and there was much fishing activity. Nevertheless, this was about 100 miles from Lusaka and Broken Hill and 22 miles from the main road joining the region to the towns. It was located about 11 miles from a chief's residence, which was periodically reached by a bus since the 1950s. The third point of entry and exit was in the northern section of the swamps where some former swamp residents lived. This was about 80 miles from Broken Hill and the nearest copperbelt town. There were no proper roads until after 1964; the bicycle remained the major mode of transport. Distances and transportation difficulties placed constraints on the frequency and quantity of the trade.

To these difficulties were added the government's negative attitude. Fish were not included in the food ration capitalists gave their workers. Consequently, the government did not subsidize fishermen who therefore could not buy more efficient instruments to raise productivity. This is also why the administration did not improve the physical infrastructure. As a result of this negative approach, participation in the market and capital formation remained low. Most did not make enough money to obtain the necessities of life, let alone to save money for investment. Poor economic opportunities resulted in the exodus of the young to other regions within the district and to urban centers, where they hoped for better economic openings.

Ecological, geographical, and marketing constraints and the lack of government financial resources rendered it impossible for some producers to increase productivity. Yet, "native life in economic and political health is not possible in this country without an increase in production which can be converted into cash," a government official had commented in 1934 (Treasurer to Chief Secretary, 24.4.34; National Archives of Zambia, Sec/1/50). Thus it was that the district's poor peasants, barely meeting their subsistence requirements, were concentrated in these regions. A very few middle peasants sold to the market when the government occasionally extended the market there. Some of these sold surpluses; others merely sold food to raise a little cash, food which they would need later in the year.

In contrast to these regions were those which participated in the market. These were regions which could grow crops needed by capitalists at home and in the metropole. These were also closer to the urban centers where buying agencies were concentrated. Proximity to towns had another advantage for producers: Main depots were located along the railway line. Until 1948, when the government legally barred Africans from delivering their maize directly to these depots, some producers avoided middlemen by "delivering" directly, thereby fetching a higher price. Some sold other produce directly to workers in Lusaka and Broken Hill. The government confined the post-1945 technical and financial schemes. The same regions monopolized the few feeder roads built after 1960.

These regions attracted more people from (1) the disadvantaged parts of the district; (2) other areas of the country, including those retiring from wage employment, thus bringing in people who had a little money and some ability to read and use modern techniques; and (3) people from Southern Rhodesia, a number of whom had already acquired new techniques from that country. The regions' opportunities for improving the productive forces were greater, the ability to raise productivity higher, and, consequently, by 1964 the rich and the majority of middle peasants lived here.

To gauge this differentiation more effectively, I shall take two regions: Keembe Mwachisompola from Ecosystem 3 and representing the advantaged places, and Chiyuni Muundu, representing the disadvantaged ones.

Clearly, Chiyuni Muundu's productivity was low and its ability to raise cash limited. The low buying power resulting from this rendered the region unattractive to businesses which provided basic necessities such as salt, soap, kerosene, candles, blankets, and clothing. Most people did not have the cash to get these from the few stores, and so depended on their relatives in wage employment.

The region's poverty found expression in the flight of the young. At the same time, it did not attract outside populations. This deprived the population of the necessary exploitable labor to increase productivity even for subsistence.

On the other hand, Keembe Mwachisompola was able to raise production through which it had increased its cash-earning capacities. Its buying power grew. It attracted business and many of the producers traveled to Lusaka or Broken Hill to

TABLE 2   Agriculture and the Physical Means
to Raise Productivity (1945-1964)

Technology/Techniques	Keembe Mwachisompola	Chiyuni Muunda
Oxdrawn plough (use of)	95%	27%
Tractor (use of)	35%	0%
Other implements	60%	7%[a]
Fertilizer	60%	2%
Sold to MCB; GMB	98%	14%
Average acreage (under cultivation)	40	3

a. Carts only.
SOURCES: Computed from oral interviews and Keembe Agricultural Station, 1957-1968, K 3/56; 1961-1967, K 3/30; 1959-1967, K 3/31

buy their supplies. The marked improvement in the material quality of life here is demonstrated in houses, dress, food, and general lifestyle.

Social Differentiation

There was a social differentiation between people living in regions exemplified by Chiyuni Muundu and of Keembe Mwachisompola. The first comprised almost almost exclusively the poor, while the second had a few rich, a large middle, and some poor peasants. It seems apparent that, whereas ecological and geographical factors contributed to regional differentiation, official social and economic policies were largely responsible for social differentiation in advantaged regions where all producers were in the same ecological and geographical situation. The origins of social differentiation cannot be found in psychological and anthropological assumptions that producers had an inherent desire to continue their old life or that some peasants were genetically lazy. They are to be found in the inability to increase productivity due to lack of more efficient factors of production: implements, inputs like seed and fertilizers, and in discriminatory marketing practices.

Improved factors of production depended on cash and credit. Producers got cash through wage employment, through running other businesses such as shops, and through sale of produce. The government loaned both money and implements. A few mission schools and the government taught more effective techniques, while some producers learned them from other peasants.

Between 1899 and 1929 some male producers in the district worked for wages. Most of these sold their labor to the mines, railways, and settler farmers. In all cases wages were too low for them to create any amount of investible capital. From 1930—particularly after the war—a few started to have a little surplus to channel into farming. But those who were able to do so seem to have combined wage employment and farming. Men went into wage work periodically. Away in wage labor, they left their wives to run the farms with the help of dependent relatives and, from the late 1940s, workers. They came home on some weekends and during the holidays. If they were close to their farms, they worked at both simultaneously. Because the farm provided family food requirements at a time of improving wages, they were able to save a little.

This mode of creating capital was used mostly by teachers, clerks, and native authority employees. This was because the mines, the country's major employer, encouraged labor stabilization from the late 1930s. The mines also wished their employees to take their wives with them to cook and cultivate supplementary food for the workers. The native authority was geographically closer. The preponderance of teachers and clerks further limited the number of producers adopting this method, because the number of Africans who received formal education was very small. There were few schools in the district which gave even elementary education (four years of schooling) to Africans. Until the 1940s only one gave six years and prepared students for teaching and clerical careers. There were two other schools in the central and southern provinces which gave up to eight years of academic tutoring plus two years' teacher's or industrial training. Another school in the central province gave industrial training. Only two offered secondary education from the 1940s to girls and boys. At this time, another school trained postsecondary teachers. Aside from the elementary and one upper primary school, all of the above schools catered to Africans from all over the country and the Congo, in the case of one mission school.

Government loans of money and implements were restricted to members of the "Improved" and "Peasant" Farmers' Schemes. "Improved" farmers were those who accepted the Department of Agriculture's instructions. Agricultural assistants concentrated on the few who had already started to raise productivity, the emerging rich, now called "progressive" farmers. They rarely visited producers living more than ten miles from the station and subcenter. In addition, a down payment of 50 percent on any purchase was required to secure a government loan, but this was more than most could pay.

Some producers owned retail businesses and tea rooms to create additional capital for agricultural investment. A survey I conducted in Keembe Mwachisompola showed that two-thirds of the retail business during this period was undertaken by wage employees-cum-farmers, the same people who became the rich peasants. As with farming, dependent relatives and/or workers helped; however, there was a tendency not to allow relatives to work in the supplemental businesses, where wives dominated.

More effective and reliable from the peasants' point of view was the capital created through their own production. This depended on increased productivity to which all the above plus the adoption of modern techniques contributed.

The "reinforcement of success" approach resulted in a concentration on those who already possessed some knowledge through which they had independently started to raise productivity. The ability to form capital by combining wage employment, farming, and retail business, plus access to government financial resources and technical help, contributed to increased productivity for the "progressive" farmers. By 1964 they stood out as a distinct group. They owned more labor-saving implements like tractors, planters, harrows, weeders, and shellers. Some hired permanent or seasonal labor, and a few owned automobiles to transport produce to depots and urban markets.

There were many others who formed the middle peasants. Some of these lived near the agricultural station or its subcenter. They were visited by the assistants, although less frequently than the "progressives." If assistants noted adoption of the new methods of production and good yields, the farmers received bonuses. Nevertheless, their capital and ability to create more were limited. Historically, they had not had much opportunity to create capital in the ways noted for the rich peasants. Though "improved" farmers, they could not take out government loans, as they lacked the 50 percent down payment. Assistants gave halfhearted help. While these middle peasants used the ox-drawn plough, their limited capacity to buy other implements, improved seed, and fertilizers resulted in lower yields than those of the rich peasants. They sold surpluses irregularly, and in fluctuating amounts.

Within this category there were some who lived farther from the agricultural station. Assistants did not visit them, although some producers attempted to learn new techniques from friends and relatives. They could not become "improved" farmers and thus could not qualify for government cash resources. Attempts to learn from others sometimes resulted in disaster as they misapplied the techniques. Their ability to accumulate capital and to raise productivity was less than that of the other middle peasants. They sold their surpluses more irregularly and experienced greater quantitative fluctuations.

There was as marked a difference in the material quality of life between the poor and middle peasants as there was between the rich and the poor. Some of the poor had worked in wage employment. They had received such low wages that they could not save anything. They returned to the rural base, but there they lacked the necessary productive forces to help them increase productivity: they did not own cattle or the ox-drawn plough. They continued to use the hoe. Their young left home in search of wage labor. Because they lacked the labor to extend the area of cultivation even by the hoe, they produced for subsistence only.

A greater percentage of those who migrated to towns came from this category. Others sold their labor permanently or seasonally to the rich and better-off middle peasants. Legally, "tribal" land could not be sold; but from the 1950s some poor peasants sold their plots.

There was a large percentage of women among the middle peasants, particularly in their lower strata. Women also formed the largest single group among the poor peasants. Employers did not hire women except for peak period agricultural labor and for child care (nannies). However, these jobs paid dismally low wages which left nothing for savings. A much lower percentage of women than men received formal education and training. Only one mission school, from 1928, opened its doors to girls, giving six years of academic and two of teacher training. Later, in the 1940s, they extended academic education to eight years and in the 1950s included up to four years of secondary schooling. Nevertheless, the intake was small. Few went to coeducational schools, which accepted girls up to the fourth grade. Few women, then, received any formal education, and those who did tended to marry church ministers, evangelists, or teachers who were full-time workers of the church. Others married the teachers and clerks who became rich peasants. Unlike some male producers who sought to create capital by combining wage employment and farming, women could not do so. Because most did not go to school, they could not pick up technical information through literature. The government excluded women from its agricultural schemes completely. As unrecognized producers, they could not secure loans or information from agricultural assistants. Mr. Nyirenda, the first officer in charge of Keembe Station, recalled how if the husband was absent on their visiting day, assistants left without instructing the wife and simply left a message informing the husband when they would next visit.

Unless they were married to rich peasants or to the upper-middle strata, women generally became differentiated by a lower standard of living. But even those married to the above categories of peasants became dependent on their husbands. Both men and women informants mentioned that men owned the implements and controlled technical knowledge. Therefore, they gave their wives a smaller share of the remuneration. The inequitable distribution of the family income was evident in dress, for example. Men wore decent clothes and shoes, while some women walked barefooted. In the case of polygamous households, the husband had a decent, more solid house; the wives lived in shacks. Women sought escape by migrating to towns where some became prostitutes or seasonally sold their labor to the rich and upper stratum of the middle peasants. Others sold or "loaned" their land.

CONCLUSION

Labor's productiveness was the backbone of rural differentiation. Ecological, geographical, and government social and economic policies influenced and controlled labor's productiveness. Between 1930 and 1964 these factors became most significant in production processes. The period witnessed a sharpening of regional and social differentiation.

In precolonial times ecology did not play a significant role in shaping differentiation, as the economy was dominated by exchange of use values. Nevertheless, social differentiation emerged and was connected with the ability to control exploitable labor. Political leaders were the most distinct group of beneficiaries from the system. The early colonial period saw the beginnings of ecological and geographical influences. The market was in specific geographical locations while the monocultural nature of the demand for maize was shaping. On account of the growing market with its specified demands after 1930, ecological, geographical, and governmental policies combined to, on the one hand, offer unprecedented opportunities for increased productivity and, on the other, to place severe constraints on some regions and sections of the society. Their combined effects rendered some regions structurally poor. In the advantaged regions official social and economic policies and attributes led to social differentiation in which the rich, middle, and poor peasants were clearly distinguishable. Women, the group facing the most discrimination, formed the largest component of the rural poor.

REFERENCES

Colonial Office (1938-1952). Reports on Northern Rhodesia. London: His Majesty's Stationery.

HELLEN, J. (1968). Rural economic development in Zambia, 1890-1964. Munich: Weltforum Verlag.

Keembe Agricultural Station (1930). "Marketing cooperatives, thrift societies, 1961-1967." K 3/30.

_____(1931). "Meetings: General, 1959-1967." K 3/31.

_____(1956). "Peasant farming: General, 1957-1968." K 3/56.

MUNTEMBA, M.S. (1973). "The evolution of political systems in southcentral Zambia, 1894-1953." Unpublished Master's thesis, University of Zambia. (unpublished)

_____(1977). "Rural underdevelopment in Zambia: Kabwe Rural District, 1850-1970." Ph.D. dissertation, University of California at Los Angeles (University Microfilms No. 77-30, 947).

National Archives of Zambia (0000). "Resolutions Regarding Control, Export of Maize, 1932-1935." Sec/1/50.

_____ "Central Province: Establishment and extension of native reserves V and VI, 1931-1942." Sec/SL/107.

_____ "Financial Inquiry Commission: Notes submitted by D.Cs. and memoranda by departments, 1937." ZP 11/1.

Northern Rhodesia Government (1937a). The soils, vegetation and agricultural systems of Northwestern Rhodesia, report of the Ecological Survey. Lusaka: Trapnell, C. and Clothier, J.

_____(1937b). Third report: Development and agricultural reports. Lusaka: Agricultural Advisory Board.

_____(1955). An economic survey of African commercial farming among the Sala of Mumbwa District of Northern Rhodesia. Lusaka: Rees, A. and Howard, R.

_____(1961). Report of the rural development working party. Lusaka.

Public Record Office. "Wartime conscription for farms." C.O. 795/128.

Senior Chief Chipepo (1975). Interview no. 11, HD/08/Tape 57/1. Zambia: University of Zambia Library.

Map of the Transkeian Territories

8

STATE INTERVENTION AND RURAL RESISTANCE:
The Transkei, 1900-1965

WILLIAM BEINART
COLIN BUNDY
Queen Elizabeth House, Oxford

Peasant movements tend to be localized, limited in aims and achievements, and deficient in organization and execution—and the same is frequently true of their academic investigation. South African historians have paid insufficient attention to the incidence and nature of rural resistance. A major study of the 1906 Bambatha rebellion in Zululand and a few contemporary accounts of the rebellions in the Transvaal and Transkei during the late 1950s stand virtually alone in the published literature (Marks, 1970; Hooper, 1960; Mbeki, 1964; Turok, n.d.). A recent resurgence of interest in rural movements and politics is reflected in a number of shorter studies, all dealing with the post-1948 period (Copelyn, 1977; Hirson, 1977; Moroney, 1900; Development Studies Group, 1978; Lodge, 1978; Rich, 1978; Yawitch, 1978). For the most part, how-

AUTHOR'S NOTE: This research has been greatly assisted by the award of a Social Science Research Council (U.K.) grant.

ever, rural disturbances have been treated in isolation, and a number of episodes are unrecorded in the academic literature. This chapter makes a preliminary attempt to describe and analyze a series of apparently unconnected incidents over a lengthy period in one part of the South African countryside. By placing these events within the context of structural changes in the Transkei, and relating them to the specific nature of intervention in this area by the Cape and later the South African states, we hope to achieve a greater understanding of their sequence and of the particular forms they took.

Civil unrest can be described in terms of a declension that runs from disaffection, disturbance, unrest, and rebellion to insurrection and revolution; and it is as well at the outset to make plain what we mean by the term "resistance" and what is intended by our focus on it. We are referring to instances of overt political action that protest against or attempt to end political and economic pressures, such action(s) assuming forms not recognized by the state as legal or permissible. These cases of resistance are specific, concentrated, and organized efforts by groups of Transkeians to retain such control over their activities and their environment as they could, to adjust the balance of socioeconomic forces in their own favor. It should be stressed that such acts of resistance are in no sense the only way in which members of subordinated classes assert their identity and interests; there has been a wide range of passive, isolated, or disorganized "day to day resistance" in the Transkei, as in other societies. Hobsbawm's (1973) observation that "the refusal to understand is a form of class struggle" is particularly apt in a colonial context where official annoyance at the "willful ignorance" of "recalcitrant tribal communities" who "stand in the way of progress" is a constant motif.

It should not be thought that the presentation of the empirical data in the form of a series of separate episodes betokens an episodic view of resistance; what follows is not a history of the spectacular, nor a search for a lineage of militancy. The brief case studies of resistance are intended as an aid to analysis of process and structure, not as an alternative. Nor does the focus on acts of resistance suggest that all other forms of political and social activity entered into during the same time-span are necessarily "passive" or "collaborationist." The episodes we have selected illustrate some of the changes that took place in the objectives, social composition, and organizational form of rural resistance between 1900 and 1965.

PRECOLONIAL AND COLONIAL BACKGROUND

In the precolonial period, the Transkeian area was settled by a number of independent African polities organized into chiefdoms of varying size and centralization; the largest were the Xhosa, Thembu, and Mpondo. During the latter half of the nineteenth century, the Cape Colony gradually extended its formal rule over the different chiefdoms. The process of colonization took significantly different forms ranging from military defeat and territorial expropriation in the case of the Xhosa to the piecemeal incorporation of the Thembu and eventual peaceful annexation of Pondoland in 1894. Mfengu people, originally refugees from the Zulu and allies of the colonial state in its wars against the Xhosa, were given part of the Xhosa chiefdoms' land in what became the southern part of the Transkeian Territories. Between 1877 and 1882, sections of the Xhosa, Thembu, Mpondomise, and Griqua[1] people participated in separate but linked armed uprisings against the extension of effective colonial rule. These risings (which are not examined in this chapter) marked the end of the phase of "primary" resistance: resistance largely, although not exclusively, led by chiefs at the head of the military forces of their precolonial political units. They were crushed without great difficulty by the Cape's military forces, and a unified system of administration was imposed on all the chiefdoms. The Transkeian Territories were demarcated by 1913 into 26 districts under magistrates directly responsible to a Chief Magistrate, and were to a considerable extent ruled separately from the rest of the Cape. Each magistracy was in turn divided into locations under the charge of salaried headmen. Many of the traditional chiefs became headmen (their authority officially limited to a single location), but the state reserved the right to appoint its own candidates, including commoners, where this was held to be necessary.

In the immediate precolonial period, the economies of the Transkeian chiefdoms were based on pastoralism, agriculture, hunting, and gathering. Specialization and exchange were limited, although there was some trade both in craft goods and in produce between chiefdoms. From the mid-nineteenth century, European traders moved into the region in large numbers and accelerated the process of economic change. Through them, an increasing amount of produce was exported to colonial markets and manufactured goods imported, particularly blankets and agricultural implements. Ploughs were bought in large numbers, and cattle—already important as a source of food, an item for exchange, and as the seal of many customary ceremonies—were now valued as draught animals. Sheep were introduced, and wool joined cattle hides, grain, and tobacco as the major exports. Rural producers, to whom we henceforth refer as peasants, became increasingly dependent on the white traders for the sale of manufactured goods, provision of credit, and purchase of their produce.[2]

Prior to about 1890, significant elements in colonial society, especially the large merchants in the Eastern Cape, favored the emergence and maintenance of a surplus-producing peasantry. The thrust of their policy, stated briefly and without qualifications, was to crush the chiefs, to convert and "civilize" the African population as a prerequisite to increased commerce, and to incorporate that population into the political structures of the colony. The Cape's qualified franchise was available to Africans, and in some eastern Cape areas the "native vote" was a substantial factor in electoral politics. During the last couple of decades of the nineteenth century, there was a marked shift in the alignment of dominant interests in the colony, consequent on the diamond and gold discoveries and the railway-building and industrialization that accompanied them. As merchant capital was shouldered aside by industrial capital, it was increasingly labor rather than agricultural produce that was required from the African "reserve" areas like the Transkei. The 1880s and 1890s saw amendments to the franchise qualifications that made it more difficult for Africans to register as voters, and that in particular diminished the numbers of possible voters from the newly acquired Transkeian Territories. Very rapidly, support was marshaled behind the precept that separate political institutions should be established for the Transkei.

In general terms, the period 1900 to 1960 saw, first, an intensification of the incorporation of the Transkei into the South African economy; and, second, an extension of the apparatus of political and social control, particularly the elaboration of a system of "indirect rule" in the territories. During our period, at differing speeds and levels in different districts, the fundamental transformation was from a peasant economy to a labor reserve economy; the crucial political development was the mounting involvement (in the context of greater stratification) of chiefs, headmen, and Christian, educated "progressive farmers" in the administrative system. Peasants turned to resistance in response to both of these broad sets of pressures (which, of course, interacted with and reinforced one another.) That resistance—as the following sections will demonstrate—underwent distinctive changes as the political economy of the Transkei was restructured; yet it also exhibited some striking continuities, particularly in the degree to which political action centered on issues affecting land and livestock. The terms of the Transkei's incorporation were such as to ensure a rapid transformation of the region in certain aspects, while other patterns and structures were not only preserved but consolidated. On the one hand, falling productivity, changing consumption trends, the spread of debt, and—above all—the massive increase in labor migrancy[3] signaled the decay of the peasantry and the onset of proletarianization; on the other hand, the continued availability under the state's "reserves" policies of at least small plots of land for a majority of families, and the tenacity of homestead production, contributed to the ideological persistence of a rural identity.

RESISTANCE TO THE GLEN GREY COUNCIL SYSTEM, 1902-1906

Between 1890 and 1896, Cecil Rhodes was Prime Minister of the Cape. At the height of his political and financial powers, he was the personification of the constellation of interests that sought a further restructuring of the African rural areas. His ideas were given form in the Glen Grey Act of 1894. Its major provisions were the introduction of an individual tenure scheme (to replace communal tenure) and the establishment of district councils and a general council as the basis for separate political institutions. The land provisions envisaged a stable peasantry on surveyed plots secured by title, but also the creation of a sizable and permanently landless proletariat. Individual tenure would diminish the power of the chiefs by weakening their control over land distribution. The councils, with limited local powers and an advisory function, would further undermine the political authority of the chiefs as well as reduce the costs of colonial administration. The Act was initially implemented in the Glen Grey district itself and in the four Fingoland districts of the southern Transkei, where there was a history of collaboration and an absence of powerful chieftaincies.

Both the land and council provisions—and also the Act's proposed labor tax—stimulated considerable opposition in the territories from different sections of the peasantry. Although some of the wealthier peasants welcomed security of tenure and the slackening of chiefly control over land, they considered the proposed size of the surveyed allotments—four morgen (one morgen is 2.1 acres)—too small, and feared the reduction of existing holdings. Chiefs and headmen, for their part, saw the Act as a direct threat to their power and were to some extent able to mobilize popular opinion against individual tenure. Under communal tenure, each family had the right to an arable plot and access to grazing; the new system threatened to replace guaranteed land rights for all with land titles for some and landlessness for the rest. Because of the strength and breadth of opposition and the difficulties in implementation, the state abandoned the labor tax and also decided to soft-pedal individual tenure: each district was to be permitted to decide for or against the scheme. Officials optimistically believed that as land became scarce and "civilization" advanced, more and more districts would see the wisdom of the scheme; in fact, only three other districts ever joined the original four.

By contrast, strenuous efforts were made immediately after the South African War (1899-1902) to implement the council system as widely as possible. These were countered by prolonged, elite-led opposition that used various channels of protest. There were public meetings, demonstrations, petitions, and pleas; arguments were made in evidence to commissions and in colonial courts. There were also stalling tactics that delayed elections and hindered the collection of revenue. Opposition was particularly widespread in Fingoland, where the Act was first effective: Years later a magistrate recollected the resistance to Glen Grey measures: "The people were sullen and angry. They held secret meetings and the whole of Fingoland agreed that they would do nothing and see whether the Government would get their Councils and their tax" (Transkeian Territories General Council, 1929:63). In districts like those of Fingoland and Emigrant Thembuland which were more thoroughly colonized and had a higher proportion of mission-educated progressive farmers and small businessmen, it was the "new" elite that led the protest. Its members feared that separate councils would mean the end of their participation in the broader sphere of Cape politics, and they were also anxious lest they lose control of local politics to the headmen and poorer peasants. Enoch Mamba, a labor agent in Idutywa, told a Commission of Enquiry that headmen would dominate the council, that they were unrepresentative, and that "the really efficient men"—like the other members of the Transkei Vigilance Association, of which he was chairman—would be excluded (Report of the Select Committee, 1903:155). In Xalanga, resistance to the Glen Grey Act was notably stubborn; and in 1903 the Chief Magistrate reported that "educated natives" from Xalanga were traveling to neighboring districts, urging hostility to the Act. Ten years later, the survey of the same district met with "a good deal of opposition by a large section of the people" who objected to Proclamation 141/1911 because of its "strong resemblance to the Glen Grey Act." The opposition was described as "of the passive resistance type," and "well kept up by men who are regarded by the Natives as their political leaders" (Cape Archives, Native Affairs Papers, 526/509; Native Affairs Department, V.6.33-'13). In Qumbu and Tsolo (both in East Griqualand), a complex alliance of wealthier peasants and headmen, both of whom viewed the councils as a threat to their power, was active between 1902 and 1906 in criticizing and obstructing the scheme. In Pondoland, the paramount chiefs—still more powerful there than anywhere else in the territories—were wary about the dilution of their influence through the proposed nomination of council members by the government, and felt that the councils would undermine their position as intermediaries between the administration and the people.

The manifestation of opposition tended to be localized, although similar arguments against the councils recurred from district to district. *Imvo Zabantsundu,* an African newspaper read by the elite throughout the territories, agitated against Glen Grey and no doubt helped to shape opinion. The anticouncil movement also received support from separatist churches which, by the turn of the century, were spreading through the area. Their leaders were sometimes hostile not only toward the established mission churches but also to the colonial political authorities. The magistrate in Qumbu believed that the people there had been "entirely poisoned by American ideas instilled among them by the Ethiopian section" and placed the responsibility for the stubborn refusal to work the council system on Reverend R. Damane of the Native Presbyterian Church (Cape Archives, Native Affairs Papers, 526/509; memo by Secretary of Native Affairs, July 24, 1903).

The council scheme was gradually implemented during the first decade of the century through a blend of *force majeure* and concessions. Headmen and members of the elite were assured of council membership; "agitators" were punished or deported; individual chiefs who had opted for collaboration, like Dalindyebo of the Thembu, were used to propagate the system. The paramount of West Pondoland eventually agreed to cooperate in 1911 after a series of meetings in which he managed to extract favorable terms: nomination of some councillors by the chiefs and assurance that certain customs crucial to the power of chiefs were inviolable at the hands of the council. Only in East Pondoland and in Xalanga—the most traditionalist and the most "progressive" areas, respectively—was the council system staved off until the 1920s. By then, it was clear that the union administration was going to perpetuate and insist on this element of the Glen Grey legislation.

Opposition to the council system, at its height between 1902 and 1906, was at no stage a dramatic or large-scale movement. It did not lead to violent resistance, but for several districts the evidence indicates fairly broad local support and tactics of passive resistance or noncooperation. In its most articulate forms, it was an expression of the fears of members of the upper strata—traditional leaders and educated Christian men of substance—that they would lose their political influence and be less able to defend their economic interests. When it became clear that the council system would not threaten their position radically, when headmen realized the scope offered them by magistrates and the powerful Mpondo chiefs had secured their special version of the scheme, their opposition subsided. The councils became, fairly rapidly, instruments through which the wealthier peasants and members of the local administration could advise the government of their concerns and channel off funds accumulated by the ten-shilling household tax which financed the system. Enoch Mamba and other "really efficient men" became district and general councillors; and by the end of the 1920s the Glen Grey Act was frequently cited by councillors as an exemplar of legislative generosity and wisdom.

THE ANTI-DIPPING MOVEMENT, 1913-1917

During the early years of the council system, expenditure on dipping for cattle and sheep was a major drain on local funds. Dipping was enforced by the administration to combat stock diseases, the spread of which menaced the herds of the peasantry and colonial farmers alike. Compulsory sheep dipping (to eradicate scab) began in the 1890s, and was not widely opposed; many Transkeian peasants depended heavily on the cash income derived from wool, which was threatened by the disease. During the first decade of this century the colony was faced with East Coast Fever, a cattle disease working its way southward down the east coast of Africa. It could be controlled only by regular dipping, to kill the ticks that transmitted the fever. Determined to prevent a recurrence of the devastation caused by rinderpest in 1897, the Cape administration devoted considerable effort to creating an infrastructure of tanks, supplies, veterinary staff, and dipping supervisors. The state paid the salaries of veterinary officials, but the bulk of the costs of dipping had to be met by the peasantry through council funds, stock levies, and dipping fees.

In 1909, the disease reached the border between Natal and the Transkei, and more stringent measures were adopted. A border fence was built between Pondoland and Natal, and all cattle movement between the two areas was outlawed; the passage of cattle was also prohibited between the zones into which the border districts of Pondoland were divided; dipping was made compulsory for the first time; some cattle were shot; and an annual tax replaced the sporadic dipping levy. These measures were speedily extended throughout the territories. Tank-building, however, was delayed, and even those areas with the prescribed number of tanks were not immune to the ravages of the disease: In 1912 and 1913 East Coast Fever swept through the Transkei, killing off up to 80 percent of the cattle in some districts. The impact of the disaster was compounded by the general drought conditions of 1912. Many peasants were compelled to buy grain at rising prices and internal distribution was hampered by the shortage of draught oxen and the restrictions on cattle movement. There was a large increase in 1912 of men leaving the Transkei as migrant laborers (from just under 80,000 in 1911 to over 96,000). The state responded to the spread of the disease by raising dipping fees and enforcing preventive measures even more strictly. Unlike rinderpest, which tended to blight a district and then disappear, East Coast Fever remained endemic.

The implementation of these measures provoked wide-spread popular opposition. While many recognized that regular dipping could combat the disease, people all over the Transkei objected to increased taxation at a time of severe pressure on the rural economy and also to specific features of the restrictions. They maintained that the long weekly trips to the dipping tanks enfeebled their remaining cattle, making them useless for draught or milking and that the gathering of large numbers of beasts at the tanks aided rather than prevented the spread of the disease. Furthermore, the restrictions radically disturbed patterns of transhumance and pasture usage, made it difficult to carry out cattle loans (a vital part of the grazing system), and interfered with customary ceremonies involving the passage of stock. For wealthier peasants, who still had animals to sell, the restrictions cut them off from all markets other than local traders, whose response to this monopoly was to offer very low prices. In sum, the East Coast Fever measures constituted the deepest and most serious intervention into the African rural economy since annexation, and the peasantry found itself unable to influence the ways in which the measures were imposed. The extent and effects of the measures were an expression of the relative powers of the state and Transkei peasant society.

In the face of these pressures, there was considerable passive resistance to dipping, and in some places violent action was taken against the local, visible manifestations of state intervention: the dipping tanks and sheds. The Chief Magistrate said that during 1912 "a tide of irritation and unrest" had swept across many districts, and an investigation into the anti-dipping revolt in East Griqualand in 1914 acknowledged that "discontent and opposition" existed throughout the territories (Native Affairs Department, U.G. 33-'13; Stanford Report, S.3-'15). Both before and during World War I the enforcement of the dipping and cattle movement regulations made heavy demands on magistrates and police. In Fingoland, in 1913-1914, tanks and sheds were destroyed at Nqamakwe and Tsomo, and the headmen could not control the wave of protest meetings; as late as 1917 the area was tense with friction between council rate-payers and the authorities (Cape Archives, Chief Magistrate of Transkei, 3/935/783 ①). The two areas most affected by the disease and the regulations—Pondoland and East Griqualand—both experienced intense popular disaffection, but with very different outcomes, providing an interesting contrast in local political control. In Pondoland the dipping tax increases of 1909 and 1914 fueled the two phases of greatest disturbance; both times the administration was able to secure the cooperation of the powerful paramount chiefs—in one instance by plucking Marelane from school at Lovedale and rushing him back to Pondoland—and protest dwindled to sullen acquiescence (Cape Archives, Chief Magistrate of Transkei, 3/829/567, 3/868/635; Native Affairs Papers, 75/F142; *Christian Express,* September 1, 1921). It was in the three East Griqualand districts of Matatiele, Mount Fletcher, and Mount Frere that the disturbances were most serious. In November 1914, a number of dipping tanks were destroyed, including some that were dynamited (the explosives having been taken from a road construction team), while other tanks were picketed so as to prevent their use. Trading stores were looted; telegraph lines were cut; and in Matatiele dissidents "broke up three dips and went into laager," causing an exodus of white women and children from the town (Stanford Report, 5.3-'15; *Cape Times,* November 26, 1914). In Mount Frere, a localized uprising in October 1916 commenced as a refusal to pay dipping fees or to attend subsequent court hearings. The resistance was led by a commoner named Magwana, who took his armed followers into the hills and was eventually captured after a gunfight with the police. He was described by the police inspector sent to arrest him as being "above the average native, he has plenty of stock, is a Sealawyer, has plenty of physical and moral courage and displayed no small amount of ability as a fighting man" (Cape Archives, Chief Magistrate of Transkei, 3/937/783 ⑥; C. Simpson, Police Inspector, to Deputy Commissioner, SA Police, December 17, 1916).

There are several reasons for the fact that resistance in East Griqualand was more violent than elsewhere. The districts lay inland on a high elevation and had poorer rainfall and more frequent frosts than the coastal strip of the Transkei, and it appears that peasants in the regions were more dependent on livestock for subsistence and less able in times of shortage to fall back on crops and gathering. Although they did not lose as many cattle in 1912-1913 as did people in the coastal districts, the grazing system rested on a pattern of transhumance between highlands in summer and lowland grass in winter. The disruption of this rhythm by the new regulations, the fall in the price of cattle, and the collapse in 1914 of the wool market (in districts where sheep had become a mainstay of the pastoralists) hit East Griqualand hard. Furthermore, political structures in East Griqualand differed markedly from those in Pondoland and Thembuland where there were strong paramountcies. Its population was made up of various nineteenth-century immigrant groups, each with its petty chiefs; and especially during the first decade of the twentieth century many former labor tenants and share-croppers entered the districts from neighboring white farming areas which were undergoing rapid capitalization. In Mount Frere, dipping disputes probably gained some impetus from friction between local groups. In March 1912 a detachment of Cape Mounted Riflemen was quartered in the district because of the level of "arson, pillage and armed conflicts" that attended "clannish feuds" there (Native Affairs Department Report, 1912:16).

When Walter Stanford was appointed as Commissioner to investigate the 1914 violence, he noted that "the loyal attitude of certain influential chiefs" had greatly aided the government in keeping peace in some locations—but these chiefs exercised only limited local authority and were unable to counter the popular movement more widely. The collaboration of individual chiefs could be offset by the vacillation of others. Some Bhaca subchiefs appear to have been complicit in the Mount Frere refusals to pay taxes, while even their superior, the Bhaca paramount Mncisana, was held by the police to have "encouraged opposition tacitly." Stanford also judged that rumours of a British defeat in the war and agitation by Afrikaner rebels who promised to "stop dipping and abolish the General Council" promoted disaffection in the region (Cape Archives, Chief Magistrate of Transkei, 3/937/783 (6) ; Stanford Report).

The anti-dipping movement led to a renewal of hostility to the district and general councils, which had actually executed the East Coast Fever regulations.

> At meetings which I attended [wrote Stanford] the speaker who shouted 'We do not want to dip and we do not want the Bunga' [Transkeian Territories General Council] met every time with general applause. At Mount Frere a Headman whom I have known for many years and to whose word weight attaches said 'The demands made on the people are causing them to hate both the Magistrate and the Council.'

By now, however, dislike of the councils stemmed mainly from the mass of the people. The chiefs, headmen, and leaders of the "school" people had become absorbed into the administrative structure and during the dipping crisis generally played a collaborative role. The contrast between the control of unrest in Pondoland and in East Griqualand underlines this point.

The anti-dipping movement marks a transition in rural political organization, for it had a mass base and was led from outside the elite groups who tended to be used, along with police and officials, to quell the disturbances.

THE WOMEN'S BOYCOTT MOVEMENT OF 1922

Most of the pickets at the dipping tanks during the East Griqualand revolt were women. Reporting this, the Commissioner reflected that "Women so roused form a dangerous element in any people or race," and this may serve as an introduction to a boycott of trading stations organized by women in response to the economic hardships faced by the peasantry after World War I.

By the second decade of the century, the mass annual exodus of male migrant laborers was a dominant feature of the political economy of the Transkei. The degree of dependence on wages for subsistence still varied considerably from district to district. In districts where production had been less affected by the penetration of capitalist relations, or where natural resources were more favorable, there was still a significant degree of independence from the labor market. In the more thoroughly transformed parts of the southern Transkei and East Griqualand, wage levels and the prices of trading store goods had already become of critical importance in the management of household budgets. This was more particularly so for the Christian "school" or "dressed" section of the community than for the traditionalist "reds" or amaqaba,[4] as the lifestyle of the former entailed far greater expenditure on commodities which could not be produced at home. The frequent absences of male labor meant that rural pressures were exerted especially keenly on women. Not only did they have to try and maintain agricultural production so as to supplement wages, but because of the falling size of the family (most pronounced in Christian households) each woman had to devote more time to childcare, gathering of wood and water, and household activities.

Incipient proletarianization manifested itself in consciousness of wages, job preferences, and patterns of migrancy. Nor were migrants passive at their place of work, despite the often closely controlled environment of the compound. However, so far as can yet be ascertained, wages and prices were not at the root of any organized rural protest prior to or during World War I although there were often complaints about conditions and wages by individuals. Again, chiefs and headmen tended to support the system of migrancy and the compounds—and even the pass laws—for it was in their interest to ensure that the rural family heads could control their migrant sons and have claim to the wages earned in the cities. It was only in the straitened economic situation after the war that price and wage issues became central to rurally based protest. Rapid price inflation coupled with an attempt by the Chamber of Mines to cut African miners' wages helped precipitate a major strike in 1920. Bonner (1978) has indicated that migrant workers were notably militant during this strike. There was some action in the rural areas at the same time; in 1920, for instance, a boycott lasting two weeks was mounted against a Butterworth trader who had refused to supply grain and coffin-boards on credit.

It was two years later, in 1922, that a more extensive boycott action was organized. Early that year there began "systematic boycotting of the trading stations by women" in the district of Herschel, in the north-eastern Cape Province, and not then part of the Transkeian Territories (although it has now been incorporated within the "independent" Bantustan.) Men and women were "being prevented from either buying or selling at the stores," in some cases forcibly. The local magistrate met with the traders, who reduced the prices of certain lines. By the middle of the year, apparently after news of the limited success in Herschel, the movement spread to Transkeian districts and especially to Qumbu in East Griqualand, where some of the Hlubi inhabitants had close kin relations with the people in Herschel. The boycott organized in Qumbu was (according to the magistrates) "due to feminist aspirations and agitation among the more advanced dressed women." The leaders were churchgoers, wives and daughters of wealthy peasants, teachers, and headmen, and their activities were organized mostly around the mission area in the northeast of the district. After meetings in June, pickets were mounted at the trading stations and the activists, who dubbed themselves "Police Women," were prepared to use violence against those who tried to pass them. Emissaries were sent to the contiguous districts of Mount Frere and Tsolo to spread the boycott. "The movement is very highly organised," warned the magistrate, "and therein lies its danger." In July a delegation of 300-400 well-dressed women assembled at the magistrate's office to protest against prices and to request that the state take action against the traders.[5]

One of the headmen summoned to account for the boycott emphasized that prices were at the heart of the protest:

> All we found in the locations was this complaint of the women of the high prices charged by traders in the stores. As instances, Paraffin, bottle, formerly 6d now 9d is charged; three candles formerly for 3d, now one only; cotton blankets which used to cost 1s now cost 3s; German prints 6d now 1/6d; shawls formerly costing £1 now cost £2. Further the women complain about the sale of the mealies which are useless to them as they don't get cash for them but iron tickets which entitle them to buy at that store. This makes it impossible for them to pay their taxes. Moreover the mines are closed [due to the 1922 strike by white miners] and there is no work on the goldfields.

Complaints about the terms of sale for maize had been common for many years and can be discounted as an immediate cause. Nor were the increases in commodity prices specific to 1922: indeed, prices rose most sharply immediately after the war. However, it does seem that while prices in other parts of the country were beginning to stabilize and to fall, traders in the Transkei—perhaps playing on rural ignorance, perhaps loaded with old, expensive stock—did not follow suit. It seems to have been this feature, coupled with the shortage of cash from migrant wages, against a background of poor harvests for several years, that precipitated the protest and identified its target.

The East Griqualand officials expressed puzzlement that the boycott was led by some of "the wealthier and best dressed of the more enlightened and wealthy natives of the district," and argued that "as far as the leaders are concerned the cry of poverty is not genuine." What they failed to understand was that it was precisely this group which felt the pressure of prices and cash shortages most acutely. Many of the Christian families were deeply in debt and they were threatened by an inability to educate their children—and hence by difficulty in differentiating themselves from the traditionalist peasantry around them. "Our children have no clothing to wear on account of our poverty—this is the reason for them not attending school," explained one of the women. Their very identity as dressed people was at stake: "We now *wear* blankets which we use for sleeping in and we are Christians," another asserted (Cape Archives, Chief Magistrate of Transkei, 3/951/15/411A, Resident Magistrate of Qumbu to Chief Magistrate of Transkei, July 13 and July 18, 1922).

The movement might have spread further had it not been quickly quashed by the state, again using the headmen to curb protest. Traders themselves took up the offensive by refusing to purchase produce, by withdrawing credit, and by threatening to take debtors to court. (They were normally reluctant to sue for debts, as the credit system ensured the long-term dependence of the peasantry.) What is not yet clear is to what extent the boycott movement was a mobilization of existing church groups in Qumbu district; nor is it clear whether this would have tended to localize such a movement in any case. A number of churches had established women's organizations which commanded a strong and committed membership in some rural areas; the best known of these were the Methodist Manyana groups with their distinctive uniforms and public meetings. The boycott movement appears to have been based on Methodist, Presbyterian, and Anglican groups which, in Qumbu, as elsewhere, organized burial societies and savings clubs as well as church meetings and social gatherings. It is also worth noting that the immediate postwar period saw a radicalization of black petty bourgeois groups in South African cities and the formation, at the national level, of the Women's League of the African National Congress. Knowledge of such an organization almost certainly spread among the more literate sections of the rural community.

MILLENIAL THOUGHT AND POLITICAL ACTION IN THE 1920s

During the late 1920s, there was an upsurge of millenial preaching and observance in the Transkei, largely, though not exclusively, focused on the activities of Wellington Buthelezi. Many of the actions taken by those who responded to the millenarian message were overtly hostile to the state and its institutions. Millenial beliefs and actions are one of the most distinctive ideological responses of Xhosa-speaking chiefdoms to conquest and incorporation. Recorded instances in the Cape reach back to the early nineteenth century, and millenial consciousness remained a recurrent element in the response to colonization. The most famous instance of widespread action based on millenial urgings is, of course, the cattle-killing of 1856-1857; but many lesser movements— with certain shared symbolic features, but with a great variety of local characteristics—took place. In the Transkei, for instance, in the 30 years before the Wellington Movement there were repeated flurries of millenial activity. These included the Le Fleur "forty years money" agitation in Griqualand East; the Mpondomise belief in the return of chief Mholnhlo; an earlier "Americanist" movement in Pondoland in the early 1920s; and outbreaks of pig-killing in Gcalekaland, Bomvanaland, Pondoland, and elsewhere. Clearly, political action predicated on millenerian promises between 1927 and 1930 is merely one instance of a particular form of rural protest; the question we are concerned with here is why in the late 1920s millenial thought took the form of the Wellington Movement with its distinctive ideology—an adapted and abridged Garveyism.[6]

Soon after the war ended in 1918, branches of Garvey's United Negro Improvement Association formed in urban centers of South Africa. Garvey's vision of black liberation tended to percolate into rural South Africa on a more informal network and in heavily modified form. In 1921, an Ethiopian sect under the leadership of Enoch Mgijima resisted removal from a "squatter" settlement near Queenstown in the belief that American Blacks would come to their aid in airplanes. Over 160 of the church's members were killed when police moved in, and the incident was widely discussed in the Transkei. The most successful interpreter of Garveyism in the territories was Buthelezi: Partly educated in mission schools, he dabbled in herbalism before winning a living in the 1920s by the sale of subscriptions to his movement. By the latter half of the decade he had established himself in the territories, and traveled around to speak to gatherings about the coming day of judgment when Afro-Americans would arrive in airplanes and release balls of burning charcoal on Europeans and on African nonsubscribers. Taxes and dipping would be abolished, factories established in the Transkei, and clothing distributed to the people. Believers were to identify themselves by painting their huts black and by killing their pigs.

Political allegiance to the Wellington Movement involved people in direct expression of hostility to institutions of authority and ideological control. Some headmen, for whom the defection was an emphatic political defiance and whose "disloyalty" was held to be most alarming by magistrates and missionaries, gave Buthelezi hospitality and sponsored his meetings. In some locations, the police who sought to enforce tax collection were attacked. People removed their children from the established schools (state-subsidized mission institutions) and placed them in separate schools begun by Buthelezi and other millenarian activists, while there was also a spate of separatist church formation and activity. These attempts to create an alternative African-controlled educational and religious system made significant inroads into existing schools and missions. One Maqolo (an agent of Buthelezi who commanded an independent following in Fingoland) started nine schools in the district of Nqamakwe alone, and the numbers of children fell sharply enough in some Fingoland schools to lead to the dismissal of some teachers.[7] The patterns of resistance were not wholly dependent on the charisma of the leaders: While the state could deport Buthelezi and imprison Maqolo, it could not by doing so snuff out their influence. The "Wellington schools" were still so numerous in 1932 as to pose a serious threat to the official institutions in some areas, and in 1933 small groups resorted to violence, in the name of the movement, in refusing to pay dipping fees. In Fingoland a number of women—many of them recent converts to Christianity—broke away from the Bantu Presbyterian Church and founded a movement that looked to the imprisoned Maqolo for inspiration. Apart from those who clearly threw their lot in with the Wellington Movement, many more were affected by its currents and exhibited various degrees of truculence and disaffection. Most chiefs and headmen remained on the side of authority—and were excluded from secret meetings in the locations. Their attempts, on the Chief Magistrate's instructions, to obtain evidence against certain people with a view to their deportation proved fruitless, and the indications are that they were confronted by a widespread refusal to inform. Charles Sakwe, one of the senior councillors in the Bunga, assured his colleagues and the magistrates in particular that they knew very little about the Wellington Movement; that "it was only the Natives themselves who knew about the movement thoroughly because it happened in their midst away in the locations. The movement was a great thing amongst the Native people." While chiefs and headmen and "enlightened Natives" tried to end the movement, because they realized that its adherents were trying to fight against the government, many who did not belong "supported Dr. Wellington to a certain extent" and felt "he was not altogether wrong" (*Blythswood Review,* February 1928, March 1928, March 1930; Transkeian Territories General Council, 1928-1932: passim—in particular, Sakive's speech, 1928:89).

The Wellington Movement appealed to different sections of the population in different areas. Some of the leaders in East Griqualand and in the southwestern Transkei, where the movement attained its greatest support, were educated men; in Pondoland the response was from the most traditionalist locations and led by *amaqaba*. It is difficult to relate the success of the movement to any particular state of dislocation or impoverishment, or to locate its base in a specific segment or stratum of the peasantry. Nevertheless, the droughts of 1926-1928 (very severe in the western Transkei) intensified the deepening underdevelopment of the region and must have contributed to the readiness of some individuals to join the movement. It is probable that the nature of state intervention, real and threatened, was of great importance to the forms millenialism took in the 1920s. The early years of that decade demonstrated the willingness of the white rulers of South Africa to use large-scale force against dissident force; while between 1924 and 1929 the segregationist rhetoric and measures of the Pact government stimulated extensive alarm in the Transkei.

The threat to the Cape suffrage was an issue that made "native opinion very restless" and generated many rural meetings in 1926; and a Bunga councillor advised that the Colour Bar Bill had agitated the people greatly: "Meetings had been held, and resolutions, which he would be ashamed to mention at the Council in the presence of the Chief Magistrate . . .had been passed" (Transkeian Territories General Council, 1926:212). In 1929, the four "native bills" provoked fresh waves of alarm. Most immediate in its effects was the Native Development and Taxation Act of 1927, which unified the taxes levied on Africans throughout the union. In the Transkei, it had the effect of raising the taxation paid by all adult males, and the displeasure that this aroused fed directly into Buthelezi's recruitment, as his speeches stressed release from taxes. A Blythswood teacher discerned a direct link between the new tax levels and the withdrawal of children from mission schools (*Blythswood Review,* October 1927). The appeal of the Garveyite ideology—and the image of the black American as deliverer—may also be understood, in part, as a response to segregationist rhetoric uttered by whites in these years. Garveyism, in the United States, was in significant degree a response to the high tide of segregationist ideas and statutes at the turn of the century: a set of ideas that reflected the ideological preoccupations of the segregators, but that was in opposition to it. In South Africa, too, the impetus to independent organizations and to Garveyite ideas may have derived from the hegemonic ideology of the day, albeit in dialectical counterpoise to it. Wellington Buthelezi's Garveyite message was the distorted mirror image of Hertzog's segregation.

Millenarian thought has not subsequently played a major part in political or social resistance in the Transkei, but the period of its heightened activity in the 1920s was to influence later developments. Although a small minority of the chiefs, headmen, and educated bureaucrat-farmers were attracted to it, the greater number of them demonstrated a conspicuous loyalty to the state, and effectively distanced themselves further from the mass of their people. The vigor with which the state inveighed against the movement and punished its agents may have contributed to the relative quiescence of the 1930s and also to the search for alternative strategies for self-expression and survival that characterized that decade.

UNDERDEVELOPMENT, STRATIFICATION, AND SURVIVAL

By the 1930s, the underdevelopment of the Transkei had intensified and deepened. A number of observers in that decade attested (in the words of one of them) that "poverty, a bare subsistence at a low level [was] the outstanding fact in the present economic situation" (Cook, 1934; Pim, 1934; Fox and Black, n.d.). Both in traditionalist and "school" communities, it was becoming more and more difficult to meet subsistence needs through peasant production. Land was overgrazed and its fertility diminished; crop yields began to fall on poorer and smaller arable plots; the great majority of households relied in part on remitted migrant wages for existence and reproduction. The Depression, during the early 1930s, made matters even worse. Prices of agricultural commodities, especially wool, fell; the operation of the Maize Quota Act meant that traders were extremely reluctant to buy African-grown grain; and the fall in wages and in employment opportunities cut down the amount of cash circulating in the territories even further. The sharp pinch of destitution, the burden of taxation, and the specter of starvation are graphically conveyed in the Bunga debates for 1932, the year of the greatest local hardship. "When there is famine," said one speaker, "you can see the signs of it. You see no smoke rising from the kraals, you hear no noise, and you do not see children playing about" (Transkeian Territories General Council, 1932:219).

It is relatively easy to describe the overall level of agrarian degeneration and rural poverty in the Transkei by the 1930s. It is much more difficult with the readily available data to analyze stratification there. The forms that it took were complex and were frequently misrepresented at the time. In an earlier period, when the emergence of a peasantry dissolved or weakened tribal social relations, the key factors in stratification were access to resources, the adoption of the ox-drawn plough, and the ability to produce a marketable surplus. Thoughout the twentieth century, stratification along these lines was checked and inhibited by certain factors, especially the policy of "one man, one plot," which effectively prevented accumulation on any scale and militated against the emergence of a capitalist farming sector within the Reserves. By the 1930s, with the transformation of the peasantry into a proletariat well underway, the crucial differentiating factors were the size of cash income from sources other than agricultural production and access to education and skills. The "large peasants" of the previous generation had become enmeshed in the administrative network as headmen, councillors, and the like. Those with most wealth (chiefs as well as the new elite) invested in the education of their children. Mission schools like Blythswood and Lovedale essentially educated the children of the better-off Transkeians, producing the teachers, clerks, interpreters, and agricultural demonstrators who were able to monopolize the higher-paid posts in church and state.

Yet, because of the rapidity of the transformation of the Transkei, these different stages of stratification overlapped and coincided. Thus, chiefs and headmen (and teachers and clerks) would translate their salaries into livestock; there is a good deal of evidence that cattle and sheep ownership became increasingly concentrated in the interwar period. Similarly, it is misleading to view the entry into (migrant) wage labor unambiguously as an index of rural pauperization; for many households, particularly in traditionalist communities, migrant wages represented the most feasible way of winning cash to reinvest in the productive process. Different wage levels available to various groups of migrant workers could be expressed in the countryside in terms of greater or lesser ability to maintain homestead production. The whole question of stratification is made more complex by the fact that its indices must be different for school and *amaqaba* communities, respectively. A great deal of research remains to be done on these and related issues before any detailed account of differentiation among the Transkeian rural population is possible. Indications are that differentiation was increasing during the 1930s and that the main axis of such differentiation was no longer between large and small peasants, but between a local, salaried bureaucrat-cum-farmer class and the mass of the population, dependent for subsistence in varying degrees on both migrant wages and agricultural production.

There was a comparatively low level of rural resistance during the 1930s. The major political issue of the decade—the removal of the Cape's African voters from the common roll—occasioned a good deal of anxiety among the small enfranchized minority, but their protests were self-consciously temperate and constitutional and generated no widespread popular support. The instances of dissidence and violence that do appear in the records appear to have been small-scale and quickly suppressed. In many cases, they were late flickers of previous protests: small pockets of the Wellington movement, resistance to dipping, and the like. It may be that political mobilization was rendered more difficult during the most acute pressures exerted by the Depression; or that the mild recovery experienced in some districts in the second half of the decade served to muffle protests. There is as yet no convincing evidence to make either case. Two other aspects do seem to help account for the virtual absence of overt resistance during the 1930s: an increase in other forms of political and social expression and the extent to which state intervention in rural life was relaxed during the decade.

There was a considerable growth in the late 1920s, and especially in the 1930s, of new associations and organizations in the Transkei. These were frequently created or dominated by members of the rural elite, and were perhaps an index of their greater self-awareness. By 1933, there were 61 Native Farmers Associations in the Transkei and over 30 Credit Cooperative Societies; there was also a considerable increase in the activities of African teachers' groups, church-based societies, and so on. Evidence that we have for these groups makes it clear that their founders and members were consciously dissociating themselves from mass action. At the other end of the social spectrum, their outlines and dynamics as yet barely visible, there was also considerable development of new associational forms. These included returned migrants' associations and various youth groups, of which the increasing number of amalaita[8] gangs attracted most attention.

The administration of the Transkei underwent no significant innovations during the 1930s; there were no novel or far-reaching forms of intervention by the state in rural life. Much had already been achieved to the satisfaction of those responsible for "Native Affairs." Mass migrancy was entrenched; the councils were established, and in 1930 the Pondoland General Councils merged with the rest of the Transkei; dipping was fairly generally practiced. Means to modify landholding had been dropped and communal tenure officially accepted in government locations. In the place of attempts to undermine the authority of the chiefs was a growing acceptance of their value as a means of social and political control; chiefs' courts were recognized in legislation of 1927, and in general greater freedom was permitted to traditional leaders to reassert greater local control.

Yet, beneath this surface of administrative stability, throughout the decade calls were being made for greatly increased state intervention, for new and sometimes drastic measures. From local magistrates and officials, from the 1930-1932 Natives Economic Commission, from academics and employers, there stemmed a generalized awareness of crisis in the Transkei and other Reserves. It was felt that the slide of the Reserves into agrarian decay had to be halted or reversed if they were to continue to fulfill their function within the South African capitalist economy—that is, if they were to continue to house the dependents of migrant laborers, to contribute a proportion of their means of subsistence, to keep urban wages low, and to minimize the growth of a settled urban proletariat. The prescriptions that were forthcoming tended to be formulated first at the local level and subsequently adopted by the departments concerned. One can trace a sequence in which, between the 1930-1932 Commission and the Tomlinson Commission of 1956, different elements in the dominant classes came to adhere to certain broad ideas regarding the place of migrant labor in the economy and the needs of the Reserves. In the Transkei during the 1930s, agricultural extension schemes were expanded, with much emphasis on better methods, crops, and livestock strains. The issue of overstocking emerged as the crucial one. The increase in Transkei flocks and herds was identified as the prime cause of soil erosion, as the greatest barrier to changed attitudes and methods, and as the perpetuator of retrograde land usage. By the late 1930s, the main outlines of a thesis had been formulated which pressed for a coordinated policy of betterment or rehabilitation rather than piecemeal measures to arrest erosion or the limited returns from extension work. Proponents of such schemes insisted that they were essential for the economic and social viability of the Transkei; they also maintained that shoring up or improving productivity there would not affect the supply of migrant laborers. Betterment proposals involved the concentration of scattered settlements, the demarcation and fencing of arable areas, and the division of grazing areas into fenced camps. An essential prerequisite was the reduction of livestock to a previously calculated optimum capacity in each location. A Betterment Act was passed by the South African legislature in 1939 and its measures first executed in Butterworth district. Only modest beginnings had been made when war broke out, and state spending on rural redevelopment of African areas slipped very far down the list of wartime priorities. Betterment and rehabilitation schemes are essentially a feature of the postwar years.

RESISTANCE TO BETTERMENT AND REHABILITATION, 1945-1951

The genesis of betterment proposals and their subsequent implementation should be located within the broader context of structural changes in the economy and in the nature of the state. These have been analyzed elsewhere (Legassick, 1974; Morris, 1976; Wolpe, 1972); there is room here only to summarize baldly their main features. The inflationary boom of the late 1930s in South Africa, fueled by the rise in the price of gold, led to a spectacular increase in manufacturing industry that was further accelerated by the war. There was, in consequence, a very rapid growth of the industrial labor force: the number of black workers in manufacturing industry rose from 76,000 in 1933 to 149,000 by 1945. Africans flocked into the periurban areas of the Witwatersrand and Cape Town; during the war, this urban working class enjoyed significant increases in real wages, and its members took part in a number of strikes and stoppages. The social and political implications of urbanization and industrialization were debated in the party political arena in the immediate postwar period. The key issues were the competing labor requirements of industrial and agrarian capital, the optimum level of African urbanization, the role of the pass laws and influx controls, and the means of containing the political and industrial challenge of an African working class. The 1948 election victory of the National Party—and of the white workers, farmers, and small businessmen that it represented—ensured that the solutions were sought, *inter alios*, in increased surveillance and control over African trade unions and political organizations, in the entrenchment and extension of migrant labor, and in the denial of residential rights to Africans in "white" urban areas.

Both sides in the political debate were in broad agreement that the corollary to their urban platforms was the need to intervene in the Reserves so as to increase and rationalize their carrying capacity. A few months before the end of the war the Smuts government announced its intention of "dealing with the problem on a wider footing" in the Reserves. The Minister of Native Affairs outlined in sweeping, imprecise terms a blueprint for large-scale "rehabilitation" of the Reserves: "something like a twelve year plan," the Secretary of the Department called it. It envisaged the creation of planning committees which would survey the Reserves and divide them into residential, grazing, and arable areas. "Rural villages" would be established for "the families of Natives regularly employed in industry and other services"; these families would not be allowed to own stock or granted access to arable plots. The implications were spelled out:

> It must be accepted that there will never be enough land to enable every Native in the Reserves to become a full-time peasant farmer. . . . The future of these families is not in farming. . . . The proposal is an important link between the Government's plan for rehabilitation in the Reserves and the large-scale industrial development expected after the war [statement of policies made by Secretary of Native Affairs, 1945].

For "full-time peasant farmers," improved methods and greater efficiency were to be sustained by a program of afforestation, fencing, soil conservation, and veld reclamation, preceded by stock culling. The idea of "economic units"—the provision of sufficient land to large peasants to permit a class of African farmers in the Reserves—was favored by some local Transkei officials and in the 1940s by the "liberal" wing of the United Party. It received its fullest exposition in the 1956 Tomlinson Report, commissioned by the National Party, but these particular recommendations were never implemented.

Betterment/rehabilitation schemes were welcomed by some of those Transkeians who stood to benefit by their provisions. Chiefs and headmen, and those peasants already engaged in improvements and extension schemes, were amenable to the changes, but a majority of families viewed them with suspicion and hostility. The sharpest objections were aimed at stock culling. Time and again peasants countered arguments about improved milk yield, better blood stock, and richer pasturage by pointing out that their problem was not too many cattle, but too few on too little land. Cattle played a critical part in the rural economy, in ceremonies and marriage transactions, and as savings; culling—cash compensation notwithstanding—threatened the individual's ability to plough or meet bride-wealth. In 1941, a Committee on Overstocking appointed by the Native Affairs Department traveled widely in the Transkei and took evidence from hundreds of people, to report that

> at nearly every centre visited the voice of the native people was unanimous in its opposition to any suggestion of compulsory limitation; and in many places the attitude adopted was definitely hostile and considerable patience and tact had to be exercised [quoted in Roux, 1944:3].

Other features of rehabilitation also met with opposition. Fencing interfered with traditional grazing and cattle-loan systems; the removal of people to rural villages involved the destruction of their homesteads; and the scheme meant enforced landlessness for many.

The first Transkei district to experience a betterment program was Butterworth—and it was also there that the first

resistance to the scheme was organized. Betterment surveys
and fencing were actually undertaken in Butterworth in 1939,
partly in response to initiatives by local peasants, and the more
sweeping rehabilitation procedures began when the scheme
was launched in the Transkei in 1945-1946. A survey of
Ndabakazi location in the district conducted in December
1947 provides valuable incidental details of the scheme and its
reception. Rehabilitation was "one of the most burning questions" of the day, and had been met with "spirited opposition."
Two issues generated particular bitterness: cattle culling and
the coercive nature of the policy. The Rehabilitation Scheme
Committee had abandoned its original "policy of appease-
ment" because of their lack of headway, and were now
insisting on the scheme's execution. Resistance took several
forms. As areas were fenced off during the preliminary
betterment phase, people "smashed fences by night and drove
their cattle in." There was much hostility in the location
toward the chief and the Bunga councillors, who—it was felt—
misrepresented popular opinion on rehabilitation. Opposition
to the scheme was voiced through a Vigilance Association
(*Iliso lomzi*) that had "sprung up as a check on Bunga
representatives" at "the initiative of the people themselves"
(National Union of South African Students Research Journal,
1951).

The first district to be completely "rehabilitated" was
Libode in Western Pondoland. It was chosen by officials not
because it was the most eroded district, but because it was the
home of Victor Poto, Paramount of Western Pondoland, who
threw the whole weight of his considerable authority behind
the scheme. Poto was one of the few chiefs who managed to
retain mass support *and* remain fully involved in the council
system, and Western Pondoland was an area where there had
been little open resistance to state authority in the past. In
1947, the Planning Committee designated the badly eroded
district of Mount Ayliff, with a largely Xesibe population, as
the third rehabilitation area. The local chief gave his support,
and an able "trouble-shooting" magistrate was appointed to

supervise the scheme. He organized meetings to explain the policy, but in Brooks Nek location the meetings were boycotted. When police were sent in, the headman refused to give up the men, who then armed themselves and moved into the surrounding hills. There they formed a secret movement, the *Kongo*, receiving some support from neighboring locations, and threatened to attack their collaborating chief. White residents removed hastily from the district to larger towns as rumors spread of an armed uprising. The All African Convention, which, since the beginning of 1946, had been distributing its pamphlet *The Rehabilitation Scheme: "The New Fraud"* in the Eastern Cape and Transkei, established some links with the Mount Ayliff movement. The activist I. B. Tabata was arrested in the district for "incitement to violence," and in 1948 Kongo affiliated to the All African Convention.[9]

Although resistance everywhere took on local variations, the broad pattern of events in Butterworth and Mount Ayliff was repeated in much of the Transkei. Distinctive features of the struggle against rehabilitation were political mobilization in new popular organizations, and the range of tactics deployed. In a number of districts, it was reported in 1948, people had "voluntarily formed Location Committees against their headmen and Bungas to assert their right to decide how they should own their land" (Minutes of the Non-European Unity Movement Annual Conference, December 1948). These organizations were coordinated to some extent through the Transkei Organized Bodies, of which Govan Mbeki was a founder and the General Secretary from 1943 to 1948. The implementation of rehabilitation was harried and held up by the boycott or disruption of meetings, attacks on government personnel, fence-cutting, the hiding or removal of livestock when surveys were done, political pressure on headmen and chiefs, and so on. The Native Affairs Department's administrative year 1948-1949 was reported to have been the most difficult ever experienced as, "with few exceptions, the Natives are generally less cooperative than hitherto." In that year, rehabilitation was extended to three more districts. In Qumbu, "considerable organised opposition was revealed . . . which manifested itself in the cutting of fences." Incitement to sabotage (said the Chief Magistrate) "came from outside and found fertile ground in a semi-secret organization." In Idutywa and Matatiele, too, the destruction of fences was reported. The following year (1949-1950) saw further "alarming reverses which caused a serious retardation" of the department's work, and "malicious opposition" was reported from several parts of South Africa. "Malicious agitators" were still active against rehabilitation in 1950-1951 (Native Affairs Department Reports, U.G. 14-1948:21, U.G. 51-'50:2,32, U.G. 61-'51:1, U.G. 30-1953:5)—but thereafter a blanket of secrecy was draped over rural resistance by Verwoerd, the new Minister, and maintained by his successors.

Two aspects of the resistance against rehabilitation are particularly noteworthy. First, several reports at the time noted that the most concerted opposition came from families heavily involved in migrant labor. But "migrant laborer" was a far from uniform category in the 1940s: As indicated, differentiation among migrants was promoted both by wage levels and by the strength or weakness of homestead production. Those who had most to lose by rehabilitation were "middle migrants" or "peasant migrants"—as opposed to their more thoroughly proletarianized brethren (the landless migrant), they had cattle of their own and access to grazing and arable lands. Removal to a rural village would confirm and emphasize their identity as wage laborers—at the same time, it would erase their identity as the family heads of peasant households. This hypothesis attempts to identify the key social basis of the fight against rehabilitation. It also takes account of the observation (by a political activist in the 1950s) that the 30 to 40 percent of landless people in the Reserve "have not always supported the struggle against rehabilitation" (Mettler, 1957). It was a group of migratory workers from the Transkei that produced one of the most succinct critiques of rehabilitation at the time. These workers listed their reasons for opposing the scheme (land shortage, the destruction of kraals, the culling of stock essential to their lives), and concluded:

The scheme seems to be another Cattle Killing Episode modernised. The scheme is designed to impoverish, to suppress the economic and social growth of the African in the native reserves. It is a means of preserving white superiority [Hirson, 1977:126].

Second, rehabilitation brought about a much sharper conflict between the mass of the people and the administrative elite of chiefs, headmen, and councillors. The Bunga councillors, said a commoner in 1947, "worked for their own good and that of their children" (Mqotsi, 1951). Even while the political tone of the Bunga swung sharply to the left between 1946 and 1949, popular hostility to its representatives deepened. For their part, collaborating chiefs and headmen were implicated in an extremely unpopular policy. In the 1950s, the powers of the administrative elite were consolidated and broadened in the Bantu Authorities Act. The struggle against rehabilitation measures increasingly became caught up in resistance to the new administrative system and its local agents.

RESISTANCE TO BANTU AUTHORITIES AND THE PONDO REVOLT

The struggle in the Transkei against the introduction and implementation of Bantu Authorities was waged with varying intensity throughout the period 1956-1965. Resistance in Eastern Pondoland in 1960-1961 was on a larger scale and at a politically more organized level than elsewhere: it involved thousands of activists and commanded the support of several thousand Mpondo in Bizana, Flagstaff, Lusikisiki, and Tabnakulu districts. The central popular organization attacked the local collaborators, structured its policy in opposition to the state as a whole, and set up the foundations of an alternative political system. State action to suppress it involved the imposition of a state of emergency and the dispatch of a task force of police and troops supported by armored vehicles and helicopters (Copelyn, 1977; Mbeki, 1964, 1957; Turok, n.d.). During the same decade, violent rural resistance broke out in the western and northeastern Transvaal and Natal; in urban areas the Treason Trial, the Sharpeville shootings and state of emergency, the banning of the national political organizations, and the Sabotage Act were milestones in the state's containment of the national liberation movement.

In the 1950s the Nationalist government first announced as a policy goal the future "independence" of tribally defined African homelands; and in the Bantu Authorities Act introduced significant changes in the nature of local administration in the Reserves/Homelands. The Bantu Authorities system was accepted by the Transkei's General Council in 1955, and established in the territories from 1956 onward. The act created a bureaucratic hierarchy of tribal, district, regional, and territorial authorities, the most distinct feature of which was the expansion of the powers vested in "tribal" or "traditional" chiefs, held to be "the true leaders of the Bantu people." Instead of formal responsibility over single locations only, chiefs now controlled clusters of locations; they retained their customary powers and were granted an agglomerate of new administrative roles, including powers previously executed by headmen and magistrates.

For commoners, the Bantu Authorities imposed a series of additional disabilities and burdens. Politically, the inception of Bantu Authorities reduced the weight of the elected element at every level and greatly cut back the popular participation previously enjoyed at the district council level. No public meetings of more than ten people could be held legally without the permission of a Bantu commissioner. Financially, the Bantu Authorities involved new fees and taxes: the direct taxation paid by household heads almost doubled between 1955 and 1960. The proliferation of bureaucratic posts was marked by a sharp rise in graft and corruption, with minor officials demanding cash payments before allowing commoners access to courts, licensing offices, and so on. Crucially, the powers allotted to the new authorities meant that chiefs became more visibly and directly the symbols of social control. Greater power meant diminished legitimacy. Chiefs were no longer perceived as intermediaries between the state and their followers, but unambiguously as the instruments of the South African state.

The position of the chiefs was highlighted by their greater identification with the rehabilitation programs. From the mid-1950s there were two changes in betterment/rehabilitation policy. First, the emphasis shifted from "reclamation" (intensive soil conservation and the substantial improvement of small areas) to "stabilization" (more extensive work in a larger area aimed at arresting deterioration). More importantly, in our context, the responsibility for carrying out the program was largely transferred to the new Bantu Authorities. Verwoerd, then Minister for Bantu Affairs, explained:

> I have tried to adopt a different course, and that fits in with the institution of Bantu Authorities in terms of which the responsibility was thrown onto the Bantu himself. . . . The result will be that improvements can be brought about on a tremendously larger scale and thereafter they can be left in the hands of the Bantu himself, subject to some supervision. That means colossal savings and great expedition [Copelyn, 1977].

The long-standing authority of the chiefs over land allocation had been transmuted and distorted into the execution of the state's rehabilitation schemes. The powers of the Bantu Authorities' officials involved them directly and daily in the lives of the rural people; moreover (as Govan Mbeki wrote in 1957) the chiefs were "now saddled with the responsibility of carrying out a land policy which people have opposed so strongly that Government has not been able to implement it." Chiefs had to move families under the Land Rehabilitation Scheme, to compel the culling of stock, and to dispossess some people of their arable allotments in the name of soil conservation (Mbeki, 1957).

For all these reasons, the introduction and operation of the scheme was met with hostility, overt opposition, and a good deal of violent resistance. Much research remains to be done before a full account of this resistance can be given, but it is possible to point to some of the questions that such investigation must pose. It is clear that in many cases resistance to Bantu Authorities took on new organizational forms. There is unusually detailed evidence on this for the Tsolo and Qumbu districts, where W. D. Hammond-Tooke (1975) carried out fieldwork in the early 1960s. Peasants in these districts had formed local vigilante groups to combat stock-theft, and in Tsolo several of these banded together in *Makhuluspani* ("the Big Team"). *Makhuluspani* raised funds by a levy, and meted out justice to thieves by fines and by attacks. In the late 1950s, the body "changed its tactics and began to threaten chiefs and headmen whom it regarded as collaborating too closely with the Government. The establishment of Bantu Authorities, in particular, saw an increase in its activities" (Hammond-Tooke, 1975:106). Less is known about the organizations that sprang up in 1956 in Cala and Glen Grey districts to prevent the installation of progovernment chiefs. In Glen Grey (part of the Transkei from 1958), those who opposed Bantu Authorities styled themselves "Jacobites," and hostility between them and the Nchothozas (who supported the system) ran deep, on occasion flaring into violence (*Ilizwi Lesizwe*, 1961). In Thembuland resistance to the authorities focused on Chief Kaiser Matanzima. The level of violence was high enough at the beginning of 1959 for a well-informed commentator to predict that Thembuland would become "a second Sekhukhuneland"; and, as Tom Lodge (1978) has demonstrated, between 1960 and 1965 sustained unrest punctuated with violence prevailed there. The pattern of events in Thembuland closely paralleled those in Pondoland, with a similar nexus of grievances and tactics; while in Thembuland resistance remained "sporadic and disjointed" during five years of incipient revolt, in Pondoland revolt achieved mass dimensions and relatively highly organized form.

The trigger of the wider revolt was the failure of the chief in Isikelo location, Bizana, to consult his people over his own (reluctant) acceptance of Bantu Authorities. At the first meeting of the Isikelo Tribal Authority, the members of the new body appointed by the chief were assaulted, and the rebels withdrew to the hills to hold meetings. The strategy widely adopted by these Hill Committees was to burn down the homesteads of collaborators, forcing them to flee. Such action spread to other parts of Bizana and into neighboring districts. The movement rapidly found a target in Botha Sigcau, the paramount chief, as a symbol of what was being resisted: "The people felt that chief Botha sold the Pondos and the country for his own ends—that was why they felt he had accepted all the changes for his own benefit" (*Van Heerden Commission on the Disturbances in Pondoland*, 1960). The succession dispute that had marked Botha's original appointment in the 1930s was revived, and he was denounced as an illegitimate ruler surrounded by corrupt councillors. A mass march was organized against the Paramount to burn down his Great Place, but was headed off by a detatchment of police. Popular feeling against Sigcau was only one element in the protests and direct action that developed. Other discontents included taxation (especially the levy for the unpopular Bantu Education system); rehabilitation and closer settlement villages; the lack of consultation and the ban on popular meetings: In sum, the Mpondo rebels rejected the institutions and policies of the state, and especially they denounced the collaboration of chiefs and Paramount. The organization of the revolt emerged as a series of local committees which appear to have acknowledged the leadership of the Hill Committee in Bizana. The committees held well-attended meetings, were sensitive to local opinion, and were able to direct and coordinate the political activities of large numbers; they levied taxes, dispensed justice, and devised policy. Their main tactics included attacks on the homes and persons of collaborators, boycotts of trading stores, large marches, and selective violence coupled with passive resistance.

Lodge (1978) has suggested that militant resistance in Thembuland between 1960 and 1965 was largely led by migrants returning from Cape Town who had been caught up in the broader struggle by the national democratic movements (especially the P.A.C./Poqo). Returned migrants, who came from the most traditionalist sector of the population in Pondoland, seem to have been an important factor in the Mpondo rising. As in Thembuland, this was much less the case with gold miners than with other migrants. Substantial numbers of Mpondo worked in Natal, particularly on the sugar estates. During 1959 there was a crisis of overproduction and a large percentage of the migrant labor force was laid off. The Pondoland uprising was most highly organized in the three districts that provided the bulk of sugar workers, and complaints about unemployment and the pass laws were articulated by the rebel movement. Another group active in Pondoland was composed of some members of the educated elite, especially teachers, many of whom had been involved in protests against the Bantu Education Act during the decade. There is also some evidence that political activists from Natal's urban centers effected links with the Hill Committees and helped formulate a program of action, and that their political affiliation was with the A.N.C.

During 1960, the Bantu Authorities effectively lost control over Bizana and portions of Lusikisiki and Flagstaff. As hostility and anger were consolidated and organized into structured resistance, rebel utterances were frequently couched in traditionalist phraseology; under the circumstances, this was not a conservative but a radical ideology. The attacks against rural collaborators were a rejection of state policies and agents, but also a clear expression of class antagonism. A member of a leading Bizana family gave this description of the progress of the revolt:

> The people showed a spirit of rebellion—they opposed all the measures which were for their own advancement. They rejected Bantu Authorities. One man stands up and gives orders, and then they start burning kraals. After the members of the Bantu Authorities were burnt out, they went about burning the kraals of those sympathetic to the Bantu Authorities. Then the more progressive people in the location were burnt out. Before burning the huts they took everything out. It is the more well-to-do owners who have suffered like this. Even if the poor owners were sympathetic to the Bantu Authorities, they are not burnt out. They tried to influence everyone on the location. They intimidate people to make them attend their meetings. They advised owners to pay some money to save their kraals and

their property. Then it would not be touched. I was warned that I was to be burnt out, but I was saved by paying £5. I don't know who ultimately received that money. It was passed from one to another. I was told that this money was to be paid out for the people who were charged with breaking the law. . . . The truth is this—they want to grab people's property and they want to break the law [*Van Heerden Commission on the Disturbances in Pondoland*, 1960].

CONCLUSIONS

From the incidents discussed above, four general tendencies merit recapitulation. First, in the early part of the century chiefs, headmen, and some educated, locally employed people were forced or absorbed into broadly collaborationist positions. While opposition to the Glen Grey council system was most clearly articulated by members of these groups, after the implementation of the councils rural resistance was based in, and frequently led from, the mass of people with less wealth and power. Those collaborating within the administrative system for the most part ceased to reproduce themselves purely as a wealthier peasantry; although most of them kept a stake in the land, they were absorbed into the structures of dominance as bureaucrats and salaried employees. Their ability to command mass loyalty declined steadily, if irregularly, through the period under review. It should not be thought that collaboration was unambiguous, nor that the position of the elites was cut and dried. Chiefs constantly struggled, within the limits of their amended roles, to protect their rights and to carve out a larger niche for themselves. In doing so they came into conflict with the state. Yet, they were no longer representative of the masses, and expressed more sectional interests. At times, individuals or elements of the elites— under popular pressure or through shared grievances—defected, and were influential in more widely based resistance.

Second, despite the social and economic changes in the Transkei and the entrenchment of mass labor migration, control over and access to rural resources—especially land and livestock—remained central objectives of those involved in resistance. Equally, the mass of the population continued to display great sensitivity to the nature of local political authority. It was essentially when state intervention threatened such controls or restructured the local political hierarchy that organized resistance surfaced. Locked into migrant labor as they were, those who had cattle or land to lose resisted their proletarianization by mobilizing in the countryside over rural issues. As a general observation, Eric Wolf (1969:292) writes:

> The middle peasant . . . stays on the land and sends his children to work in town; he is caught in a situation in which one part of the family retains a footing in agriculture, while the other undergoes "the training of the cities.". . . It is probably not so much the growth of an industrial proletariat as such which produces revolutionary activity, as the development of an industrial work force still closely geared to life in the villages. . . . It is the very attempt of the middle and free peasant to remain traditional which makes him revolutionary.

Third, and related to the above, is the importance in the Transkei of different cultural identities. The process of transformation in the subregions of the Transkei was uneven, but within each region occurred the cultural divide commonly typified as "school" and "red." That is, at the two poles of cultural identity were those who broadly accepted the ideology and culture of the colonial state and those who rejected it. The origins of this cleavage go back to the era of intense missionary activity in the nineteenth century, to the formation of a surplus-producing peasantry, to the wars of conquest which were waged for political and cultural independence and bequeathed great bitterness, and to the historical conflicts between Xhosa and Mfengu. By the beginning of the twentieth century, a complex interweaving of these and other experiences had produced two social groupings that tended to reproduce themselves and their specific cultural adhesions. The differences existed not only in cultural forms, but also in family structure, patterns of investment, and especially patterns of consumption. School people were more dependent on the purchase of manufactured commodities; their children wore clothes from the trader's store and attended school, while those of the *amaqaba* donned the less expensive blanket and tended to be engaged in herding duties. Before 1930, it was the school people who felt most acutely the pinch of declining rural independence and the limits on African advancement. Except for the highly educated few, they had no access to better jobs, yet were involved in greater local expenditure. Their sensitivity to wages and prices was very clear during the women's boycott movement described earlier. They felt menaced by the segregationist policies and rhetoric of the early twentieth century (the 1920s in particular), and responded by creating institutions that drew on the forms of the colonizers: separatist and Zionist churches. The Wellington Movement of the 1920s attracted many school people, although it also drew deeply on traditionalist symbolism, and attracted adherents from right across the cultural spectrum.

For the *amaqaba*, the segregationist era was less disruptive. In a sense it provided some elements of what they sought: the entrenchment of communal tenure for the masses and greater emphasis on traditional structures. At the economic level, hardship and poverty confirmed their attempts to reject imported commodities as far as possible. From the 1930s onward, the core of militant resistance in the Transkei appears to have been provided by traditionalist middle migrants or peasant-migrants. Their rejection of the dominant culture did not necessarily lead to organized political action, but served as a powerful ideological force when rural resources or local political structures came under threat.

Fourth, the form and aims of rural organization changed significantly in the period under consideration. In broad, crude outline, movements in the first three decades of the century tended to be based on specific "grievances" and to be directed against immediate targets: dipping tanks, traders' stores, and so on. The Wellington Movement signified a more general rejection of the state's apparatus of political and ideological control, while after World War II large-scale state intervention was met with political action aimed against the state as a whole, more violent in character than earlier episodes, and with some conception of an alternative political system. Action no longer sought the rectification of grievances by the state, but challenged or impeded its agents, aiming directly at collaborating groups within the society.

None of the movements described in these pages succeeded in altering the balance of power in the state; at best, they could dilute or delay the execution of rural policy. Events in the Transkei provide a further illustration of the weakness of peasant movements as analyzed by others. The peasantry's sense of its own weakness and inferiority, the tendency of peasant movements to remain localized, the role of kinship and mutual aid in spreading distress evenly, the dictates of the harvest and the herd, and the backwardness of communications and other technology vis-à-vis the dominant classes—all these are attested in the literature of peasant studies, and all are true of the Transkei in our period.

NOTES

1. A non-Bantu-speaking community which established a considerable polity in the northwestern part of the territories in the 1860s, but which had largely been dispossessed of its land during the late 1870s.

2. For fuller discussions of these processes, see Bundy (1979) and Beinart (1979).

3. Although permanent migration from the Transkei to urban areas also took place, the characteristic form of migrancy was that of frequently repeated departures in search of wage labor (on the gold mines and elsewhere) by the men, commonly for periods of up to a year at a time.

4. The terms "school" and "red" are well established in the South African literature, and are used to distinguish between those whose lifestyle expressed cultural acceptance of western dress and manufactured goods, and those who adhered to the cultural symbols of traditionalism. We have adopted this terminology, although we are conscious of its limitations and of the need for a reexamination of the concepts.

5. For Herschel, Cape Archives, Chief Magistrate of Transkei, 3/951/15/411A, Resident Magistrate of Herschel to Secretary of Native Affairs, August 28, 1922; for Qumbu, Cape Archives, Chief Magistrate of Transkei, 3/824/558, report of meeting of July 24, 1922, and Chief Magistrate of Transkei, 3/951/15/411A, native unrest and boycotting of stores, Acting Resident Magistrate to Chief Magistrate, July 19, 1922.

6. Wellington Buthelezi's life and career have been studied by Edgar (1975, 1976). Unfortunately, we have not had access to his doctoral thesis (UCLA, 1976) on Buthelezi.

7. For an account of Maqolo's trial, see *Blythswood Review*, November 1927. For creation of separate schools, see *Blythswood Review*, September 1927 and October 1927; Transkeian Territories General Council, 1928:72-73; 1929:44-45, 75, 146-147; 1932: 78-79.

8. *Amalaita* were groups of young men who banded together in Johannesburg; their existence can be traced back to early in the century.

9. For Mount Ayliff disturbances, we have used an interview with V.M.P. Leibbrandt (in 1947, Resident Magistrate at Mount Ayliff and later Chief Magistrate of Transkei), recorded in Durban in 1976. For AAC involvement, see Tabata (1974), Clark (1977), and Hirson (1977).

REFERENCES

BEINART, W.J. (1979). "Production, labour migrancy, and chieftaincy: Aspects of the political economy of Pondoland, 1860-1930." Ph.D. dissertation. London: University of London.

BONNER, P.C. (1978). "The 1920 Black mineworkers' strike." University of Witwatersrand. (unpublished)

BUNDY, C.J. (1979). The Rise and Fall of the South African Peasantry. Berkeley: University of California Press.

CLARK, A. (1977). "The Non-European Unity Movement, 1943-1952." M.A. dissertation. York: University of York.

COOK, P.A.W. (1934). The Education of a South African Tribe. Cape Town and Johannesburg: Juta.

COPELYN, J. (1977). "The Mpondo Revolt of 1960-61." B.A. Hons. dissertation. Johannesburg: University of Witwatersrand.

Development Studies Group (1978). Conference on the History of Opposition in South Africa. Johannesburg: University of Witwatersrand.

EDGAR, R. (1976). "Garveyism in Africa: Dr. Wellington and the 'American Movement' in the Transkei, 1925-40." Institute of Commonwealth Studies, Collected Seminar Papers on the Societies of Southern Africa 6. London: University of London.

_____(1975). "The strange career of Wellington Buthelezi, or Bantu profits in South Africa." Los Angeles: University of California, Los Angeles. (unpublished)

HAMMOND-TOOKE, W.D. (1975). Command or Consensus: The Development of Transkeian Local Government. Cape Town: David Philip.

HIRSON, B. (1977). "Rural revolt in South Africa, 1937-1951." Institute of Commonwealth Studies, Collected Seminar Papers on the Societies of Southern Africa 8. London: University of London.

HOBSBAWM, E.J. (1973). "Peasants and politics." Journal of Peasant Studies 1:3-22.

HOOPER, C. (1960). Brief Authority. London.

Ilizwi Lesizwe (1961). "A village mourns." I(September).

LEGASSICK, M. (1974). "Legislation, ideology and economy in post-1948 South Africa." Journal of Southern African Studies 1:5-35.

LODGE, T. (1978). "The rural struggle: Poqo and Transkei Resistance, 1960-1965." In Development Studies Group, Conference on the History of Opposition in South Africa. Johannesburg: University of Witwatersrand.

MARKS, S. (1970). Reluctant Rebellion: The 1906-8 Disturbances in Natal. London: Oxford University Press.

MBEKI, G. (1964). The Peasants' Revolt. Harmondsworth: Penguin.

_____(1957). "The Transkei Tragedy." Liberation 23 (Johannesburg).

METTLER, R. (1957). "It Is Time To Awake." Johannesburg. (pseudonym for B. Hirson)

MORONEY, S. (1900). "The 1950 Witzieshoek Rebellion." Africa Perspective 1.

MORRIS, M.L. (1976). "Apartheid, agriculture and the state: The farm labour question." Southern Africa Labour & Development Research Unit Working Paper 8. Cape Town: University of Cape Town.

National Union of South African Students Research Journal (1951). The Transkei Survey. (ed. P. Tobias) Cape Town.

Report of the Select Committee on the Glen Grey Act, 1903 (1903). Minutes of evidence. (Capetown): Cape Parliamentary Papers, A.1-'03.

RICH, R. (1978). "Black peasants and Ethiopianism in South Africa, 1896-1915." In Development Studies Group, Conference on the History of Opposition in South Africa. Johannesburg: University of Witwatersrand.

ROUX, E. (1944). The Native Reserves and Post-War Reconstruction. Cape Town.

Secretary of Native Affairs (1945). A New Era of Reclamation. Pretoria, South Africa: Government Printers.

Stanford Report (1914). Report of the Government's Special Commissioner, Sen. Col. the Hon. W.E.M. Stanford, with regard to the Matatiele Disturbances.

TABATA, I.B. (1974). The Awakening of a People. Nottingham: Spokesman Books.

TUROK, B. (n.d.). The Pondo Revolt. Johannesburg.

WOLF, E. (1971). Peasant Wars of the Twentieth Century. London: Faber.

WOLPE, H. (1972). "Capitalism and cheap labour-power: From segregation to apartheid." Economy and Society 1.

YAWITCH, J. (1978). "Natal 1959: The women's protests." In Development Studies Group, Conference on the History of Opposition in South Africa. Johannesburg: University of Witwatersrand.

ABOUT THE CONTRIBUTORS

WILLIAM BEINART was educated at the Universities of Cape Town and London. He has held research posts at the Centre for Intergroup Studies, University of Cape Town, and the Institute for Social and Economic Research, Rhodes University; he is currently involved in the research project on rural history in Southern Africa at Queen Elizabeth House, Oxford. He has published articles dealing with the history of the Transkeian Territories and the economic situation in South Africa's African homelands. His doctoral thesis analyzed social and economic changes in Pondoland (part of the Transkei) between 1860 and 1913.

COLIN BUNDY is Staff Tutor in History in the Department for External Studies, Oxford University, and Associate Fellow of Queen Elizabeth House, Oxford. Born and raised in South Africa, he studied at the Universities of Natal, the Witwatersrand, and Oxford. He has taught in South Africa, England, and the United States. He is author of *The Rise and Fall of the South African Peasantry* and a co-editor of the *Journal of Southern African Studies*. He is currently working on a joint research project with William Beinart.

JULIAN CLARKE teaches sociology at the University of Liverpool. His thesis on "Agricultural Production in a Rural Yoruba Community" was defended at the University of London in 1978. It is primarily concerned to document the political economy of land tenure and to relate this to the development of small-scale farming enterprises. Clarke's major interests are in the sociopolitical dimensions of agricultural development in Nigeria, the development of appropriate notions of farming enterprise, and possession and control of means of production.

JEAN-PIERRE CHAUVEAU is Research Associate (Chargé de Recherches) with the Office de Recherches Scientifiques et Techniques Outre-Mer in Paris. His own research has been done among the Gban in the Ivory Coast, in Baule country, in collaboration with Jacques Richard. His research deals principally with the economic and social history of precolonial structures, with the contemporary plantation economy, and with colonial and present-day "development" policies.

JEAN COPANS has studied in Paris and conducted fieldwork in the Ivory Coast and Senegal. He teaches at l'Ecole des Hautes Etudes en Sciences Sociales, where he has a position since 1970. He has also taught at the Johns Hopkins University and at l'Université Laval, Québec. His main interests are in the history and criticism of anthropological theory and practice and in the nature of contemporary West African nations. He has published *Critique et Politique de l'anthropologie* (1974) and *Les Saintes Huiles* (1980). He has edited *Secheresses et Famines du Sahel* (1975), co-edited with J. Jamin, *Aux origines de l'Anthropologie francaise* (1979) and with P. Gutkind and R. Cohen, *African Labor History* (Volume 2 in this series).

ELIANE DE LATOUR DEJEAN is a French anthropologist who has done research on the history of the Mawri of Niger. She is a researcher with the Centre National de la Recherche Scientifique.

BOGUMIL JEWSIEWICKI was born in Poland, where he received his doctorate in 1968 from the University of Lodz. He taught in Zaire at the Institut Pedagogique Supérieur in Mbandaka, at Lovanium University in Kinshasa, and at the Université Nationale du Zaire. At the latter institution, he supervised a program of research on the social and economic history of modern Zaire. He has written widely in this area.

MARTIN A. KLEIN teaches African history at the University of Toronto. He is the author of *Islam and Imperialism in Senegal: Sine-Saloum 1847—1914* (Stanford, 1968), and has been working on a study of slavery and French colonial rule and on the transition from slave labor to free labor. He is also editing, with Claire Robertson, a collection of articles on women and slavery in Africa.

MICHAEL D. LEVIN has taught social anthropology at the State University of New York at Buffalo, and in 1978 and 1979 at the University of Calabar, Nigeria. He is presently teaching social anthropology at the University of Toronto. His fieldwork has been undertaken in the southwestern province of Cameroun and the Cross River State of Nigeria. His main academic interests are in problems of social change and economic development in West African communities.

MAUD SHIMWAAYI MUNTEMBA is Senior Lecturer and Chair of the Department of History at the University of Zambia (Lusaka). She graduated from the University of Nottingham and from 1967 to 1973 was Keeper of History at the National Museum in Livingstone. She received her M.A. from the University of Zambia in 1973 and her Ph.D. from the University of California in Los Angeles in 1977. Her thesis was entitled "Rural Underdevelopment in Zambia: Kabwe Rural District, 1850-1970."